William Faulkner's
Absalom, Absalom!

A CASEBOOK

CASEBOOKS IN CRITICISM

General Editor, William L. Andrews

WILLIAM FAULKNER'S
Absalom, Absalom!

◆ ◆ ◆

A CASEBOOK

Edited by
Fred Hobson

OXFORD
UNIVERSITY PRESS

2003

OXFORD

UNIVERSITY PRESS

Oxford   New York

Auckland   Bangkok   Buenos Aires   Cape Town   Chennai
Dar es Salaam   Delhi   Hong Kong   Istanbul   Karachi   Kolkata
Kuala Lumpur   Madrid   Melbourne   Mexico City   Mumbai   Nairobi
São Paulo   Shanghai   Taipei   Tokyo   Toronto

Copyright © 2003 by Oxford University Press, Inc.

Published by Oxford University Press, Inc.
198 Madison Avenue, New York, New York 10016

www.oup.com

Oxford is a registered trademark of Oxford University Press

Library of Congress Cataloging-in-Publication Data
William Faulkner's Absalom, Absalom! : a casebook / edited by Fred
Hobson.
p. cm. — (Casebooks in criticism)
ISBN 0-19-515477-0; 0-19-515478-9 (pbk.)
1. Faulkner, William, 1897–1962. Absalom, Absalom! 2. Historical
fiction, American—History and criticism. 3. Plantation life in
literature. 4. Mississippi—In literature 5. Family in literature.
6. Race in literature. I. Hobson, Fred C., 1943– II. Series.
PS3511.A86 A775 2003
813'.52—dc21   2002013988

1 3 5 7 9 8 6 4 2

Printed in the United States of America
on acid-free paper

Acknowledgments

For invaluable assistance with this book, I wish to thank Bryan Giemza. I am indebted as well to William Andrews, Barbara Bennett, Frances Coombs, David Davis, George Lensing, John Lowe, Susan Marston, Lewis P. Simpson, Linda Wagner-Martin, Nina Wallace, and John Michael Walsh. Most of all, I thank the authors of the essays that appear in this collection; in several cases, they revised earlier essays to fit the length requirements of this volume.

Credits

Contents

The Signifyin' Monkey

William Faulkner's
Absalom, Absalom!

A CASEBOOK

Introduction

FRED HOBSON

❖ ❖ ❖

ONE HARDLY NEEDS TO MAKE a case for the promi-
nence of William Faulkner and his novel *Absalom, Absalom!* in
the American literary canon. Harold Bloom may not have spoken
for everyone—but he certainly did for many—when he wrote
in 1986, "By universal consent of critics and common readers,
Faulkner now is recognized as the strongest American novelist of
this century." As for *Absalom*, Cleanth Brooks, writing in 1963,
considered the work "the greatest of [Faulkner's] novels," and
Joseph Urgo, in *American Literature* in 1990, pronounced it Faulkner's
"greatest novel, his most complex and rewarding literary work."
Dirk Kuyk, Jr., in *Sutpen's Design* (1990) goes even further: not only
does *Absalom, Absalom!* "tower among" Faulkner's work, but "we
can now hear it described as the greatest American novel of the
century . . . joining *Moby Dick* and *Huckleberry Finn* at the pinnacle
of American fiction." Faulkner himself had a similar view. In January 1936, just as he was wrapping up the novel, he said to a
friend, "I think it's the best novel yet written by an American."[1]
   Not everyone, of course, would go as far as Kuyk, or as Faulk-

ner; among the author's own work, *The Sound and the Fury* would also get a few votes as his greatest. The two novels—*The Sound and the Fury* coming at the beginning (1929) of Faulkner's greatest creative period, *Absalom* at the end (1936) of that period—are closely linked. Not only are both tragedies nearly on the Greek scale—concerning the decline and fall of a notable family—but each has at its center young Quentin Compson who, carrying the weight of family and region, commits suicide in the first novel but is brought back by Faulkner—at a point less than a year before his death—to serve as primary narrator for the latter. Either novel, then, could be seen as Faulkner's masterpiece; I finally choose *Absalom, Absalom!* not only because of the richness of its story (of Thomas Sutpen and his attempt to create a dynasty), its tragic dimension, its prose, and its narrative complexity (*The Sound and the Fury* shares these, after all) but also because of its keen historical sense. *Absalom* is the Faulkner novel that (along with *Go Down, Moses*) deals most centrally with what C. Vann Woodward called "the burden of southern history"[2]—that is, the racial burden—and it is a work that paints, in many particulars, a realistic picture of antebellum life in the Deep South and explores the origins and the meaning of "aristocracy" in that region. In no other Faulkner novel, perhaps no American novel, are all elements of that critical triumvirate, race, class, and gender, explored so compellingly. For this reason, among others, historians and scholars in various disciplines, not just literary scholars, teach it in their undergraduate and graduate classes.

Absalom, Absalom! was written between 1934 and early 1936 during an unusually stressful period for Faulkner. In his late thirties, he found himself in financial straits (which necessitated periodic trips to Hollywood to make quick money by writing screenplays), an unstable marriage, and—in late 1935 and early 1936—an emotionally charged relationship with a young woman in Hollywood. During the latter stages of the novel's composition, Faulkner's younger brother Dean died in a plane crash; Faulkner felt responsible since he had bought the plane and paid for his brother's flying lessons. In addition, just before he began the novel he first called "The Dark House," his writing had not gone particularly well. Despite the publication between 1929 and 1932 of such novels as *The Sound and the Fury*, *As I Lay Dying*, and *Light in August* (all later to be hailed as classics), he had achieved neither financial nor widespread critical success. In the beginning, in 1934 and early 1935, he had a difficult time with *Absalom, Absalom!* as well: in the novel, which drew on earlier, shorter pieces of Faulkner's—stories in which one finds early versions of Sutpen and his daughter Judith and son Henry, as well as Charles Bon and Sutpen's poor white companion Wash Jones[3]—he had problems with tone, point of view, and devising a means for early twentieth-century narrators to know details of the life of a mid–nineteenth-century protagonist. Not until the early spring of 1935 did he hit his stride, and then he wrote in nine or ten months what became the final version of the novel. When it appeared in October 1936, however, it did not meet with the reception Faulkner had desired. Major reviews in the *Saturday Review* and the *New Yorker* were harsh, and other reviews were mixed. Random House issued fewer than ten thousand copies, and by early 1940 the novel was out of print. Its fate was dramatically different from that of another southern novel, also published in 1936, set in the same time period, and treating many of the same subjects, including the Civil War, the plantation South, and decline and fall—*Gone with the Wind.*

The great success of *Absalom, Absalom!* then—as would also be the case with Faulkner's other major work of the 1930s—came later, after Malcolm Cowley and other critics began to champion Faulkner in the late 1940s and particularly after Faulkner was awarded the Nobel Prize in 1950. Critics, scholars, and general readers came to appreciate the richness of a work that, in 1936, had been seen largely as a particularly harrowing specimen of southern Gothic or, in some circles, as a work of southern "social realism" to be placed alongside Erskine Caldwell's *Tobacco Road* and other novels chronicling multiple southern depravities and crimes against humanity. In his Yoknapatawpha novels, Faulkner was indeed a chronicler of the American South, particularly that part of it centered around his own "little postage stamp of native soil" (as he famously called it), and in those works he wrote—among other things—a kind of social history of the South from the early nineteenth century to the mid-twentieth. Just how accurate he was, historically if not always psychologically, in his portrait of Thomas Sutpen can be seen by comparing Sutpen to W. J. Cash's representative southern planter in Cash's classic work *The Mind of the South* (1941)—a raw, crude man who started with nothing except energy, determination, "innocence" (Cash's word as well as Faulkner's), and a capacity for hard work; who came into the upcountry and made his way on the frontier where shrewdness was more important than refinement (where refinement was, in fact, a liability); who acquired land and slaves, grew cotton, soon became wealthy, and eventually built a big house that some called a mansion. And he dreamed. Though uneducated and unacquainted with formal culture, he aped Tidewater manners, ways foreign to him, made himself an "aristocrat," and set out to found a dynasty. Such was Cash's "man at the center," and such was Faulkner's Sutpen—with the mythic proportions and the ruthlessness of Faulkner's character added to the mix.

Thus *Absalom, Absalom!* is a "southern" novel, but it is much more than that—it is, indeed, a novel about the American dream just as fully as *The Great Gatsby* is a novel about that dream. Like Fitzgerald, Faulkner created a character who refuses to be bound by background, by social class, by *time*—and in the end is, as is Gatsby, a victim of his own innocence. Like Hawthorne, Faulkner deals with the sins of the fathers (his own antebellum white southern ancestors filling the role of Hawthorne's seventeenth-century Puritan ancestors) and the burdens of the regional past, and he views that past with a mixture of love and hate, pride, shame, and guilt; like Hawthorne as well, he is fascinated with the head-centered man, the *abstracted* man, who is deficient in things of the heart. Like Melville in his portrait of Ahab, Faulkner creates in Sutpen a character who lives altogether by design, disregarding the aspirations, the dignity—the humanity—of others in his pursuit of that design. And, like any number of American writers, from Melville to Ellison and beyond, Faulkner in *Absalom, Absalom!* illustrates the subjectivity of history—making clear that one's understanding of what happened in the past depends largely on how it is told in the present.

Such themes suggest the richness and fullness of Faulkner's text and the varied directions one might take in approaching it—and I have not yet touched on the narrative complexity of the work, the multiple tellers of what is, among other things, a great detective story. Such richness explains why *Absalom* has attracted the attention of literally hundreds of critics and scholars in the past half century (for most of the critical attention began in the early 1950s, not in 1936 when the novel was published). Elisabeth Muhlenfeld noted in 1984 that "some three hundred critical essays and chapters in books" had been devoted to *Absalom*,[4] and without undertaking a precise current count, I can say with certainty that the number has now far more than doubled. The tenor of these essays and chapters reflects in great measure the direction of Faulkner criticism as a whole—not to mention a broader American and European literary criticism and scholarship—since the 1950s. Up until the 1970s, most of the work on *Absalom* was formalist, "New Critical," although, in their treatments of Faulkner, such leading scholars as Cleanth Brooks, Olga Vickery, Richard Poirier, and Michael Millgate were hardly so limited (i.e., to the text) in their approaches as that term might suggest. (Brooks was equally concerned with the texture of a place—"The Yoknapatawpha Country"—as his subtitle had it.) In 1975, John Irwin, in *Doubling and Incest/Repetition and Revenge*, took a psychoanalytic approach to *Absalom* and *The Sound and the Fury* in a work that has since become a classic of *Absalom* studies. In the mid-and late 1970s and early 1980s, other scholars—primary among them André Bleikasten, Donald Kartiganer, and, especially, John T. Matthews—incorporated contemporary critical theory into their work on *Absalom*, as have many other critics since then. The other prevailing approach to contemporary Faulkner studies—that is, placing Faulkner more fully in historical and cultural context, focusing more closely on issues of race, class, and gender—was anticipated by Eric Sundquist's *Faulkner: The House Divided* in 1983. Historical and cultural criticism has become perhaps the dominant approach in Faulkner studies since 1990.[5]

In this collection, I have brought together eight of the most insightful essays on *Absalom, Absalom!* as well as the closest thing to an interview Faulkner ever gave concerning the novel: his responses to students' questions at the University of Virginia and Washington and Lee University in 1957 and 1958, published in *Faulkner in the University* (1959). Choosing from hundreds of essays has not been easy, but I have tried to strike a balance between the "classics" and more recent essays and approaches. One of the essays I have selected, Brooks's "History and the Sense of the Tragic," comes from the 1960s; another, Irwin's "Repetition and Revenge," from the 1970s; two others are from the 1980s, and four from the 1990s. In so choosing, I have had to omit several notable early treatments—including those by Vickery, Millgate, Poirier, and James Guetti—as well as excellent treatments from the 1970s and 1980s, including those by Matthews, Kartiganer, and Bleikasten, in order to include (often) lesser known but equally stimulating essays from the 1990s by Minrose Gwin, Dirk Kuyk, Barbara Ladd, and Richard Godden.[6] (Another reason for choosing, in these cases, near-contemporary essays over older ones is that many of the older ones have been reprinted in other Faulkner collections published in the 1960s, 1970s, and 1980s.) I should add that all but two of the essays originated as chapters in books devoted to Faulkner; in several cases the chapters needed to be condensed for this collection. In one case (Irwin) the original book treatment had already been condensed; in four other cases— Sundquist, Thadious Davis, Gwin, and Godden—the authors undertook for this volume revisions and of their original treatments.

Cleanth Brooks's "History and the Sense of the Tragic" (from Brooks's 1963 study *William Faulkner: The Yoknapatawpha Country*) is one of several lengthy essays in which Brooks examines *Absalom, Absalom!* Here he sets forth many of the ideas we have come to accept about *Absalom*: that Thomas Sutpen's "innocence" is the moral innocence of modern man; that Sutpen lives altogether in the realm of abstraction; that Charles Bon, another stranger with a mysterious past, an octoroon wife, and a great insult in his youth, is Sutpen's "mirror image"; that Judith, "one of Faulkner's finest characters of endurance," is perhaps the most admirable Sutpen; and that the community functions nearly as a single character in its approach to Sutpen—first suspicious and hostile, then grudgingly accepting. The first part of Brooks's essay deals largely with characterization, the latter half with narrative technique, particularly Quentin's and Shreve's roles in telling the story. *Absalom, Absalom!* is a "wonderful detective story," Brooks writes, and most of all, the novel is "a persuasive commentary upon the thesis that much of 'history' is really a kind of imaginative construction."

John Irwin's psychoanalytic reading, "Repetition and Revenge" (condensed from Irwin's 1975 study, *Doubling and Incest/Repetition and Revenge*), takes up the subject of the relationship between narrator and story, particularly Quentin and the Henry–Judith–Charles Bon triangle. Perhaps the single most widely cited treatment of *Absalom*, Irwin's essay focuses on Quentin and his protective—and incestuous—love for his sister Caddy (as revealed in *The Sound and the Fury*), which is mirrored by Henry Sutpen's love for and protectiveness toward his sister Judith, as well as his strong and conflicted feelings for his half brother Charles Bon. Irwin also treats Sutpen's "revenge against time," the will's "titanic, foredoomed struggle to repeat the past and alter it," and the Nietzschean connection of the revenge against time with "the envy that a son feels for his father." Drawing on both Freud and Nietzsche, Irwin examines Sutpen's relationship both with his own father and with the surrogate father from whose mansion door he was turned away, as well as Quentin's tortured relationship—and narrative competition—with his father.

Thadious Davis's "The Signifying Abstraction: Reading 'The Negro' in *Absalom, Absalom!*" is an updated version of the treatment in her insightful 1983 study, *Faulkner's "Negro": Art and the Southern Context*. Focusing on "the Negro [as] an abstract force confounding southern life both past and present even while, paradoxically, stimulating much of [southern] life and art," Davis contends that "the Negro"—primarily "a social rather than a racial concept"— "shapes, motivates, and determines Sutpen's design from the beginning." In one of the finest treatments of blackness in *Absalom*, she holds that the "metaphorical presence of the enigmatic 'Negro' pervades the entire novel." From her discussion of the black house servant (the "monkey nigger") who turns away Sutpen at the front door to Rosa Coldfield's construction of Sutpen's original band of "wild niggers" to the "illusive, disturbing" Jim Bond as "metaphor perhaps for the unknowable, or the contradictions, inherent in southern life, and in life generally," Davis is interested in "Negro" not so much as reality as perception: what "the Negro" represents to the white South. She includes in her discussion the fullest treatment of Sutpen's neglected (by critics as well as by Sutpen) "other" child, Clytie, offspring of his liaison with one of his slaves and, along with Judith, eventual keeper of the Sutpen house.

With her successful attempt to read race in Faulkner, Davis moves in the direction in which Eric Sundquist, in "*Absalom, Absalom!* and the House Divided," turns even more emphatically in the same year, 1983. Focusing largely on race and miscegenation, as well as the North-South conflict of the mid–nineteenth century, Sundquist examines *Absalom* in relation to Lincoln, Mary Chesnut, Melville, and proslavery apologists, and brings into his discussion historians such as Eugene Genovese and Winthrop Jordan and students of the southern mind such as W. J. Cash. In many ways, as André Bleikasten has argued in an insightful assessment of Faulkner scholarship, Sundquist's treatment—with his attention to placing *Absalom, Absalom!* and other novels in a larger historical, social, and cultural context—has pointed the way in Faulkner studies over the past two decades. Sundquist, he writes, was "the first critic to reassess Faulkner's achievement and to reorder the Faulkner canon according to extraliterary criteria. Faulkner's importance, [Sundquist] argued, is not to be sought in his contribution to the art of the novel but in the seriousness with which he addresses social and historical themes"; "nearly all recent Faulkner criticism starts from similar premises"—that is, social and cultural issues. In many respects I agree with Bleikasten's assessment (although I believe he overstates the shift in direction), but my estimate of the value of that turn in Faulkner studies is different from his. For the most part, he disapproves, seeing a "regression to a naively realistic conception of literature," in short, a movement "from poetics to mimetics."[7] It seems to me, however, that Sundquist and numerous other critics in the two decades since he published *Faulkner: The House Divided* view

Faulkner not only in his own time and place but in our own—
not solely in Mississippi in the early twentieth century but rather
in the larger world of ideas, social and political currents, and
unresolved issues of race and class, which Faulkner also inhabited.
In Sundquist's condensed version of his 1983 treatment of *Absalom*,
he sees Faulkner's work in the larger dimension of American civil
discord and racial politics.

Minrose Gwin's "The Silencing of Rosa Coldfield"—condensed
from her chapter on *Absalom* in her 1990 study, *The Feminine and
Faulkner*—is both informed by contemporary critical theory (in
fact, is probably the most theoretical essay in this collection) and
engaged with social issues. Gwin's feminist reading, which focuses
on Faulkner's early narrator, the ridiculed and finally "silenced"
Rosa Coldfield, draws not only on such feminist scholars as Hélène Cixous and Mary Jacobus but also, to a lesser extent, on
Freud, Derrida, and Lacan. "The bisexual space of the narrative,"
Gwin writes, is "shaped by the struggle between the male desire
(Quentin's, Mr. Compson's, Shreve's) to make Rosa disappear (or
at least to make her shut up) and *her* narrative desire to speak
madness, to say the feminine difference within a masculinist culture, to tell a story of her own." Since Rosa "threatens and disrupts southern white patriarchy," Gwin holds, "it is no surprise
that the novel's males are often ambushing her text, marginalizing and diminishing it." Thus, Quentin's father's "masculinist
text" challenges Rosa's for narrative authority; he, Quentin's
grandfather, Sutpen, Shreve, and Quentin himself speak "the
grand narrative of white patriarchy." They all, quite literally,
speak the same language, and they judge Rosa's narrative "illegitimate, unreadable, hysterical." But Rosa "will not shut up and
she will not stay put": she speaks "the madness of the Father's
House."

If Gwin recasts Rosa Coldfield—redeems her from the charges
of many earlier critics, both male and female, that Rosa is a bitter,
unreliable narrator whose judgments are completely untrustwor-
thy—Dirk Kuyk, in "Sutpen's Design," gives us an even more
revisionist reading of Thomas Sutpen. In an essay from his 1990
book of the same title, Kuyk challenges the traditional view (in-

deed, a view never before seriously disputed) that Sutpen, in response to being turned away from the front door of a Tidewater mansion as a child, vows to do all he can to *become* the planter who will then be in a position to turn away others from the front door. The accepted view, thus, has been that Sutpen, in the deepest sense, is the ultimate conformist: rather than contesting the system that rejected him, he would succeed within that system. To the contrary, Kuyk contends—proposing a thesis that is intriguing, if arguable—that Sutpen, far from wanting to model himself after the Virginia aristocrat from whose house he was turned away, desired to own a plantation and create a dynasty "so that he could turn it against dynastic society itself," could "take in" the poor boy who knocked at his door. His is a reading that Kuyk links in some measure to the decade of the 1930s in which the novel was written, a decade in which any number of poor boys—and men and women—were knocking on doors, front and back. In his discussion, Kuyk anticipates and contests nearly every possible objection to his thesis (e.g., why did not Sutpen, then, take in Charles Bon?) and changes not precisely the direction of *Absalom* scholarship but at least the ways in which its protagonist (and thus its author) might be viewed.

Barbara Ladd's 1994 *American Literature* article, " 'The Direction of the Howling': Nationalism and the Color Line," also expands the horizons of *Absalom* scholarship. In one of the finest recent treatments of the work, Ladd places the novel—and the idea of the octoroon in particular—in historical and cultural context: she accomplishes this in part by examining "racial classification in the creole Deep South." Such an approach helps the reader to understand more fully the mysterious figure of Charles Bon, a native of Haiti (or so the narrators believe) who had taken a mixed-blood wife in New Orleans before he arrives in racially—and morally—rigid northern Mississippi. Another contribution of Ladd's essay is that it anticipates the direction of much future Faulkner scholarship (as well as southern literary scholarship in a more general sense) by seeing Faulkner and Deep South writing not so much in relation to "American" (i.e., U.S.) literature but rather in relation to the plantation economy and culture of the

Caribbean with which the Deep South has a great deal in common—a colonial, then a postcolonial, culture, as much French
and Spanish as English, looking toward Haiti as much as Virginia.

Richard Godden, in his 1994 article, *"Absalom, Absalom!*
Haiti, and Labor History"* (which became part of Godden's 1997 book,
Fictions of Labor: William Faulkner and the South's Long Revolution), turns to
the Caribbean as well, but for a somewhat different reason. He
points in the beginning to a historical "error" in *Absalom*: Faulkner
portrays Sutpen, in the third decade of the nineteenth century,
as the overseer of a plantation in Haiti who puts down a slave
uprising—when, in fact, slavery had been abolished in Haiti decades earlier, at the founding of the independent republic of Haiti.
But Godden goes on to contend that this was not an "error" after
all, that Faulkner knew full well that slavery had been abolished
by the 1820s but that he also knew that in the antebellum South,
Haiti had been "synonymous with revolution," with slave uprisings, since the 1791 San Domingo revolt and that it was very
much to his purpose to use Haiti and the Haitian slaves Sutpen
brings with him to suggest the wildness and the potential for
revolution in the plantation South. From here, Godden turns to
relations between masters and slaves, to Sutpen's boyhood awakening to the differences between master and worker. Sutpen, indeed, comes to see all humans (slaves, but also free men and
women, including Charles Bon) as "real property" or, in another
sense, as one more "crop that could be taken to market." His
essay is, quite literally, a study of labor relations, and as Godden
proceeds he focuses as much on class as on race.

After these eight critics, over a span of nearly four decades,
investigate *Absalom*, Faulkner has his own say, in comments to
students at the University of Virginia (and, on one occasion,
Washington and Lee University) in the late 1950s. What strikes
the reader in these remarks—in which Faulkner addresses narrative technique, the figures of Sutpen and Quentin, and several
other subjects—is that the author himself, viewing his novel
nearly a quarter century after he wrote it, seems to be another
interested but at times confused reader of his own text. When
asked whether Charles Bon ever had suspicions of who his father

was, Faulkner answered, "I think he knew. I don't know whether he—his mother probably told him." Or whether Bon loved Judith: "I think he loved her." Or "what sort of deal" was made between Sutpen and Goodhue Coldfield before Sutpen's marriage to Ellen: "I don't remember. That book is so long ago to me." Asked when, in his composition of the novel, he laid aside *Absalom*, not knowing how to proceed, he answered, "I can't say just where it was that I had to put it down." And so on. At other times— for example, in his statement that, in the latter stages of the novel, Shreve holds the novel "to something of reality"—Faulkner seems to be altogether wrong. But if, at times, Faulkner causes us to heed the adage "trust the tale, not the teller," at other times he provides us with valuable information about the writing of his novel and what he intended it to say.

In his remarks at the University of Virginia, Faulkner picks up on a suggestion from a student questioner that, for the four primary narrators in *Absalom*, understanding Thomas Sutpen is "more or less a case of thirteen ways of looking at a blackbird with none of them right." In this collection, we have eight ways of looking at a blackbird—nine, if we include Faulkner's own— and if space permitted we could open up still other lines of vision. But, as Faulkner added, "The truth, I would like to think, comes out, that when the reader has read all these thirteen different ways of looking at the blackbird, the reader has his own fourteenth image of the blackbird which I would like to think is the truth." The reader of the novel, then, is the fifth narrator of Sutpen's story, the tenth interpreter of this collection, the final viewer of the blackbird.

Notes

1. Harold Bloom, introduction to *William Faulkner*, ed. Harold Bloom (New York: Chelsea House, 1986), 1; Cleanth Brooks, *William Faulkner: The Yoknapatawpha Country* (New Haven, Conn.: Yale University Press, 1963), 295; Joseph Urgo, "*Absalom, Absalom!* The Movie," *American Literature* 62 (March 1990): 56; Dirk Kuyk, Jr., *Sutpen's Design: Interpreting Faulkner's Absalom, Absalom!* (Charlottesville: University Press of Virginia, 1990), 2; and Faulkner,

quoted in Joseph Blotner, *Faulkner: A Biography* (New York: Random House, 1974), 927.

2. C. Vann Woodward, *The Burden of Southern History* (New York: Viking, 1960).

3. For an excellent examination of the earlier work on which Faulkner drew in *Absalom, Absalom!* see Elisabeth Muhlenfeld's introduction to *William Faulkner's "Absalom, Absalom!" A Critical Casebook* (New York: Garland, 1984), xv–xxiv.

4. Ibid., ix.

5. For valuable discussions of recent directions in Faulkner criticism, see Donald M. Kartiganer, "In Place of an Introduction: Reading Faulkner," in *Faulkner at 100: Retrospect and Prospect*, ed. Donald M. Kartiganer and Ann J. Abadie (Jackson: University Press of Mississippi, 2000), xii–xxvi; and André Bleikasten, "Faulkner in the Singular," also in *Faulkner at 100*, 204–18.

6. Several other excellent treatments of *Absalom* from the 1970s and 1980s—by Carolyn Porter, David Krause, Myra Jehlen, François Pitavy, Peter Brooks, Elisabeth Muhlenfeld, Linda Kauffman, Warwick Wadlington, and Wesley Morris—were also difficult to leave out, as were, from the 1990s, treatments by Doreen Fowler and Karl Zender. See suggested reading.

7. Bleikasten, "Faulkner in the Singular," 206–7.

History and the Sense of the Tragic

CLEANTH BROOKS

◆　◆　◆

*A*BSALOM, *ABSALOM!* in my opinion the greatest of Faulkner's novels, is probably the least well understood of all of
his books. The property of a great work, as T. S. Eliot remarked
long ago, is to communicate before it is understood, and *Absalom,
Absalom!* passes this test triumphantly. It has meant something
very powerful and important to all sorts of people, and who is
to say that, under the circumstances, this something was not the
thing to be said to that particular reader? To the young Frenchman who had served in the *maquis*, to the young writer in New
York interested in problems of technique, a little weary from
having given his days and nights to the prose of Henry James, to
the Shrevlin McCannons all over Canada and the United States
with their myths of the South compounded out of *Uncle Tom's
Cabin* and *Strange Fruit*—to all of these, *Absalom, Absalom!* had something to give. That is important, and I do not mean to disparage
it. Yet the book has its own rights, as it were, and in proportion
as we admire it, we shall want to see not merely what we can
make of it but what it makes of itself. In any case, the book is

more than a bottle of Gothic sauce to be used to spice up our own preconceptions about the history of American society.

Harvey Breit's sympathetic introduction to the Modern Library edition provides a useful—because it is not an extreme—instance of the typical misreading that I have in mind. Breit writes:

> It is a terrible Gothic sequence of events, a brooding, tragic fable. . . . Was it the "design" that had devoured Sutpen and prevented him from avowing the very thing that would have saved the design? Was it something in the South itself, in its social, political, moral, economic origins that was responsible for Sutpen and for all the subsequent tragedy? Quentin can make no judgment: Sutpen himself had possessed courage and innocence, and the same land had nourished men and women who had delicacy of feeling and capacity for love and gifts for life.

These are questions which the typical reader asks. Shreve, the outsider, implies them. But it is significant that Quentin does not ask them. The questions are begged by the very way in which they are asked, for, put in this way, the questions undercut the problem of tragedy (which is the problem that obsesses Quentin). They imply that there is a social "solution." And they misread Sutpen's character in relation to his society and in relation to himself.

It is the quality of Sutpen's innocence that we must understand if we are to understand the meaning of his tragedy, and if we confuse it with innocence as we ordinarily use the term or with even the typical American "innocence" possessed by, say, one of Henry James's young heiresses as she goes to confront the corruption of Europe, we shall remain in the dark. Sutpen will be for us, as he was for Miss Rosa, simply the "demon"—or, since we lack the justification of Miss Rosa's experience of personal horror, we shall simply appropriate the term from her as Shreve, in his half-awed, half-amused fashion, does.

Faulkner has been very careful to define Sutpen's innocence for us. "Sutpen's trouble," Quentin's grandfather observed, "was innocence" (p. 220). And some pages later, Mr. Compson elaborates the point: "He believed that all that was necessary was courage and shrewdness and the one he knew he had and the other he believed he could learn if it were to be taught" (p. 244). It is this innocence about the nature of reality that persists, for Sutpen "believed that the ingredients of morality were like the ingredients of pie or cake and once you had measured them and balanced them and mixed them and put them into the oven it was all finished and nothing but pie or cake could come out" (p. 263). That is why Sutpen can ask Quentin's grandfather, in his innocence, not "Where did I do wrong" but "Where did I make the mistake . . . what did I do or misdo . . . whom or what injure by it to the extent which this would indicate? I had a design. To accomplish it I should require money, a house, a plantation, slaves, a family—incidentally of course, a wife. I set out to acquire these, asking no favor of any man" (p. 263).

This is an "innocence" with which most of us today ought to be acquainted. It is par excellence the innocence of modern man, though it has not, to be sure, been confined to modern times. One can find more than a trace of it in Sophocles' Oedipus, and it has its analogies with the rather brittle rationalism of Macbeth, though Macbeth tried to learn this innocence by acts of the will and proved to be a less than satisfactory pupil. But innocence of this sort can properly be claimed as a special characteristic of modern man, and one can claim further that it flourishes particularly in a secularized society.

The society into which Sutpen rides in 1833 is not a secularized society. That is not to say that the people are necessarily "good." They have their selfishness and cruelty and their snobbery, as men have always had them. Once Sutpen has acquired enough wealth and displayed enough force, the people of the community are willing to accept him. But they do not live by his code, nor do they share his innocent disregard of accepted values. Indeed, from the beginning they regard him with deep suspicion and some consternation. These suspicions are gradually mollified; there is a kind of acceptance; but as Quentin tells Shreve, Sutpen had only one friend, Quentin's grandfather, General Compson, and this in spite of the fact that the society of the lower South in the nineteenth century was rather fluid and that class lines were flexible. Men did rise in one generation from log cabins to great landed estates. But the past was important, blood was important, and southern society thought of itself as traditional.

That Sutpen does remain outside the community comes out in all sorts of little ways. Mr. Compson describes his "florid, swaggering gesture" with the parenthetical remark: "yes, he was underbred. It showed like this always, your grandfather said, in all his formal contacts with people" (p. 46). And Mr. Compson goes on to say that it was as if John L. Sullivan "having taught himself painfully and tediously to do the schottische, having drilled himself and drilled himself in secret . . . now believed it no longer necessary to count the music's beat, say." Yet though Sutpen's manners have been learned painfully, Sutpen has complete confidence in them: "He may have believed that your grandfather or Judge Benbow might have done it a little more effortlessly than he, but he would not have believed that anyone could have beat him in knowing when to do it and how" (p. 46).

Mr. Compson is not overrating the possession of mere manners. More is involved than Miss Rosa's opinion that Sutpen was no gentleman. For Sutpen's manners indicate his abstract approach to the whole matter of living. Sutpen would seize upon "the traditional" as a pure abstraction—which, of course, is to deny its very meaning. For him the tradition is not a way of life handed down or transmitted from the community, past and present, to the individual nurtured by it. It is an assortment of things to be possessed, not a manner of living that embodies certain values and determines men's conduct. The fetish objects are to be gained by sheer ruthless efficiency. (Sutpen even refers to "my schedule.") Thorstein Veblen would have understood Sutpen's relation to traditional culture. Sutpen is on all fours with the robber baron of the Gilded Age building a fake Renaissance palace on the banks of the Hudson. The New York robber baron's acquiring a box at the opera did not usually spring from a love of music, and one is tempted to say that Sutpen's unwillingness to acknowledge Charles Bon as his son does not spring from any particular racial feeling. Indeed, Sutpen's whole attitude toward the Negro has to be reinspected if we are to understand his relation to the southern community into which he comes.

It would seem that the prevailing relation between the races in Jefferson is simply one more of the culture traits which Sutpen takes from the plantation community into which he has come as a boy out of the mountains of western Virginia. Sutpen takes over the color bar almost without personal feeling. His attitude toward the Negro is further clarified by his attitude toward his other part-Negro child, Clytie. Mr. Compson once casually lets fall the remark that Sutpen's other children "Henry and Judith had grown up with a negro half sister of their own" (p. 109). The context of Mr. Compson's remarks makes it perfectly plain that Henry and Judith were well aware that Clytie was indeed their half sister, and that Clytie was allowed to grow up in the house with them. This fact in itself suggests a lack of the usual southern feeling about Negroes. Miss Rosa is much more typically southern when she tells Quentin, with evident distaste, that Clytie and Judith sometimes slept in the same bed.

After Sutpen has returned from the war, Clytie sits in the same room with Judith, Rosa, and Sutpen and listens each evening to the sound of Sutpen's voice. When Sutpen proposes to Rosa, he begins, " 'Judith, you and Clytie—' and ceased, still entering, then said, 'No, never mind. Rosa will not mind if you both hear it too, since we are short for time' " (p. 164). Clytie is accepted naturally as part of the "we." She can be so accepted because acceptance on this level does not imperil Sutpen's "design." But acceptance of Charles Bon, in Sutpen's opinion, would. For Sutpen, the matter is really as simple as that. He does not hate his first wife nor feel repugnance for her child. He does not hate just as he does not love. His passion is totally committed to the design. Not even his own flesh and blood are allowed to distract him from that. As for slavery, Sutpen does not confine himself to black chattel slavery. He ruthlessly bends anyone whom he can to his will. The white French architect whom he brings into

Yoknapatawpha County to build his house is as much a slave as
any of his black servants: Sutpen hunts him down with dogs
when he tries to escape.

The trait that most decisively sets Sutpen apart from his neighbors in this matter of race is his fighting with his slaves. Sutpen
is accustomed to stripping to the waist and fighting it out with
one of his slaves, not with rancor, one supposes, and not at all
to punish the slave but simply to keep fit—to prove to himself
and incidentally to his slaves that he is the better man. Some of
Sutpen's white neighbors come to watch the fights as they might
come to watch a cockfight. But it is significant that they come
as to something extraordinary, a show, an odd spectacle; they
would not think of fighting with their own slaves. To Miss Rosa,
Sutpen's sister-in-law, the ultimate horror is that Sutpen not only
arranges the show but that he enters the ring himself and fights
with no holds barred—not even eye gouging.

Sutpen is not without morality or a certain morality of a certain code of honor. He is, according to his own lights, a just man.
As he told Quentin's grandfather with reference to his rejection
of his first wife:

> Suffice that I . . . accepted [my wife] in good faith, with no res-
> ervations about myself, and I expected as much from [her par-
> ents]. I did not [demand credentials], as one of my obscure
> origin might have been expected to do. . . . I accepted them at
> their own valuation while insisting on my part upon explaining
> fully about myself and my progenitors: yet they deliberately
> withheld from me one fact which I have reason to know they
> were aware would have caused me to decline the entire matter.
> (p. 264)

But Sutpen, as he tells General Compson, "made no attempt to
keep . . . that [property] which I might consider myself to have
earned at the risk of my life . . . but on the contrary I declined
and resigned all right and claim to this in order that I might
repair whatever injustice I might be considered to have done [in
abandoning my wife and child] by so providing for" them.

Moreover, Sutpen is careful to say nothing in disparagement of his first wife. Quentin's grandfather comments upon "that morality which would not permit him to malign or traduce the memory of his first wife, or at least the memory of the marriage even though he felt that he had been tricked by it" (p. 272). It is Sutpen's innocence to think that justice is enough—that there is no claim that cannot be satisfied by sufficient monetary payment. Quentin imagines his grandfather exclaiming to Sutpen: "What kind of abysmal and purblind innocence would that have been which someone told you to call virginity? what conscience to trade with which would have warranted you in the belief that you could have bought immunity from her for no other coin but justice?" (p. 265).

Sutpen thinks of himself as strictly just, and he submits all of his faculties almost selflessly to the achievement of his design. His attitude toward his second wife conforms perfectly to this. Why does he choose her? For choose he does: he is not chosen—that is, involved with her through passion. The choice is calculated quite cold-bloodedly (if, to our minds, naively and innocently). Ellen Coldfield is not the daughter of a planter. She does not possess great social prestige or beauty, and she does not inherit wealth. But as the daughter of a steward in the Methodist church, she possesses in high degree the thing that Sutpen most obviously lacks—respectability. Mr. Compson sees the point very clearly. He describes Mr. Coldfield as "a man with a name for absolute and undeviating and even Puritan uprightness in a country and time of lawless opportunity, who neither drank nor gambled nor even hunted" (p. 43). For Sutpen, respectability is an abstraction like morality: you measure out so many cups of concentrated respectability to sweeten so many measures of disrespectability—"like the ingredients of pie or cake."

The choice of a father-in-law is in fact just as symbolically right: the two men resemble each other, for all the appearance of antithetical differences. Mr. Coldfield is as definitely set off from the community as is Sutpen. With the coming of the Civil War, this rift widens to an absolute break. Mr. Coldfield denounces secession, closes his store, and finally nails himself up in the attic of his house, where he spends the last three years of his life. No more than Sutpen is he a coward: like Sutpen, too, his scheme of human conduct is abstract and mechanical. "Doubtless the only pleasure which he had ever had . . . was in [his money's] representation of a balance in whatever spiritual counting-house he believed would some day pay his sight drafts on self-denial and fortitude" (p. 84).

This last is Mr. Compson's surmise, but I see no reason to question it or to quarrel with the motive that Mr. Compson assigns for Coldfield's objection to the Civil War: "not so much to the idea of pouring out human blood and life, but at the idea of waste: of wearing out and eating up and shooting away material in any cause whatever" (p. 83). Mr. Coldfield is glad when he sees the country that he hates obviously drifting into a fatal war, for he regards the inevitable defeat of the South as the price it will pay for having erected its economic edifice "not on the rock of stern morality but on the shifting sands of opportunism and moral brigandage" (p. 260).

Some critics have been so unwary as to assume that this view of the Civil War is one that the author would enjoin upon the reader, but William Faulkner is neither so much of a Puritan nor so much of a materialist as is Mr. Coldfield. The truth of the matter is that Mr. Coldfield's morality is simply Sutpen's turned inside out. Faulkner may or may not have read Tawney's *Religion and the Rise of Capitalism*, but on the evidence of *Absalom, Absalom!* he would certainly have understood it.

Sutpen is further defined by his son Charles Bon. Bon is a mirror image, a reversed shadow of his father. Like his father, he suddenly appears out of nowhere as a man of mystery: "a personage who in the remote Mississippi of that time must have appeared almost phoenix-like, fullsprung from no childhood, born of no woman and impervious to time" (p. 74). Like his father, Bon has an octoroon "wife," whom he is prepared to repudiate along with his child by her. Like his father, he stands beyond good and evil. But Bon is Byronic, rather than a go-getter; spent, rather than full of pushing vitality; sophisticated, rather than confidently naïve.

Sutpen is the secularized Puritan; Bon is the lapsed Roman Catholic. Whereas Sutpen is filled with a fresh and powerful energy, Bon is world-weary and tired. Bon is a fatalist, but Sutpen believes in sheer will: "anyone could look at him and say, *Given the occasion and the need, this man can and will do anything*" (p. 46). Bon possesses too much knowledge; Sutpen on the other hand is "innocent." The one has gone beyond the distinction between good and evil; the other has scarcely arrived at that distinction. The father and the son define the extremes of the human world: one aberration corresponds to—and eventually destroys—the other. The reader is inclined to view Bon with sympathy as a person bravely wronged, and he probably agrees with Quentin's interpretation of Bon's character: that Bon finally put aside all ideas of revenge and asked for nothing more than a single hint of recognition of his sonship. Faulkner has certainly treated Bon with full dramatic sympathy, as he has Sutpen, for that matter. But our sympathy ought not to obscure for us Bon's resemblances to his father, or the complexity of his character. Unless we care to go beyond Quentin and Shreve in speculation, Charles Bon displays toward his octoroon mistress and their son something of the cool aloofness that his father displays toward him. If he is the instrument by which Sutpen's design is wrecked, his own irresponsibility (or at the least, his lack of concern for his own child) wrecks his child's life. We shall have to look to Judith to find responsible action and a real counter to Sutpen's ruthlessness.

These other children of Sutpen—Judith and Henry—reflect further light upon the character of Sutpen, upon his virtues, and upon his prime defect. They represent a mixture of the qualities of Sutpen and Coldfield. Judith, it is made plain, has more of the confidence and boldness of her father; Henry, more of the conventionality and the scruples of his maternal grandfather. It is the young Henry who vomits at the sight of his father stripped to the waist in the ring with the black slave. Judith watches calmly. And it is Judith who urges the coachman to race the coach on the way to church.

Henry is, of the two, the more vulnerable. After Sutpen has forbidden marriage between Bon and Judith and during the long period in which Henry remains self-exiled with his friend Bon, he is the one tested to the limit by his father's puzzling silence and by his friend's fatalistic passivity. But he has some of his father's courage, and he has what his father does not have: love. At the last moment he kills though he kills what he loves and apparently for love. It is the truly tragic dilemma. Faulkner has not chosen to put Henry's story in the forefront of the novel, but he has not needed to do so. For the sensitive reader the various baffles through which that act of decision reaches us do not muffle but, through their resonance, magnify the decisive act.

Henry's later course is, again, only implied. We know that in the end—his last four years—he reverted to the course of action of his grandfather Coldfield and shut himself up in the house. But there is a difference. This is no act of abstract defiance and hate. Henry has assumed responsibility, has acted, has been willing to abide the consequences of that action, and now, forty years later, has come home to die.

If it is too much to call Henry's course of action renunciation and expiation, there is full justification for calling Judith's action just that. Judith has much of her father in her, but she is a woman, and she also has love. As Mr. Compson conjectures:

> And Judith: how else to explain her but this way? Surely Bon could not have corrupted her to fatalism in twelve days. . . . No: anything but a fatalist, who was the Sutpen with the ruthless Sutpen code of taking what it wanted provided it were strong enough. . . . [Judith said] *I love, I will accept no substitute; something has happened between him and my father; if my father was right, I will never see him again, if wrong he will come or send for me; if happy I can be I will, if suffer I must I can.* (p. 121)

It is Judith who invites Charles Bon's octoroon mistress to visit Bon's grave. It is Judith who, on his mother's death, sends to New Orleans for Bon's son and tries to rear him. Some years later she also tries to free him (as Quentin conjectures) by promising to take care of his Negro wife and child if he will go to the North to pass as white, and Quentin imagines her saying to him: "Call me Aunt Judith, Charles" (p. 208). But Quentin's conjectures aside, we know that Judith did take him into the house when he was stricken with yellow fever and that she died nursing him. The acknowledgment of blood kinship is made; Sutpen's design is repudiated; the boy, even though he has the "taint" of Negro blood, is not turned away from the door.

Both Henry's action, the violent turning away from the door with a bullet, and Judith's, the holding open the door not merely to Bon, her fiancé, but literally to his part-Negro son, are human actions, as Sutpen's actions are not. Both involve renunciation, and both are motivated by love. The suffering of Henry and Judith is not meaningless, and their very capacity for suffering marks them as having transcended their father's radical and disabling defect.

Faulkner has not put the contrast between the children and their father explicitly nor with quite this emphasis. In the first place, it is Sutpen's story that he is telling (or rather, it is Sutpen's story that Quentin and Shreve are trying to recreate). The stories of Judith and, particularly, Henry are dealt with only obliquely. But the Judith, who, in the hard and poverty-stricken years after the war, learns to plow like a man and who collects the dimes and quarters in the rusty can to pay for the headstone for Charles Bon's grave and who asks Bon's son to call her Aunt Judith is a very different person from the dreamy and willful girl to whom Henry introduced Bon at Sutpen's Hundred. And on the night when Quentin and Miss Rosa break into the decaying mansion and find Henry, who has come home to die, what looks out from Henry's eyes is not "innocence." Faulkner does not name it, but he does dramatize for us Quentin's reaction to it. At the least, it is knowledge, a fearful knowledge bought with heroic suffering.

One must not alter the focus of the novel by making wisdom won through suffering the issue. But the consequences entailed upon Judith and Henry have to be mentioned if only to discourage a glib Gothicizing of the novel or forcing its meaning into an overshallow sociological interpretation.

Miss Rosa feels that the Coldfields are all cursed, and certainly the impact of Sutpen upon her personally is damning: she remains rigid with horror and hate for forty-three years. But it is Miss Rosa only who is damned. Judith is not damned, nor am I sure that Henry is. Judith and Henry are not caught in an uncomprehending stasis. There is development: they grow and learn at however terrible a price. Uncle Ike in "The Bear" also inherits a curse: an ancestral crime that, for him at least, involves the necessity for renunciation and expiation. I cannot see that the "curse" inherited by Judith and Henry is essentially different in nature or that the general moral pattern in *Absalom, Absalom!* differs radically from that in "The Bear."

Sutpen, as has been pointed out, never learns anything; he remains innocent to the end. As Quentin sees the character: when Charles Bon first comes to his door, Sutpen does not call it "retribution, no sins of the father come home to roost; not even calling it bad luck, but just a mistake . . . just an old mistake in fact which a man of courage and shrewdness . . . could still combat if he could only find out what the mistake had been" (p. 267). I have remarked that Sutpen's innocence is peculiarly the innocence of modern man. For like modern man, Sutpen does not believe in Jehovah. He does not believe in the goddess Tyche. He is not the victim of bad luck. He has simply made a "mistake." He "had been too successful," Mr. Compson tells Quentin; his "was that solitude of contempt and distrust which success brings to him who gained it because he was strong instead of merely lucky" (p. 103).

Marshall McLuhan has somewhere pointed out that the more special feats of James Fenimore Cooper's woodsmen are always attributed to their skill, but those of William Gilmore Simms's woodsmen, to their luck. On this perhaps whimsical test of the sectional character, Sutpen turns out to be a Yankee, not a southerner at all. At any rate, Sutpen resembles the modern American, whose character, as Arthur M. Schlesinger has put it, "is bottomed on the profound conviction that nothing in the world is beyond [his] power to accomplish."[1] Sutpen is a "planner" who works by blueprint and on a schedule. He is rationalistic and scientific, not traditional, not religious, not even superstitious.

We must be prepared to take such traits into account if we attempt to read the story of Sutpen's fall as a myth of the fall of the Old South. Unless we are content with some rather rough and ready analogies, the story of the fall of the house of Sutpen may prove less than parallel. The fall of the house of Compson as depicted in *The Sound and the Fury* is also sometimes regarded as a kind of exemplum of the fall of the old aristocratic order in the South, and perhaps in some sense it is. But the breakups of these two families come from very different causes, and if we wish to use them to point a moral or illustrate a bit of social history, surely they point to different morals and illustrate different histories. Mr. Compson, whose father, General Compson, regarded Sutpen as a "little underbred," has failed through a kind of overrefinement. He has lost his grip on himself; he has ceased finally to believe in the values of the inherited tradition. He is a fatalist and something of an easy cynic. His vices are diametrically opposed to those of Thomas Sutpen, and so are his virtues.

One could even argue that Faulkner's most pertinent account of the fall of the Old South is set forth in his story of the rise of the Snopes clan. The latter-day Compsons, Sartorises, and Benbows lack the requisite resolution and toughness to cope with the conditions of the modern world. The Snopeses, therefore, because they recognize no values but self-interest and have unlimited vitality, threaten to take over the modern South. But the story of Flem Snopes is a kind of success story, not a tragedy; and if Snopesism is destroying the older aristocracy, it is not Snopesism that destroys Sutpen. Indeed, Sutpen is at some points more nearly allied to Flem than he is to the Compsons and the Sartorises. Like Flem, he is a new man with no concern for the past and has a boundless energy with which to carry out his aggressive plans.

Yet to couple Sutpen with Flem calls for an immediate qualification. Granting that both men subsist outside the community and in one way or another prey upon the community, Sutpen is by contrast a heroic and tragic figure. He achieves a kind of grandeur. Even the obsessed Miss Rosa sees him as great, not as petty and sordid. His innocence resembles that of Oedipus (who, like

him, had been corrupted by success and who put his confidence
in his own shrewdness). His courage resembles that of Macbeth,
and like Macbeth he is "resolute to try the last." Perhaps the
most praiseworthy aspect of Faulkner is his ability to create a
character of heroic proportions and to invest his downfall with
something like tragic dignity. The feat is, in our times, sufficiently
rare.

Faulkner's concern with innocence runs through all of his
novels. One of General Compson's impressions of Sutpen is that
he spoke "with that frank innocence which we call 'of a child'
except that a human child is the only living creature that is never
either frank or innocent" (p. 246). Nor, as we have seen, are Faulkner's women innocent. The only people in Faulkner who are
"innocent" are adult males, and their innocence amounts finally
to a trust in rationality—an overweening confidence that plans
work out, that life is simpler than it is.

But though Faulkner criticizes rationalism, he never glorifies
irrationality. Even Uncle Isaac in "The Bear" does not merely
accept nature, content to contemplate its richness and perennial
vitality. He does not argue that because the spoliation of the
wilderness is a rape that brings its own curse, man ought to cut
no trees. He does not believe that it is possible for man to go
back to Adam's existence in the happy garden. Uncle Isaac acts;
he helps kill the bear; he goes on the hunt to the end of his
days. But he knows that efficiency as an end in itself is self-
defeating. It is man's fate to struggle against nature; yet it is
wisdom to learn that the fight cannot finally be won and that
the contest has to be conducted with love and humility and in
accordance with a code of honor. Man realizes himself in the
struggle, but the ultimate to be gained in the struggle is wisdom.
Sutpen never really acquires wisdom, for he never loses his innocence. He will never learn. The figure of Time with his scythe
never received a more grim embodiment than it does in the
grizzled Wash Jones raising his rusty implement to strike Sutpen
down.

Sutpen belongs to the company of Conrad's Kurtz (though
perhaps Kurtz did learn something at the very end; Marlow

thinks that he did). But it is not difficult to find his compeers closer to home. I have already suggested that we might search for them with good hope of success among the brownstone mansions of post–Civil War New York. But it is easy to locate them in recent fiction. The southern novelists of our time have been fascinated by this kind of character, perhaps because for them he still has some aura of the monstrous and is still not quite to be taken for granted.

Up to this point we have been concerned with the character of Thomas Sutpen, especially in his relation to the claims of the family and the community. We have treated him as if he were a historical figure, but of course he is not. More than most characters in literature, Thomas Sutpen is an imaginative construct, a set of inferences—a hypothesis put forward to account for several peculiar events. For the novel *Absalom, Absalom!* does not merely tell the story of Thomas Sutpen, but dramatizes the process by which two young men of the twentieth century construct the character Thomas Sutpen. Fascinated by the few known events of his life and death, they try, through inference, conjecture, and guesswork, to ascertain what manner of man he was. The novel then has to do not merely with the meaning of Sutpen's career but with the nature of historical truth and with the problem of how we can "know" the past. The importance of this latter theme determines the very special way in which the story of Sutpen is mediated to us through a series of partial disclosures, informed guesses, and constantly revised deductions and hypotheses.

Young Quentin Compson, just on the eve of leaving Mississippi for his first year at Harvard, is summoned by Miss Rosa Coldfield and made to listen to the story of her wicked brother-in-law, Thomas Sutpen. Sutpen had been a friend of Quentin's grandfather, General Compson, and as Quentin waits to drive Miss Rosa out to Sutpen's Hundred after dark, as she has requested, Quentin's father tells him what he knows about the Sutpen story.

Nobody had really understood the strange events that had occurred at Sutpen's Hundred—the quarrel between Thomas Sutpen and Henry, the disappearance of Henry with his friend

Charles Bon, the forbidding of the marriage between Judith and Bon, and later, and most sensational of all, Henry's shooting of his friend Charles Bon at the very gates of Sutpen's Hundred in 1865. Mr. Compson makes a valiant effort to account for what happened. What evidently sticks in his mind is the fact that Charles Bon had an octoroon mistress in New Orleans. Presumably Judith had told General Compson or his wife about finding the octoroon's picture on Charles Bon's dead body. But in any case the visit, at Judith's invitation, of the woman to Charles Bon's grave would have impressed the whole relationship upon General Compson and upon his son, Mr. Compson. Mr. Compson thinks that it was the fact of the mistress that made Thomas Sutpen oppose Bon's marriage to his daughter, but that Henry was so deeply committed to his friend that he refused to believe what his father told him about Bon's mistress, chose to go away with Charles, and only at the very end, when Charles Bon was actually standing before his father's house, used the gun to prevent the match.

It is not a very plausible theory. For though it could account for Sutpen's opposition to Bon, it hardly explains Henry's violent action, taken so late in the day. Mr. Compson does the best that he can with this aspect of the story and says: "[Henry] loved grieved and killed, still grieving and, I believe, still loving Bon the man to whom he gave four years of probation, four years in which to renounce and dissolve the other marriage, knowing that the four years of hoping and waiting would be in vain" (p. 97). But Mr. Compson has to concede that, after all, "it's just incredible. It just does not explain. . . . something is missing" (p. 100).

Quentin's other informant about the Sutpens is Miss Rosa Coldfield, Sutpen's sister-in-law. Miss Rosa clearly does not understand what happened. She exclaims that "Judith's marriage [was] forbidden without rhyme or reason" (p. 18), and her only theory to account for the murder is that Sutpen was a demon and, as a demon, dowered his children with a curse which made them destroy themselves. Even Judith evidently did not know why her marriage was forbidden nor did she know why her brother killed Charles Bon. After the murder and Henry's flight,

Judith tells Mrs. Compson, the general's wife, that the war will soon be over now because "they [the Confederate soldiers] have begun to shoot one another" (p. 128). The remark indicates her bafflement as well as her despair.

By the time we have reached the end of section 5—that is, halfway through the book—we have been given most of the basic facts of the Sutpen story but no satisfactory interpretation of it. We know the story of Sutpen's life in the Mississippi community pretty much as the community itself knew it, but the events do not make sense. The second half of the book may be called an attempt at interpretation When section 6 opens, we are in Quentin's room at Harvard, and Quentin is reading a letter from his father telling about the death of Miss Rosa Coldfield. From this time on until past midnight, Quentin and Shreve discuss the story of Sutpen and make their own conjectures as to what actually happened. In this second half of the book there are, to be sure, further disclosures about Sutpen, especially with reference to his early life before he came to Mississippi. Sutpen, it turns out, had once told the story of his early life to General Compson, and his information had been passed on to Quentin through Mr. Compson. As Shreve and Quentin talk, Quentin feeds into the conversation from time to time more material from his father's and grandfather's memories of events and one very brilliant scene which he himself remembers: how, hunting quail on a gray autumn day, he and his father came upon the graves in the Sutpen family graveyard and his father told him the touching story of Judith's later life. But as the last four sections of the book make plain, we are dealing with an intricate imaginative reconstruction of events leading up to the murder of Charles Bon—a plausible account of what may have happened but not what necessarily did happen.

If the reader reminds himself how little hard fact there is to go on—how much of the most important information about the motivations of the central characters comes late and is, at best, vague and ambiguous—he will appreciate how much of the story of Sutpen and especially of Sutpen's children has been spun out of the imaginations of Quentin and Shreve.

Absalom, Absalom! is indeed from one point of view a wonderful detective story—by far the best of Faulkner's several flirtations with this particular genre. It may also be considered to yield a nice instance of how the novelist works, for Shreve and Quentin both show a good deal of the insights of the novelist and his imaginative capacity for constructing plausible motivations around a few given facts. This theme would obviously be one dear to Faulkner's heart. Most important of all, however, *Absalom, Absalom!* is a persuasive commentary upon the thesis that much of "history" is really a kind of imaginative construction. The past always remains at some level a mystery, but if we are to hope to understand it in any way, we must enter into it and project ourselves imaginatively into the attitudes and emotions of the historical figures. Both of the boys make this sort of projection, though one would expect it to be easy for Quentin and difficult for Shreve. Actually, it does not work out in this way, for Shreve enters into the reconstruction of the past with ardor. He finds it, in his lack of any serious emotional commitment, a fascinating game—in fact, he consistently treats it as a game, saying, "Let me play now." The novelty of fitting actual human beings into roles that he had earlier connected only with the stage intrigues him. At one point he teases Quentin by saying, "Jesus, the South is fine, isn't it. It's better than the theatre, isn't it. It's better than Ben Hur, isn't it" (p. 217). Quentin, on the other hand, is too much involved—too fully committed to the problems and the issue—actually to enjoy the reconstruction. He feels a compulsion to do so, of course, the same compulsion that had caused him, against his better judgment, to go up into the bedroom at Sutpen's Hundred and look upon the wasted face of Henry Sutpen.

To note that the account of the Sutpens which Shreve and Quentin concoct is largely an imaginative construct is not to maintain that it is necessarily untrue. Their version of events is plausible, and the author himself—for whatever that may be worth—suggests that that some of the scenes which they palpably invented were probably true, for example, "the slight dowdy woman ... whom Shreve and Quentin had ... invented" and who was probably "true enough" (p. 335). But it is worth remarking that we do not "know," apart from the Quentin-Shreve semifictional process, many events which a casual reader assumes actually happened.

To provide some illustrations: Charles Bon's telling Henry, "So it's the miscegenation, not the incest, which you cant bear" (p. 356) is a remark that rests upon no known fact. It is a conjecture though a plausible one. Again, Bon's agonized waiting for his father to give him the merest hint of a father's recognition and Bon's comment that this was all that Sutpen needed to do to stop his courtship of Judith are both surmises made by Quentin and Shreve. So too is the scene in which the boys imagine the visit of Bon and Henry to New Orleans and hear Bon's mother's bitter question, "So she [Judith] has fallen in love with him" (p. 335), and listen to her harsh laughter as she looks at Henry. The wonderfully touching scene in which Judith asks Charles Bon's son to call her Aunt Judith is presumably an imaginative construction made by Quentin.

One ought to observe in passing that in allowing the boys to make their guesses about what went on, Faulkner plays perfectly fair. Some of their guesses have the clear ring of truth. They are obviously right. On the other hand, some are justified by the flimsiest possible reasoning. For example, notice Shreve's argument (p. 344) that it was Bon, not Henry, who was wounded at the battle of Shiloh.

One of the most important devices used in the novel is the placing of Shreve in it as a kind of sounding board and mouthpiece. By doing so, Faulkner has in effect acknowledged the attitude of the modern, "liberal," twentieth-century reader, who is basically rational, skeptical, without any special concern for history, and pretty well emancipated from the ties of family, race, or section. In fact, Shreve sounds very much like certain literary critics who have written on Faulkner. It was a stroke of genius on Faulkner's part to put such a mentality squarely inside the novel, for this is a way of facing criticism from that quarter and putting it into its proper perspective.

Shreve teases Quentin playfully and even affectionately, but it is not mere teasing. When Shreve strikes a pose and in his best theatrical manner assigns a dramatic speech to Wash, Faulkner, in one of his few intrusions as author, observes: "This was not flippancy. . . . It too was just that protective coloring of levity behind which the youthful shame of being moved hid itself." The author remarks on Quentin's "sullen bemusement" but also on the "flipness, the strained clowning" (p. 280) on the part of both.

It is curious that Shreve, all of whose facts have been given him by or through Quentin, is allowed in the later chapters to do most of the imaginative work—far more, I should say, than is allowed to Quentin. This is the more interesting since Quentin has met three of the participants in the tragedy face to face and is filled with vivid impressions of the scene. Perhaps the fact that Quentin is so involved makes it difficult or distasteful for him to talk. At any rate, it is the "outsider" who does most of the imaginative reconstruction. Quentin's role at times becomes merely that of a check or brake upon Shreve's fertile imagination.

The last sections of the novel tell us a great deal about Shreve's and Quentin's differing attitudes toward history and of their own relation to history. Shreve has been genuinely moved by the story of Sutpen. For all of his teasing, he is concerned to understand, and late in the evening he says to Quentin: "Listen. I'm not trying to be funny, smart. I just want to understand it if I can and I don't know how to say it better. Because it's something my people haven't got" (p. 361). And though he cannot suppress his bantering tone in alluding to the southern heritage—it is "a kind of entailed birthright . . . of never forgiving General Sherman, so that forevermore as long as your children's children produce children you wont be anything but a descendant of a long line of colonels killed in Pickett's charge"—Shreve's question is seriously put. What is it that Quentin as a southerner has that Shreve does not have? It is a sense of the presence of the past and with it an access to a tragic vision. For the South has experienced defeat and guilt and has an ingrained sense of the stubbornness of human error and of the complexity of history. The matter has been recently put very well in C. Vann Woodward's *The Burden of Southern History:* "The experience of evil and the experience of tragedy," he writes,

"are parts of the Southern heritage that are as difficult to reconcile with the American legend of innocence and social felicity
as the experience of poverty and defeat are to reconcile with the
legends of abundance and success."[2]

In remarking on how little of hard fact one has to go on, we
should bear in mind particularly the question of Bon's Negro
blood and of his kinship to Henry. Quentin says flatly that "nobody ever did know if Bon ever knew Sutpen was his father or
not" (p. 269). Did anyone ever know whether Bon knew that he
was part Negro? In their reconstruction of the story, Shreve and
Quentin assume (p. 356) that Bon was aware that he was Henry's
part-Negro half brother (though on page 327 Quentin and Shreve
assume that Bon did not know that he had Negro blood). If in
fact Bon did have Negro blood, how did Shreve and Quentin
come by that knowledge? As we have seen, neither Judith nor
Miss Rosa had any inkling of it. Nor did Mr. Compson. Early in
the novel he refers to Bon's "sixteenth part negro son." Since
Bon's mistress was an octoroon, his son could be one-sixteenth
Negro only on the assumption that Charles Bon was of pure
white blood—and this is evidently what Mr. Compson does assume. Mr. Compson, furthermore, knows nothing about Bon's
kinship to Henry.

The conjectures made by Shreve and Quentin—even if taken
merely as conjectures—render the story of Sutpen plausible.
They make much more convincing sense of the story than Mr.
Compson's notions were able to make. And that very fact suggests
their probable truth. But are they more than plausible theories?
Is there any real evidence to support the view that Bon was
Sutpen's son by a part-Negro wife? There is, and the way in which
this evidence is discovered constitutes another, and the most decisive, justification for regarding *Absalom, Absalom!* as a magnificent
detective story. Precisely what is revealed and how it is revealed
are worth a rather careful review.

In the course of his conversation with Quentin, Shreve objects
that Mr. Compson "seems to have got an awful lot of delayed
information awful quick, after having waited forty-five years"
(p. 266). Quentin confirms the fact that his father *had* got delayed

information—had got it from Quentin himself—and had got it the day after "we" (that is, Quentin and Miss Rosa) had gone out to Sutpen's Hundred. A little later (p. 274), when Quentin tells Shreve of Sutpen's long conversation with General Compson about his "design" and about the "mistake" that Sutpen had made in trying to carry it out, Shreve asks Quentin whether General Compson had then really known what Sutpen was talking about. Quentin answers that General Compson had not known; and Shreve, pressing the point, makes Quentin admit that he himself "wouldn't have known what anybody was talking about" if he "hadn't been out there and seen Clytie." The secret of Bon's birth, then, was revealed to Quentin on that particular visit. Shreve's way of phrasing it implies that it was from Clytie that Quentin had got his information, but, as we shall see, it is unlikely that Clytie was Quentin's informant. In any case, when Shreve puts his question about seeing Clytie, he did not know that another person besides Clytie and her nephew was living at Sutpen's Hundred.

Miss Rosa has sensed that "something"—she does not say "someone"—was "living hidden in that house." When she and Quentin visit Sutpen's Hundred, her intuition is confirmed. The hidden something turns out to be Henry Sutpen, now come home to die. Presumably, it was from Henry Sutpen that Quentin learned the crucial facts. Or did he? Here again Faulkner may seem to the reader either teasingly reticent or, upon reflection, brilliantly skillful.

We know from the last section of the book that after Miss Rosa had come down from the upstairs room with her "eyes wide and unseeing like a sleepwalker's" (p. 370), Quentin felt compelled to go up to that room and see what was there. He does go, though Faulkner does not take us with him into the room. He descends the stairs, walks out of the house, overtakes Miss Rosa, and drives her home. Later that night, however, after he has returned to his own home and is lying sleepless, he cannot—even by clenching his eyelids—shut out his vision of the bed with its yellowed sheets and its yellowed pillow and the wasted yellow face lying upon it, a face with closed "almost transparent eyelids" (p. 373). As Quentin tosses, unable to erase the picture from his eyes, we are vouchsafed one tiny scrap of his conversation with Henry, a conversation that amounts to no more than Quentin's question, "And you are—?" and Henry's answer that he is indeed Henry Sutpen, that he has been there four years, and that he has come home to die. How extended was the conversation? How long did it last? Would Henry Sutpen have volunteered to a stranger his reason for having killed Charles Bon? Or would Quentin Compson, awed and aghast at what he saw, put such questions as these to the wasted figure upon the bed? We do not know, and Faulkner—probably wisely—has not undertaken to reconstruct this interview for us. (It is possible, of course, that Henry did tell Miss Rosa why he had killed Bon and that Miss Rosa told Quentin in the course of their long ride back to Jefferson.)

At all events, the whole logic of *Absalom, Absalom!* argues that *only* through the presence of Henry in the house was it possible for Quentin—and, through Quentin, his father and Shreve and those of us who read the book—to be made privy to the dark secret that underlay the Sutpen tragedy.

At the end of the novel Shreve is able to shrug off the tragic implications and resume the tone of easy banter. His last comment abounds with the usual semisociological clichés: the Negroes "will bleach out again like the rabbits and the birds. . . . In a few thousand years, I who regard you will also have sprung from the loins of African kings" (p. 378). Though the spell of the story has been powerful enough to fire his imagination and involve all his sympathies, he is not personally committed, and we can see him drawing back from the tragic problem and becoming again the cheery, cynical, commonsense man of the present day. In the long perspective of history, how few issues really matter! The long perspective is antihistorical: make it long enough and any sense of history evaporates. Lengthen it further still and the human dimension itself evaporates.

From his stance of detachment, Shreve suddenly, and apropos of nothing, puts to Quentin the question "Why do you hate the South?" And Quentin's passionate denial that he hates it tells its own story of personal involvement and distress. The more naive reader may insist on having an answer: "Well, does he hate it?" And the response would have to be, I suppose, another question: "Does Stephen Daedalus hate Dublin?" Or, addressing the question to Stephen's creator, "Did James Joyce hate Ireland?" The answer here would surely have to be yes and no. In any case, Joyce was so obsessed with Ireland and so deeply involved in it that he spent his life writing about it.

At this point, however, it may be more profitable to put a different question. What did the story of Sutpen mean to Quentin? Did it mean to him what it has apparently meant to most of the critics who have written on this novel—the story of the curse of slavery and how it involved Sutpen and his children in ruin? Surely this is to fit the story to a neat and oversimple formula. Slavery was an evil. But other slaveholders avoided Sutpen's kind of defeat and were exempt from his special kind of moral blindness.

What ought to be plain, in any event, is that it is Henry's part in the tragic tale that affects Quentin the most. Quentin had seen Henry with his own eyes and Henry's involvement in slavery was only indirect. Even Henry's dread of miscegenation was fearfully complicated with other issues, including the problem of incest. In view of what we learn of Quentin in *The Sound and the Fury*, the problem of incest would have fascinated him and made him peculiarly sensitive to Henry's torment. Aside from his personal problem, however, Sutpen's story had for Quentin a special meaning that it did not have for Shreve.

The story embodied the problem of evil and of the irrational; Henry was beset by conflicting claims; he was forced to make intolerably hard choices—between opposed goods or between conflicting evils. Had Henry cared much less for Bon, or else much less for Judith, he might have promoted the happiness of one without feeling that he was sacrificing that of the other. Or had he cared much less for either and much more for himself, he might have won a cool and rational detachment, a coign of vantage from which even objections to miscegenation and incest would appear to be irrational prejudices, and honor itself a quaint affectation whose saving was never worth the price of a bullet. Had Henry been not necessarily wiser but simply more cynical, more gross, or more selfish, there would have been no tragedy.

To say that Quentin was peculiarly susceptible to this meaning of Henry's story is not to make of Shreve a monster of inhumanly cool irrationality. But Shreve is measurably closer to the skepticism and detachment that allow modern man to dismiss the irrational claims from which Quentin cannot free himself and which he honors to his own cost.

The reader of *Absalom, Absalom!* might well follow Quentin's example. If he must find in the story of the House of Sutpen something that had special pertinence to the tragic dilemmas of the South, the aspect of the story to stress is not the downfall of Thomas Sutpen, a man who is finally optimistic, rationalistic, and afflicted with elephantiasis of the will. Instead, he ought to attend to the story of Sutpen's children.

The story of Judith, though muted and played down in terms of the whole novel, is one of the most moving that Faulkner has ever written. She has in her the best of her father's traits. She is the stout-hearted little girl who witnesses without flinching scenes which force poor Henry to grow sick and vomit. She is the young woman who falls in love with a fascinating stranger, the friend of her brother, who means to marry him in spite of her father's silent opposition, and who matches her father's strength of will with a quiet strength of her own. She endures the horror of her fiancé's murder and buries his body. She refuses to commit suicide; she keeps the place going for her father's return. Years later it is Judith who sees to it that Bon's mistress has an opportunity to visit his grave, who brings Bon's child to live with her after his mother's death and, at least in Quentin's reconstruction of events, tries to get the little boy to recognize her as his aunt and to set him free, pushing him on past the barriers of color. When she fails to do so, she still tries to protect him. She nurses him when he sickens of yellow fever, and she dies with him in the epidemic. She is one of Faulkner's finest characters of endurance—and not merely through numb, bleak stoicism but also through compassion and love. Judith is doomed by misfortunes not of her making, but she is not warped and twisted by them. Her humanity survives them.

Because Henry knew what presumably Judith did not know, the secret of Bon's birth, his struggle—granted the circumstances of his breeding, education, and environment—was more difficult than Judith's. He had not merely to endure but to act, and yet any action that he could take would be cruelly painful. He was compelled to an agonizing decision. One element that rendered tragic any choice he might make is revealed in Henry's last action, his coming home to die. One might have thought that after some forty years, Henry would have stayed in Mexico or California or New York or wherever he was, but the claims of locality and family are too strong, and he returns to Sutpen's Hundred.

Absalom, Absalom! is the most memorable of Faulkner's novels— and memorable in a very special way. Though even the intelligent reader may feel at times some frustration with the powerful but darkly involved story, with its patches of murkiness and its almost willful complications of plot, he will find himself haunted by individual scenes and episodes, rendered with almost compulsive force. He will probably remember vividly such a scene as Henry's confrontation of his sister Judith after four years of absence at war—the boy in his "patched and faded gray tunic" crashing into the room in which his sister stands clutching against her partially clothed nakedness the yellowed wedding dress and shouting to her: "Now you cant marry him . . . because he's dead . . . I killed him" (p. 172). Or there is Miss Rosa's recollection of the burial of Charles Bon. As she talks to Quentin, she relives the scene: the "slow, maddening rasp, rasp, rasp, of the saw" and "the flat deliberate hammer blows" as Wash and another white man work at the coffin through the "slow and sunny afternoon," with Judith in her faded dress and "faded gingham sunbonnet . . . giving them directions about making it." Miss Rosa, who has never seen Bon alive and for whom he is therefore a fabulous creature, a mere dream, recalls that she "tried to take the full weight of the coffin" as they carried it down the stairs in order "to prove to myself that he was really in it" (p. 151).

There is the wonderful scene of Thomas Sutpen's return to

Sutpen's Hundred, the iron man dismounting from his "gaunt and jaded horse," saying to Judith, "Well, daughter," and touching his bearded lips to her forehead. There follows an exchange that is as laconically resonant as any in Greek tragedy: " 'Henry's not—?' 'No. He's not here.' '—Ah. And—?' 'Yes. Henry killed him' " (p. 159). With the last sentence Judith bursts into tears, but it is the only outburst of which Judith is ever guilty.

The reader will remember also the scenes of Sutpen's boyhood and young manhood—perhaps most vivid of all of them, that in which the puzzled boy is turned away from the plantation door by the liveried servant. Sometimes the haunting passage is one of mere physical description: the desolate Sutpen burial ground with the

> flat slabs ... cracked across the middle by their own weight (and vanishing into the hole where the brick coping of one vault had fallen in was a smooth faint path worn by some small animal—possum probably—by generations of some small animal since there could have been nothing to eat in the grave for a long time) though the lettering was quite legible: *Ellen Coldfield Sutpen. Born October 9, 1817. Died January 23, 1863.* (p. 188)

One remembers also the account of something that had taken place earlier in this same graveyard, when Bon's octoroon mistress, a "magnolia-faced woman a little plumper now, a woman created of by and for darkness whom the artist Beardsley might have dressed, in a soft flowing gown designed not to infer bereavement or widowhood ... knelt beside the grave and arranged her skirts and wept," while beside her stood her "thin delicate child" with its "smooth ivory sexless face" (p. 193).

There is, too, the ride out to Sutpen's Hundred in the "furnace-breathed" Mississippi night in which Quentin shares his buggy with the frail and fanatical Miss Rosa and smells her "fusty camphor-reeking shawl" and even her "airless black cotton umbrella." On this journey, as Miss Rosa clutches to her a flashlight and a hatchet, the implements of her search, it seems to Quentin that he can hear "the single profound suspiration of the parched earth's agony rising toward the imponderable and aloof stars" (p. 362). Most vivid of all is the great concluding scene in which Clytie, seeing the ambulance approaching to bear Henry away, fires "the monstrous tinder-dry rotten shell" (p. 375) of a house, and from an upper window she defies the intruders, her "tragic gnome's face beneath the clean headrag, against a red background of fire, seen for a moment between two swirls of smoke, looking down at them, perhaps not even now with triumph and no more of despair than it had ever worn, possibly even serene above the melting clapboards" (p. 376).

These brilliantly realized scenes reward the reader and sustain him as he struggles with the novel, but it ought to be remembered that they are given their power by the way in which the novel is structured and thus constitute a justification of that peculiar structure. For example, consider Henry's confrontation of Judith with the word that he has killed her lover. The incident is alluded to in remarks made to Quentin by Miss Rosa (section 1) and later by Mr. Compson as he talks to Quentin on the porch of their home in the fading daylight (section 2). But the first major preparation for this scene does not occur until the end of section 3 with Wash's riding up to Miss Rosa's house on a saddleless mule and shouting, "Hello, hello," at intervals until she comes to the door. Whereupon, "he lowered his voice somewhat, though not much. 'Air you Rosie Coldfield?' he said" (p. 133). But what he had to tell her is not stated. The reader may very well guess what it was, but if he wants to hear the rest of Wash's speech, he must read on all the way through section 4 to find, at the very end: "Air you Rosie Coldfield? Then you better come on out yon. Henry has done shot that durn French feller. Kilt him dead as a beef." But the postponement of what Wash had to impart is, of course, no mere teasing of the reader. Because of what we learn in section 4, the episode becomes invested with tremendously increased power. The repetition with added and altered detail functions somewhat like the folk-ballad device of incremental repetition.

The conclusion of section 5 brings us up to the confrontation scene itself. For this scene, the sequel to the murder so tersely reported by Wash, is now visualized for us through Quentin's imagination: our own imaginations have been prepared for the presentation, and we are likely to hear the brother and sister, as Quentin does, speaking to one another in "brief staccato sentences like slaps, as if they stood breast to breast striking one another in turn neither making any attempt to guard against the blows" (p. 172).

The ending of section 5, however, does something more than bring to climactic focus the meeting of Henry and Judith: it generates a new line of suspense. For Quentin is jerked out of his abstracted reverie by suddenly apprehending the significance of something Miss Rosa has been saying. He asks her to repeat, and section 5 closes with her words: "There's something in that house. . . . Something living in it. Hidden in it. It has been out there for four years, living hidden in that house" (p. 172).

Section 6 resumes other narrative lines of the story and describes the decaying mansion at Sutpen's Hundred as Quentin had seen it a few years earlier on a hunt. But at the end of the section Shreve returns to the possibility of something hidden at Sutpen's Hundred and of the journey that Quentin made with Rosa to test her intuition that this was so. The section ends with Shreve's excited query: " 'and so you went out there, drove the twelve miles at night in a buggy and you found Clytie and Jim Bond both in it and you said You see? and she (the Aunt Rosa) still said No and so you went on: and there was?' 'Yes.' 'Wait then. . . . For God's sake wait' " (p. 216).

Shreve is here the proper surrogate for the reader. The reader too wants to know the secret, but he does not want (or ought not to want) to know too quickly. Shreve, who is in some sense the perfect audience, yearns to know the secret, but only at the proper time when the revelation can come with full significance. Scattered through sections 7 and 8 there are a number of references to what Quentin's journey to Sutpen's Hundred revealed, though each of these sections ends with another and less important disclosure. The account of Quentin's journey is reserved for the last pages of the book. Indeed, though Quentin must have at some point during the evening told Shreve what he found at Sutpen's Hundred, his recounting it to Shreve is in fact never presented in this book. Instead, there is a compulsive reenactment of the episode as Quentin lies in his bed, unable to sleep, feeling, even with the "chill pure weight of the snow-breathed New England air on his face," the dust of that "breathless . . . Mississippi September night" (p. 362).

Absalom, Absalom! is in many respects the most brilliantly written of all of Faulkner's novels, whether one considers its writing line by line and paragraph by paragraph, or its structure, in which we are moved up from one suspended note to a higher suspended note and on up further still to an almost intolerable climax. The intensity of the book is a function of the structure. The deferred and suspended resolutions are necessary if the great scenes are to have their full vigor and significance. Admittedly, the novel is a difficult one, but the difficulty is not forced and factitious. It is the price that has to be paid by the reader for the novel's power and significance. There are actually few instances in modern fiction of a more perfect adaptation of form to matter and of an intricacy that justifies itself at every point through the significance and intensity which it makes possible.

Notes

1. Arthur M. Schlesinger, "What Then Is the American, This New Man," *American Historical Review* 48 (1943): 244.
2. C. Vann Woodward, *The Burden of Southern History* (Baton Rouge: Louisiana State University Press, 1960), 21.

Repetition and Revenge

JOHN T. IRWIN

◆ ◆ ◆

IN THE STORY OF THE SUTPENS, the threat of miscegenation between Bon and Judith is also a threat of brother-sister
incest, and it is another brother, Henry, who acts to stop these
threats. This archetype of the brother who must kill to protect
or avenge the honor of his sister pervades *Absalom, Absalom!* It
occurs, first of all, in the very title of the novel. In the Old
Testament (2 Sam. 13), Absalom, one of David's sons, kills his
brother Amnon for raping their sister Tamar. The archetype presents itself again in Quentin Compson, the principal narrator of
Absalom, Absalom! From *The Sound and the Fury* we know that Quentin
is in love with his own sister Candace and that he is tormented
by his inability to play the role of the avenging brother and kill
her seducer. Of the many levels of meaning in *Absalom, Absalom!*
the deepest level is to be found in the symbolic identification of
incest and miscegenation and in the relationship of this symbolic
identification both to Quentin Compson's personal history in *The
Sound and the Fury* and to the story that Quentin narrates in *Absalom,
Absalom!*

There are, of course, four narrators in the novel—Quentin, his father, his roommate Shreve, and Miss Rosa Coldfield—but of these four certainly Quentin is the central narrator, not just because he ends up knowing more of the story than do the other three, but because the other three only function as narrators in relation to Quentin. When Mr. Compson or Shreve or Miss Rosa Coldfield tell what they know or conjecture of the Sutpens' story, they are talking, either actually or imaginatively, to Quentin. One reason that the voices of the different narrators sound so much alike is that we hear those voices filtered through the mind of a single listener: Quentin's consciousness is the fixed point of view from which the reader overhears the various narrators, Quentin included. Since Quentin is the principal narrative consciousness in *Absalom, Absalom!* and since the story of the Sutpens contains numerous gaps that must be filled by conjecture on the part of the narrators, it is not surprising that the narrative bears a striking resemblance to Quentin's own personal history and that of his family. Quentin uses his own experience of family life in a small southern town to try to understand the motives for events in the story of Thomas Sutpen and his children, particularly that central enigmatic event to which the narration continually returns—the murder of Charles Bon by his best friend, Henry Sutpen. This is not to imply that the factual similarities between the stories of the Sutpen and Compson families are a product of Quentin's imagination, but to point out that, given these similarities of fact, Quentin as creative narrator could easily presume similarity of motivation. It is a mutual process in which what Quentin knows of the motivations in his own family life illuminates the story of the Sutpens and, in turn, the events in the Sutpens' story help Quentin to understand his own experiences. . . .

To what extent, then, does the story that Quentin tells in *Absalom, Absalom!* resemble his own life story in *The Sound and the Fury?* We noted first of all that Quentin's failure to kill Candace's seducer and thus fulfill the role of protective brother has its reverse image in Henry's murder of Bon to safeguard the honor of their sister. Also, Quentin's incestuous love for Candace is mirrored by Bon's love for Judith. That Quentin identifies with both

Henry, the brother as protector, and Bon, the brother as seducer, is not extraordinary, for in Quentin's narrative they are not so much two separate figures as two aspects of the same figure. Quentin projects onto the characters of Bon and Henry opposing elements in his own personality—Bon represents Quentin's unconsciously motivated desires for his sister Candace, while Henry represents the conscious repression or punishment of that desire. . . .

In the story of the Sutpens, Quentin also finds a reenactment of the way that the fate of a father is passed on to a son. When Sutpen was a child, he received an affront from the black servant of a rich plantation owner. He was told that he could not come to the front door of the planter's house but had to go around to the back because he was white trash, because he and his family were not as good as the plantation owner. Comparing the plantation owner with his own father, Sutpen rejects his father as a model and adopts the plantation owner as his surrogate father, as his model for what a man should be. And Sutpen feels the same ambivalence toward him that a son would feel for a father. At first, he considers killing him, but then he realizes that he does not want to do away with the plantation owner, he wants to become the plantation owner. The ruthless odyssey on which Sutpen embarks is a quest for revenge for the affront that he suffered as a boy—not revenge against a system in which the rich and powerful can affront the poor and powerless but against the luck of birth that made him one of the poor when he should have been one of the rich. Like Gatsby, Sutpen distinguishes between the "Platonic" and the "merely personal." Ideally, he accepts the justice of that mastery which the powerful have over the powerless, which the rich planter has over the poor boy, a father over his son. The fact that circumstance happened to start Sutpen off by casting him in the role of the powerless, poor boy is merely personal. A mere stroke of chance does not invalidate that hierarchy—or rather, patriarchy—of power. Sutpen seeks revenge within the rules of patriarchal power for the affront that he suffered; he does not try to show the injustice of the system, but rather to show that he is as good as any man in the system.

If the planter is powerful because he is rich, then Sutpen will have his revenge by becoming richer and more powerful than the planter. And he will pass that wealth and power on to his son, doing for his son what his own father could not do for him. Sutpen comes to terms with the traumatic affront that he suffered as a boy by accepting the impersonal justice of it even though he feels its personal inappropriateness. He incorporates into himself the patriarchal ideal from which that affront sprang in much the same way that a son comes to terms with the image of his father as a figure of mastery and power by impersonalizing and internalizing that image as the superego, accepting the justice of the father's mastery even though that mastery has been exercised against the son. It is a mechanism by which the son tries to overcome the mastery of the personal father while maintaining the mastery of fatherhood—a mechanism in which the personal father dies without the son having to kill him. Accepting this idea of patriarchal power, Sutpen determines his fate—to repeat periodically that traumatic affront but in a different. role. Henceforth, he will no longer receive the affront, he will deliver it. Thus, he rejects his first wife and son because they are not good enough to share the position to which he aspires. And he passes that fated repetition on to his sons—to Charles Bon, who returns thirty years later seeking admittance to the rich plantation owner's "house" (and thereby represents the return of the repressed traumatic affront of Sutpen's boyhood), and to Henry, who, acting as his father's surrogate, delivers the final affront to Bon, killing him at the gates of the house to prevent him from entering.

In his interviews at the University of Virginia, Faulkner repeatedly pointed out that *Absalom* is a revenge story—indeed, a double revenge story: Sutpen's revenge for the affront that he suffered as a boy and Bon's revenge for the affront that he and his mother suffered at Sutpen's hands during Sutpen's quest for revenge. Faulkner said of Sutpen:

> He wanted revenge as he saw it, but also he wanted to establish the fact that man is immortal, that man, if he is man, cannot

be inferior to another man through artificial standards or circumstances. What he was trying to do—when he was a boy,
he had gone to the front door of a big house and somebody,
a servant, said, Go around to the back door. He said, I'm going
to be the one that lives in the big house, I'm going to establish
a dynasty, I don't care how, and he violated all the rules of
decency and honor and pity and compassion, and the fates
took revenge on him.[1]

Sutpen wants revenge not against the injustice of that mastery
which the powerful have over the powerless, but against those
"artificial standards or circumstances" that determine who are the
powerful and who the powerless, against the artificial standard of
inherited wealth and the circumstances of one's birth. Faulkner
says that Sutpen in his quest for revenge "violated all the rules
of decency and honor and pity and compassion," but there is one
rule that Sutpen does not violate, and that is the rule of power.
For the rule that Sutpen follows is that real power springs not
from the external, artificial advantages of birth and inherited
wealth but from something internal: for Sutpen, the source of
real power is the force of the individual will. In any group of
men, power belongs to the man whose will is strong enough to
seize that power and hold it against his fellow men. But that
brings us face to face with the central paradox of Sutpen's quest—
that he seeks revenge on the artificial standards of birth and inherited wealth as the determinants of power by setting out to
establish a dynasty—that is, by trying to confer those very same
artificial advantages on his son. Faulkner gives us the key to this
paradox when he says that Sutpen "wanted revenge as he saw it,
but also he wanted to establish the fact that man is immortal,
that man, if he is man, cannot be inferior to another man
through artificial standards or circumstances." It is a puzzling
statement. First of all, what does it mean to equate Sutpen's attempt to establish that man is immortal with his effort to prove
that one man cannot be inferior to another through artificial
standards or circumstances? And then, what does it mean to link
these two with the quest for revenge?

The idea that lies behind Faulkner's statement is what Nietzsche called "the revenge against time."[2] To understand what this idea involves, let us compare for a moment the careers of Jay Gatsby and Thomas Sutpen. Clearly, what Gatsby and Sutpen both seek in their quests is to alter the past—to repeat the past and correct it. As Sutpen in the role of the poor boy suffered an affront from the rich plantation owner, so Gatsby as the poor boy was rejected by the rich girl Daisy Buchanan, and as the former affront initiated Sutpen's grand design to get land, build a mansion, and establish a dynasty, that is, to repeat the past situation but with Sutpen now in the role of the affronter rather than the affronted and to pass on to his son the rich man's power to affront the poor and powerless, so Daisy's rejection of Gatsby initiates Gatsby's dream: of acquiring a fortune, owning a great house, and winning Daisy back, his dream of repeating the past by marrying Daisy this time and obliterating everything that occurred between that rejection and his winning her back. When Nick Carraway realizes the enormity of Gatsby's dream, he tells him, "You can't repeat the past," and Gatsby with his Sutpenlike innocence replies, "Why of course you can." As Sutpen rejected his powerless, real father as a model in favor of the powerful plantation owner, so Gatsby rejected his father, who was a failure, changed his name from Gatz to Gatsby, and adopted the self-made man Dan Cody as his surrogate father. But now the question arises, Why does the attempt to repeat the past and correct it turn into the revenge against time? Nietzsche's answer is worth quoting at length:

> To redeem those who lived in the past and to recreate all "it was" into a "thus I willed it"—that alone should I call redemption. Will—that is the name of the liberator and joy-bringer; thus I taught you, my friends. But now learn this too: the will itself is still a prisoner. Willing liberates; but what is it that puts even the liberator himself in fetters? "It was"—that is the name of the will's gnashing of teeth and most secret melancholy. Powerless against what has been done, he is an angry spectator—of all that is past. The will cannot will back-

wards; and that he cannot break time and time's covetousness, that is the will's loneliest melancholy.

Willing liberates; what means does the will devise for himself to get rid of his melancholy and to mock his dungeon? Alas, every prisoner becomes a fool; and the imprisoned will redeems himself foolishly. That time does not run backwards, that is his wrath; "that which was" is the name of the stone he cannot move. And so he moves stones out of wrath and displeasure, and he wreaks revenge on whatever does not feel wrath and displeasure as he does. Thus the will, the liberator, took to hurting; and on all who can suffer he wreaks revenge for his inability to go backwards. This, indeed this alone, is what *revenge* is: the will's ill will against time and its "it was." (pp. 251–52)

Since the will operates in the temporal world and since time moves only in one direction, the will can never really get at the past. The will's titanic, foredoomed struggle to repeat the past and to attempt to alter it is simply the revenge that the will seeks for its own impotence in the face of what Nietzsche calls the "it was" of time. Nietzsche connects this revenge against time with the envy that a son feels for his father. In a passage on the equality of men, Zarathustra says:

"What justice means to us is precisely that the world be filled with the storms of our revenge"—thus they speak to each other. "We shall wreak vengeance and abuse on all whose equals we are not"—thus do the tarantula-hearts vow. "And 'will to equality' shall henceforth be the name of virtue; and against all that has power we want to raise our clamor!"

You preachers of equality, the tyrannomania of impotence clamors thus out of you for equality: your most secret ambitions to be tyrants thus shroud themselves in words of virtue. Aggrieved conceit, repressed envy—perhaps the conceit and envy of your fathers—erupt from you as a flame and as the frenzy of revenge.

What was silent in the father speaks in the son; and often I found the son the unveiled secret of the father.

They are like enthusiasts, yet it is not the heart that fires
them—but revenge. (p. 212)

Clearly, the doctrine of the equality of men is at odds with the
patriarchal principle that fathers are inherently superior to sons,
for obviously the doctrine of equality is the doctrine of a son.
The son, finding himself powerless in relation to the father, yet
desiring power, admits that mastery inheres in the role of the
father but disputes the criteria that determine who occupies that
role. The doctrine of the son is simply the doctrine of the son's
equality of opportunity to assume the role of the father through
a combat with the father that will show who is the better man.
But that doctrine of equality the father must reject, for from the
father's point of view the authority which he holds as the father
is not open to dispute; it is not subject to trial by combat because
that authority is not something that the father could ever lose,
it is not accidental to fatherhood, it inheres in its very nature.
That authority is something which has been irrevocably conferred
on the father by the very nature of time, for the essence of the
authority, the mastery, that a father has over his son is simply
priority in time—the fact that in time the father always comes
first. And against that patriarchal authority whose basis is priority
in time, the son's will is impotent, for the will cannot move
backward in time, it cannot alter the past. In his rivalry with the
father for the love of the mother, the son realizes that no matter
how much the mother loves him, she loved the father first. Indeed, the son carries with him in the very fact of his own existence inescapable proof that she loved the father first and that
the son comes second. Any power that the son has, he has not
in his own right, but by inheritance from the father, by being a
copy of the father, who has supreme authority because he comes
first, who has power because of the very nature of time. No
wonder, then, that the envy of the son for the father takes the
form of the revenge against time.

When Nietzsche speaks of the "envy of your fathers," the
phrase is intentionally ambiguous, for it is not just the envy that
a son feels for his father, it is as well the envy that the son inherits

from his father, who was himself a son once. The targets of Sutpen's revenge for the affront that he suffered as a boy are the
artificial advantages of high birth and inherited wealth (or the
artificial disadvantages of low birth and inherited poverty), that
is, generation and patrimony—those modes of the son's dependence on his father, those expressions of the fact that whatever
the son is or has, he has received from his father and holds at
the sufferance of the father. But again we confront the paradox
of Sutpen's solution—that he seeks revenge on the artificial standards that make one man inferior to another, not by trying to
do away with those standards, but rather by founding a dynasty,
by establishing that same artificial standard of superiority for his
family and bequeathing it to his son. Put in that way, the paradox
seems clearer: it is the paradox that sons turn into fathers by
trying to forget (albeit unsuccessfully) that they were once sons.
When Sutpen began his quest for revenge, his quest to supplant
the father, his attitude was that of a son: that the authority and
power of the father obey the rule of power, that they are subject
to a trial by combat, and if the son's will proves the stronger,
belong to the son not as a gift or inheritance (which would entail
his dependence on the father) but as a right, a mark of his independence. Yet (and here is the paradoxical shift) the proof of
the son's success in his attempt to become the father will be the
son's denial of the attitude of the son (the rule of power) in favor
of the attitude of the father. The proof that Sutpen has achieved
his revenge, that he has become the father, will be his affirmation
that the authority and power of the father obey not the rule of
power but the rule of authority, that is, that they are not subject
to dispute or trial by combat since they belong irrevocably to the
father through priority in time, that to oppose the father is to
oppose time, that authority and power cannot be taken from the
father by the son but can only be given as a gift or inheritance
by the father to the son. We see why Sutpen's revenge requires
that he found a dynasty, for the proof that he has succeeded in
becoming the father will finally be achieved only when he be-
queaths his authority and power to his son as an inheritance (a
gift, not a right), thereby establishing the son's dependence on

his father and thus the father's mastery. That proof, of course, Sutpen never achieves, though he dies trying. . . .

When Sutpen returns from the Civil War to find one son dead and the other gone, he starts over a third time in his design to found a dynasty, to get the son who will inherit his land and thereby prove, through dependence, that Sutpen has succeeded in his quest to be the son who seized the power of the father and then, as the father, kept that power from being seized by his own son in turn. For Sutpen can only prove that he is a better man than his father if he proves that he is a better man than his son, since Sutpen's father would have been defeated by his son in that very act. In Sutpen's final attempt to achieve his design, the battle against time receives its most explicit statement: "He was home again where his problem now was haste, passing time, the need to hurry. *He was not concerned, Mr. Compson said, about the courage and the will, nor even about the shrewdness now. He was not for one moment concerned about his ability to start the third time. All that he was concerned about was the possibility that he might not have time sufficient to do it in, regain his lost ground in.*"[3] But then, "*he realized that there was more in his problem than just lack of time, that the problem contained some super-distillation of this lack: that he was now past sixty and that possibly he could get but one more son, had at best but one more son in his loins, as the old cannon might know when it had just one more shot in its corporeality*" (p. 279). The problem is not just too little time; it is also the physical impotence that time brings, a physical impotence symbolic of Sutpen's "old impotent logic" (p. 279), of the impotence of the son's will in the face of the "it was" of time. Rosa says that when Sutpen gave her her dead sister's wedding ring as a sign of their engagement, it was "as though in the restoration of that ring to a living finger he had turned all time back twenty years and stopped it, froze it" (p. 165).

Sutpen's concern that he might be able to get only one more son leads him to suggest to Rosa that they try it first, and if the child is a male, that they marry. That suggestion drives Rosa from Sutpen's home and leads Sutpen to choose for his partner in the last effort to accomplish his design the only other available woman on his land, Milly Jones, the granddaughter of the poor white Wash Jones, and that choice brings Sutpen to the final repetition of the traumatic affront. In fact, Sutpen had reenacted that affront from the very start of his relationship with Wash Jones, never allowing Jones to approach the front of the mansion. When Sutpen seduces Milly and when her child is a daughter rather than the required son, Sutpen rejects mother and child as he had rejected his first wife and child. He tells Milly that if she were a mare he could give her a decent stall in his stable—a remark that Wash Jones overhears and that makes Jones realize for the first time Sutpen's attitude toward him and his family. Jones confronts the seducer of his granddaughter and kills him with a scythe. The irony of Sutpen's final repetition of the affront is that, though he delivers the affront in the role of a father rejecting his child, in order to get that child he had to assume the role of the son, he had to become the seducer; and Wash Jones, the poor white who had been the object of Sutpen's paternalism, now assumes the role of outraged father in relation to Sutpen. It is emblematic of the fate of the son in his battle against time that Sutpen, struggling in his old age to achieve his revenge, must again become the son and in that role be struck down by an old man with a scythe. . . .

The struggle between Quentin and his father that runs through the stream-of-consciousness narrative of Quentin's last day (in *The Sound and the Fury*) is primarily a dispute about time. The narrative begins with Quentin's waking in the morning ("I was in time again")[4] to the ticking of his grandfather's watch, the watch that his father had presented to him, saying, "I give it to you not that you may remember time, but that you may forget it now and then for a moment and not spend all your breath trying to conquer it" (p. 95). Quentin twists the hands off his grandfather's watch on the morning of the day when he forever frees himself and his posterity from the cycles of time and generation. When Quentin is out walking that morning, he passes the shop window of a watch store and turns away so as not to see what time it is, but there is a clock on a building and Quentin sees the time in spite of himself. He says, "I thought about how, when you dont want to do a thing, your body will try to trick you into doing it, sort of unawares" (p. 102). And that, of course, is precisely Quentin's sense of time—that it is a compulsion, a fate. For his father has told him that a man is the sum of his misfortunes and that time is his misfortune like "a gull on an invisible wire attached through space dragged" (p. 123). In his struggle against his father and thus against time, Quentin must confront the same problem that he faces in the story of Sutpen and his sons—whether a man's father is his fate. In *Absalom, Absalom!* when Shreve begins to sound like Quentin's father, Quentin thinks, "*Am I going to have to hear it all again. . . . I am going to have to hear it all over again. I am already hearing it all over again I am listening to it all over again I shall have to never listen to anything else but this again forever so apparently not only a man never outlives his father but not even his friends and acquaintances do*" (p. 277).

In *The Sound and the Fury,* when Quentin demands that his father act against the seducer Dalton Ames, Quentin, by taking this initiative, is in effect trying to supplant his father, to seize his authority. But Quentin's father refuses to act, and the sense of Mr. Compson's refusal is that Quentin cannot seize his father's authority because there is no authority to seize. Quentin's alcoholic, nihilistic father presents himself as an emasculated son, ruined by General Compson's failure. Mr. Compson psychologically castrates Quentin by confronting him with a father figure, a model for manhood, who is himself a castrated son. Mr. Compson possesses no authority that Quentin could seize because what Mr. Compson inherited from the general was not power but impotence. If Quentin is a son struggling in the grip of Father Time, so is his father. And it is exactly that argument that Mr. Compson uses against Quentin. When Quentin demands that they act against the seducer, Mr. Compson answers in essence:

Do you realize how many times this has happened before and how many times it will happen again? You are seeking a once-and-for-all solution to this problem, but there are no once-and-for-all solutions. One has no force, no authority to act in this matter because one has no originality. The very repetitive nature of time precludes the existence of originality within its

cycles. You cannot be the father because I am not the father—
only Time is the father.

When Quentin demands that they avenge Candace's virginity, his
father replies, "Women are never virgins. Purity is a negative state
and therefore contrary to nature. Its nature is hurting you not
Caddy and I said That's just words and he said So is virginity and
I said you dont know. You cant know and he said Yes. On the
instant when we come to realize that tragedy is second-hand"
(p. 135). In essence Quentin's father says:

> We cannot act because there exists no virginity to avenge and
> because there exists no authority by which we could avenge
> since we have no originality. We are second-hand. You are a
> copy of a copy. To you, a son who has only been a son, it
> might seem that a father has authority because he comes first,
> but to one who has been both a father and a son, it is clear
> that to come before is not necessarily to come first, that pri-
> ority is not necessarily originality. My fate was determined by
> my father as your fate is determined by yours.

Quentin's attempt to avenge his sister's lost virginity (proving
thereby that it had once existed) and maintain the family honor
is an attempt to maintain the possibility of "virginity" in a larger
sense, the possibility of the existence of a virgin space within
which one can still be first, within which one can have authority
through originality. . . .

Mr. Compson's denial of the existence of an authority by
which he could act necessarily entails his denial of virginity, for
there is no possibility of that originality from which authority
springs if there is no virgin within which one can be first. For
the same reason, Quentin's obsession with Candace's loss of virginity is necessarily an obsession with his own impotence, since
the absence of the virgin space renders him powerless. When Mr.
Compson refuses to act against Dalton Ames, Quentin tries to
force him to take some action by claiming that he and Candace
have committed incest—that primal affront to the authority of

the father. But where there is no authority, there can be no affront, and where the father feels his own inherited impotence, he cannot believe that his son has power. Mr. Compson tells Quentin that he does not believe that he and Candace committed incest, and Quentin says, "If we could have just done something so dreadful and Father said That's sad too, people cannot do anything that dreadful they cannot do anything very dreadful at all they cannot even remember tomorrow what seemed dreadful today and I said, You can shirk all things and he said, Ah can you" (p. 99). Since Mr. Compson believes that man is helpless in the grip of time, that everything is fated, there is no question of shirking or not shirking, for there is no question of willing. In discussing the revenge against time, Nietzsche speaks of those preachers of despair who say, "Alas, the stone *It was* cannot be moved" (p. 252), and Mr. Compson's last words in Quentin's narrative are "was the saddest word of all there is nothing else in the world its not despair until time its not even time until it was" (p. 197).

Is there no virgin space in which one can be first, in which one can have authority through originality? This is the question that Quentin must face in trying to decide whether his father is right, whether he is doomed to be an impotent failure like his father and grandfather. And it is in light of this question that we can gain an insight into Quentin's act of narration in *Absalom, Absalom!* for what is at work in Quentin's struggle to bring the story of the Sutpens under control is the question of whether narration itself constitutes a space in which one can be original, whether an "author" possesses "authority," whether that repetition which in life Quentin has experienced as a compulsive fate can be transformed in narration, through an act of the will, into a power, a mastery of time. Indeed, Rosa Coldfield suggests to Quentin when she first involves him in the story of the Sutpens that becoming an author represents an alternative to repeating his father's life in the decayed world of the postwar South:

"Because you are going away to attend the college at Harvard they tell me," Miss Coldfield said. "So I dont imagine you will ever come back here and settle down as a country lawyer in a little town like Jefferson, since Northern people have already seen to it that there is little left in the South for a young man. So maybe you will enter the literary profession as so many Southern gentlemen and gentlewomen too are doing now and maybe some day you will remember this and write about it." (pp. 9–10)

We noted earlier that the dialogue between Quentin and his father about virginity that runs through the first part of *Absalom, Absalom!* appears to be a continuation of their discussions of Candace's loss of virginity and Quentin's inability to lose his virginity contained in Quentin's section of *The Sound and the Fury*. Thus, the struggle between father and son that marked their dialogue in *The Sound and the Fury* is continued in their narration of *Absalom*. For Quentin, the act of narrating Sutpen's story, of bringing that story under authorial control, becomes a struggle in which he tries to best his father, a struggle to seize "authority" by achieving temporal priority to his father in the narrative act. At the beginning of the novel, Quentin is a passive narrator. The story seems to choose him. Rosa involves him in the narrative against his will, and he spends the first half of the book listening to Rosa and his father tell what they know or surmise. But in the second half, when he and Shreve begin their imaginative reconstruction of the story, Quentin seems to move from a passive role to an active role in the narrative repetition of the past.

So far I have mainly discussed the experience of repetition as a compulsion, as a fate, using Freud's analysis of the mechanism of the repetition compulsion in *Beyond the Pleasure Principle* as the basis for my remarks. But in that same text, Freud also examines the experience of repetition as a power—repetition as a means of achieving mastery. He points out that in children's play an event that the child originally experienced as something unpleasant will be repeated and now experienced as a source of pleasure, as a game. He describes the game of *fort/da* that he had observed being played by a little boy of one and a half. The infant would throw away a toy and, as he did, utter a sound that Freud took to be the German word *fort*, "gone." The child would then recover the toy and say the word *da*, "there." Freud surmised that the child had created a game by which he had mastered the traumatic event of seeing his mother leave him and into which he had incorporated the joyful event of her return. Freud points out that the mechanism of this game in which one actively repeats an unpleasant occurrence as a source of pleasure can be interpreted in various ways. First of all, he remarks that at the outset the child

> was in a *passive* situation—he was overpowered by the experience; but, by repeating it, unpleasurable though it was, as a game, he took on an *active* part. These efforts might be put down to an instinct for mastery that was acting independently of whether the memory was in itself pleasurable or not. But still another interpretation may be attempted. Throwing away the object so that it was "gone" might satisfy an impulse of the child's, which was suppressed in his actual life, to revenge himself on his mother for going away from him. In that case it would have a defiant meaning: "All right, then, go away! I don't need you. I'm sending you away myself."[5]

Freud makes a further point about the nature of children's games that has a direct bearing on our interest in the son's effort to become his father:

> It is obvious that all their play is influenced by a wish that dominates them the whole time—the wish to be grown-up and to be able to do what grown-up people do. It can also be observed that the unpleasurable nature of an experience does not always unsuit it for play. If the doctor looks down a child's throat or carries out some small operation on him, we may be quite sure that these frightening experiences will be the subject of the next game; but we must not in that connection overlook the fact that there is a yield of pleasure from another source. As the child passes over from the passivity of the experience to the activity of the game, he hands on the dis-

agreeable experience to one of his playmates and in this way
revenges himself on a substitute. (S.E., 18:17)

Significantly, Freud refers to this mastery through repetition as
"revenge," and his remarks suggest that this revenge has two
major elements—repetition and reversal. In the game of *fort/da*
the child repeats the traumatic situation but reverses the roles.
Instead of passively suffering rejection when his mother leaves,
he actively rejects her by symbolically sending her away. In the
other case, the child repeats the unpleasant incident that he experienced but now inflicts on a playmate, on a substitute, what
was formerly inflicted on him.

In this mechanism of a repetition in which the active and
passive roles are reversed, we have the very essence of revenge.
But we must distinguish between two different situations. In the
ideal situation, the revenge is inflicted on the same person who
originally delivered the affront—the person who was originally
active is now forced to assume the passive role in the same scenario; in the other situation, the revenge is inflicted on a substitute. This second situation sheds light on Sutpen's attempt to
master the traumatic affront that he suffered as a boy from the
man who became his surrogate father, to master it by repeating
that affront in reverse, inflicting it on his own son Charles Bon.
This scenario of revenge on a substitute sheds light as well on
the connection between repetition and the fantasy of the reversal
of generations and on the psychological mechanism of generation
itself. The primal affront that the son suffers at the hands of the
father and for which the son seeks revenge throughout his life is
the very fact of being a son—of being the generated in relation
to the generator, the passive in relation to the active, the effect
in relation to the cause. He seeks revenge on his father for the
generation of an existence which the son, in relation to the father,
must always experience as a dependency. But if revenge involves
a repetition in which the active and passive roles are reversed,
then the very nature of time precludes the son's taking revenge
on his father, for since time is irreversible, the son can never
really effect that reversal by which he would become his father's

father. The son's only alternative is to take revenge on a substitute, that is, to become a father himself and thus repeat the generative situation as a reversal in which he now inflicts on his own son, who is a substitute for the grandfather, the affront of being a son, the affront that the father had previously suffered from his own father. We can see now why Nietzsche, in connecting the revenge against time with the "envy of your fathers" (that envy which the son feels for his father and which the son has inherited from his father, who was himself a son), says, "What was silent in the father speaks in the son; and often I found the son the unveiled secret of the father."

When Sutpen takes revenge on a substitute for the affront that he received as a boy, he takes revenge not just on Charles Bon but on Henry as well. For if the primal affront is the very fact of being a son, then acknowledgment and rejection, inheritance and disinheritance are simply the positive and negative modes of delivering the affront of the son's dependency on the father. . . .

Keeping in mind this notion of revenge on a substitute, we can now understand how Quentin's act of narration in *Absalom, Absalom!* is an attempt to seize his father's authority by gaining temporal priority. In the struggle with his father, Quentin will prove that he is a better man by being a better narrator—he will assume the authority of an author because his father does not know the whole story, does not know the true reason for Bon's murder, while Quentin does. Instead of listening passively while his father talks, Quentin will assume the active role, and his father will listen while Quentin talks. And the basis of Quentin's authority to tell the story to his father is that Quentin, by a journey into the dark, womblike Sutpen mansion, a journey back into the past, has learned more about events that occurred before he was born than either his father or grandfather knew:

> "Your father," Shreve said. "He seems to have got an awful lot of delayed information awful quick, after having waited forty-five years. If he knew all this, what was his reason for telling you that the trouble between Henry and Bon was the octoroon woman?"

"He didn't know it then. Grandfather didn't tell him all of it either, like Sutpen never told Grandfather quite all of it."

"Then who did tell him?"

"I did." Quentin did not move, did not look up while Shreve watched him. "The day after we—after that night when we—"

"Oh," Shreve said. "After you and the old aunt. I see. Go on." (p. 266)

In terms of the narrative act, Quentin achieves temporal priority over his father, and within the narrative Quentin takes revenge against his father, against time, through a substitute—his roommate Shreve. As Quentin had to listen to his father tell the story in the first half of the novel, so in the second half Shreve must listen while Quentin tells the story. But what begins as Shreve listening to Quentin talk soon turns into a struggle between them for control of the narration with Shreve frequently interrupting Quentin to say, "Let me tell it now." That struggle, which is a repetition in reverse of the struggle between Mr. Compson and Quentin, makes Quentin realize the truth of his father's argument in *The Sound and the Fury*—that priority is not necessarily originality, that to come before is not necessarily to come first. For Quentin realizes that by taking revenge against his father through a substitute, by assuming the role of active teller (father) and making Shreve be the passive listener (son), he thereby passes on to Shreve the affront of sonship, the affront of dependency, and thus ensures that Shreve will try to take revenge on him by seizing authority, by taking control of the narrative. What Quentin realizes is that generation as revenge on a substitute is an endless cycle of reversibility in which revenge only means passing on the affront to another who, seeking revenge in turn, passes on the affront, so that the affront and the revenge are self-perpetuating. Indeed, the word "revenge," as opposed to the word "vengeance," suggests this self-perpetuating quality—*re-*, again, + *venger*, to take vengeance—to take vengeance again and again and again, because the very taking of revenge is the passing on of an affront that must be revenged. . . .

In his narrative struggle with Shreve, Quentin directly experiences the cyclic reversibility involved in revenge on a substitute—he experiences the maddening paradox of generation in time. At the beginning of their narrative, Quentin talks and Shreve listens, and in their imaginative reenactment of the story of the Sutpens, Quentin identifies with Henry, the father surrogate, and Shreve identifies with Charles Bon, the son, the outsider. But as the roles of brother avenger and brother seducer are reversible (precisely because the roles for which they are substitutes—father and son—are reversible through substitution), so Quentin and Shreve begin to alternate in their identifications with Henry and Bon, and Quentin finds that Shreve is narrating and that he (Quentin) is listening and that Shreve sounds like Quentin's father. Quentin not only learns that *"a man never outlives his father"* and that he is going to have to listen to this same story over and over again for the rest of his life, but he realizes as well that in their narration he and Shreve *"are both Father"*—*"Maybe nothing ever happens once and is finished. . . . Yes, we are both Father. Or maybe Father and I are both Shreve, maybe it took Father and me both to make Shreve or Shreve and me both to make Father or maybe Thomas Sutpen to make all of us"* (p. 210). In terms of a generative sequence of narrators, Mr. Compson, Quentin, and Shreve are father, son, and grandson (reincarnation of the father). Confronting that cyclic reversibility, Quentin realizes that if sons seek revenge on their fathers for the affront of sonship by a repetition in reverse, if they seek to supplant their fathers, then the very fathers whom the sons wish to become are themselves nothing but sons who had sons in order to take that same revenge on their own fathers. Generation as revenge against the father, as revenge against time, is a circular labyrinth; it only establishes time's mastery all the more, for generation establishes the rule that a man never outlives his father, simply because a man's son will be the reincarnation of that father. If for Quentin the act of narration is an analogue of this revenge on a substitute, then narration does not achieve mastery over time; rather, it traps the narrator more surely within the coils of time. What Quentin realizes is that the solution he seeks must be one that frees him alike from time and generation, from fate and revenge: he must die childless, he must free himself from time without having passed on the self-perpetuating affront of sonship.

Notes

1. Frederick L. Gwynn and Joseph L. Blotner, eds., *Faulkner in the University* (New York: Vintage, 1959), p. 71.

2. Friedrich Nietzsche, *Thus Spoke Zarathustra*, in *The Portable Nietzsche*, trans. Walter Kaufman (New York: Viking, 1954), pp. 249–54. All subsequent quotations from *Zarathustra* are taken from this edition.

3. William Faulkner, *Absalom, Absalom!* (New York: Random House, 1964), p. 278. All subsequent quotations from *Absalom, Absalom!* are taken from this edition.

4. William Faulkner, *The Sound and the Fury* (New York: Random House, 1946), p. 95. All subsequent quotations from *The Sound and the Fury* are taken from this edition.

5. Sigmund Freud, *The Standard Edition of the Complete Psychological Works of Sigmund Freud*, trans. James Strachey et al. (London: Hogarth, 1953), 18: 16. All subsequent quotations from Freud are taken from this edition, which will be cited hereafter as S.E.

The Signifying Abstraction

Reading *"the Negro" in* Absalom, Absalom!

THADIOUS DAVIS

◆　◆　◆

Aʙʟᴀᴄᴋ ᴘʀᴇꜱᴇɴᴄᴇ ᴅᴏᴍɪɴᴀᴛᴇꜱ *Absalom, Absalom!* as it
does perhaps no other Faulkner novel. Nowhere else is it so
apparent that the Negro is an abstract force confounding southern life both past and present even while, paradoxically, stimulating much of that life and art. The material or experiential
realities of black people do not figure into the conception of "the
Negro," an essentialized, always already "typed" configuration. A
symbolic statement of this idea is suggested by the action of Miss
Rosa Coldfield, one of the participants and narrators, who attempts to lift the weight of a coffin bearing the body of Charles
Bon (whom she has never seen either alive or dead) in order to
ascertain whether Bon's body is, in fact, inside. In essence, she
desires to validate Bon's existence from sensory evidence; she is
determined to know whether he is flesh or an imaginative construct. However, Miss Rosa is forced to apply not the most expedient sensory mechanism (that is, sight) but the only one available to her, and that one is insufficient for such a determination.
She recalls:

I tried to take the full weight of the coffin to prove to myself
that he was really in it. And I could not tell.... Because I
never saw him.... There are some things which happen to us
which the intelligence and the senses refuse ... occurrences
which stop us dead as though by some impalpable interven-
tion, like a sheet of glass through which we watch all subsequent events transpire as though in a soundless vacuum, and
fade, vanish; are gone, leaving us immobile, impotent, helpless;
fixed, until we can die.[1]

Her metaphorical language suggests the white South confronted with the Negro—its morally paralyzing abstraction. No
one sensory test is capable of validating the existence of the Negro;
even sight has traditionally been insufficient, not only because
blacks who are visibly white in color exist, but also because the
white southerner has persistently refused to see blacks, despite
living and dying with the effects of their presence. In Rosa Coldfield's mind, Charles Bon becomes "the abstraction which we
nailed into a box" (153), but like the Negro in the South, the
abstraction in this novel refuses to remain in a box. Bon is always
flesh *and* imaginative construct, both of which excite the rational
and creative faculties of the narrators. His presence, whether seen
or felt, is an inescapable reality. He becomes, like the Negro in
general, the metaphorical embodiment of all that is invisible in
southern life.

The Negro supplies the central focus—albeit the most illusive—and the major tensions in the pre- and postwar South of
Thomas Sutpen, a man born into the poor white mountain culture of western Virginia. Sutpen formulates a grand design for
living, labors to execute his design, and comes extremely close to
completing it. A synopsis of the Sutpen legend without the inclusion of the Negro is a story without motivation or significant
meaning. In June 1833, Sutpen mysteriously arrives in Jefferson
and resolutely establishes a plantation, wealth, and respectability.
He marries Ellen Coldfield, whose sister Rosa is one of the principal narrators, and he begets two children, Henry and Judith.

Prior to the outbreak of the Civil War, Sutpen's son renounces his birthright and departs from Sutpen's Hundred, his father's plantation, with a University of Mississippi classmate, Charles Bon, a New Orleans Creole and Judith Sutpen's intended husband. The two youths do not reappear until the end of the war when Henry shoots Bon at Sutpen's Hundred and then disappears. Sutpen himself returns from the war a decorated colonel but poverty ridden (having lost both his only son and most of his plantation). He salvages a mile of land, consorts with a poor white, Wash Jones, and opens a small store with Jones as partner; he is eventually killed by Jones.[2]

The addition of the Negro lifts the Sutpen legend from a flat canvas and transforms it into a powerful vehicle of individual will, of complex human motives and emotions, of personal, social, historical interactions. From the beginning, the Negro shapes, motivates, and determines Sutpen's design. As a boy of thirteen or fourteen, Sutpen approaches the big house on a Tidewater Virginia plantation with a message from his father to the owner, Pettibone. He is thwarted in his attempt to deliver the message (and see the inside of the house) by a black house slave who turns Sutpen away from the front entrance and directs him to the back door. The black man becomes the "monkey nigger" in Sutpen's accounts, and the young Sutpen becomes "the boy-symbol."

According to Sutpen's own version, which he gave to General Compson, Quentin's grandfather and Sutpen's sole confidant if not friend:

> He had never thought about his own hair or clothes or anybody else's hair or clothes until he saw that monkey nigger, who through no doing of his own happened to have had the felicity of being housebred in Richmond maybe, looking at them and he never even remembered what the nigger said, how it was the nigger told him, even before he had had time to say what he came for, never to come to that front door again but to go around to the back. (232)

Sutpen regards the incident as a denial of his individual value by the "monkey-dressed nigger butler" and the plantation owner and the system he represents. This recognition forces Sutpen to evaluate his personal and societal estimations of human worth. He has an epiphany regarding himself and his society:

Not the monkey nigger. It was not the nigger anymore than it had been the nigger that his father had helped to whip that night. The nigger was just another balloon face slick and distended with that mellow loud and terrible laughing so that he did not dare to burst it, looking down at him from within the half-closed door during that instant in which, before he knew it, something in him had escaped and—he unable to close the eyes of it—was looking out from within the balloon face just as the man who did not even have to wear the shoes he owned, whom the laughter which the balloon held barricaded and protected from such as he, looked out from whatever invisible place he (the man) happened to be at the moment, at the boy outside the barred door in his patched garments and splayed bare feet, looking through and beyond the boy, he himself seeing his own father and sisters and brothers as the owner, the rich man (not the nigger) must have been seeing them all the time—as cattle, creatures heavy and without grace, brutely evacuated into a world without hope or purpose for them, who would in turn spawn with brutish and vicious prolixity, populate, double treble and compound, fill space and earth with a race whose future would be a succession of cut-down and patched and made-over garments bought on exorbitant credit because they were white people, from stores where niggers were given the garments free, with for sole heritage that expression on a balloon face bursting with laughter which had looked out at some unremembered and nameless progenitor who had knocked at a door when he was a little boy and had been told by a nigger to go around to the back. (234–35)

Compressed into Sutpen's epiphany are all the tensions of caste and class struggles in the South, the brutalization of human beings, black and white, inherent in the slave system, and the moral ambiguities engendered by social problems. In closing the door, the "monkey nigger" opened the young Sutpen to a painful awareness of the inner dynamics of southern life. Because of his action, the "monkey nigger" balloons up larger than life; he becomes at once a visible metaphor for social reality and an allusive, invisible presence in the boy's life. The incident precipitates Sutpen's rejection of his family's simple way of life in favor of all that the "monkey nigger" held the door against. As a result, Sutpen desires not simply wealth, but slaves and a plantation, all the trappings designating the value of a human being in the antebellum world. He realizes, " 'You got to have land and niggers and a fine house to combat them with' " (238). He works for the indisputable, visible and material, right to assert his superiority over the "monkey nigger" and his kind, whom he further abstracts by means of the "balloon" metaphor. The intent, then, of Sutpen's design is to elevate himself into the landed gentry against whom no "nigger" can close doors. Sutpen feels compelled to prove that he is better than the "monkey nigger" and of course better than his owner. His self-image, personality, and life goals are shaped by the "monkey nigger," who is ultimately the personification of an entire society, its values and ideology.

Sutpen's eventual downfall may be read as inevitable because he substitutes his personal design in place of an existing moral and social order; however, his encounter with the "monkey nigger," as well as the resulting self-debate, leads to a recognition of his design as one complying with the existing social order and the prevalent moral order. In fact, because Sutpen's way of life is so in tune with the dominant southern way, his personal history can become one, in Quentin and Shreve's construction, with the progress of southern history. The South's retreat and surrender, in particular, are imagined as occurring simultaneously with the failure of Sutpen's design (347–50). What Sutpen violates in accepting the principles of the "monkey nigger" and plantation-society Virginia is precisely a personal code of honor and moral behavior derived from the social and ethical order of his own mountain society.

Sutpen's design is preeminently a drive toward completion of self. The irony is that he strives to complete an image of self constructed from models alien to his "natural" state. His failure is ordained from the moment he loses touch with that inner self which demands of the aware individual a completing of self. That initial loss of harmony is irreparable. Sutpen strives vaingloriously to complete Pettibone and his kind. Like those slave owners who upon seeing the African's black skin deemed him animal rather than human, Sutpen settles for appearance rather than substance as an estimate of human worth. Thus, he is essentially always about the business of duplication instead of true self-completion. Because an imitation is, by its very nature in the usual order of things, less than the original, his process of duplication, despite its unfinished state, can never attain the status, albeit morally questionable, of the model.

Moreover, because Sutpen's understanding of completion is literally a body fitted to the prescribed mold of Pettibone's kind, his design has as its ultimate goal the heir, the male figure, a replica of the model, which is again Pettibone's kind, not Sutpen himself but the Sutpen who is an imitation of Pettibone. Therefore, Charles Bon appears as a threat to Sutpen's design, not simply because Bon himself by virtue of his blood from the slave class cannot duplicate Pettibone's model, but primarily because Bon exercises such a powerful hold over Henry Sutpen, the heir apparent to Sutpen's design, that Bon possesses the potential of becoming himself a Pettibone, a model for Henry instead of the one laid out for Henry by his father.

Because he bases his design mimetically upon a negative, unwholesome model, Sutpen lacks the stature of a man who has failed in the attempt to achieve something magnificent or laudable. He, finally, can be reduced to a pathetic old man literally killing himself by trying to place his seed in an available and remotely acceptable (that is, "white") female in order to produce a male child. His ultimate failure is not a tragedy; he has denied his "central I-Am" (139). Yet because Faulkner presents that poignant boy symbol and with it the possibility of harmonious self-completion, he shows in that moment of faulty, but private, individual choice, Sutpen's lost potential. Though haunted by the boy symbol and the "monkey nigger," Sutpen understands neither the proportions nor the implications of his choice. Consequently, he never knows that his choice of Pettibone as a model for self-completion corrupts the boy symbol and signals waste and loss, which ultimately justify the laughter of the balloon-face "monkey nigger."

THE NEGRO PROVIDES the modern survivors of Sutpen's South (specifically, three of the four narrators: Jason Compson, his son Quentin, and Rosa Coldfield) with one means of approaching, understanding, and living with their past, the collective southern past, if they prove capable of reading the meaning of Sutpen's story. The opportunity that the story represents for them is reminiscent of an observation on race relations made by Joel Chandler Harris: "The problems of one generation are the paradoxes of a succeeding one, particularly if war, or some such incident intervenes to clarify the atmosphere and strengthen the understanding."[3]

The four narrators help to clarify the novel's intricate design and to determine the Negro's relationship to the verbal design, because narrating or "telling" in this novel is a way of establishing the concrete reality of narrator characters, both those participating in the legend and those attending its recreation. At the same time, the lack of telling by the blacks who inhabit the world of *Absalom, Absalom!* reduces them to an involved dependency upon the actual narrators, and their lack of telling functions, inversely, to establish the abstract quality of their existences.

Mr. Compson suggests the narrative method in his attempt to grasp the reality of the legend from "a few old mouth-to-mouth tales" and "letters without salutation or signature" exhumed "from old trunks and boxes and drawers" (100–101). He recognizes that fragments from the past are "almost indecipherable, yet meaningful" (101) and that the "living blood and seed" of people "in this shadowy attenuation of time" (101) create him and generate his absorption in their lives. He tells and sees both as himself, a sardonic and disillusioned southerner (an image which results from narrative voice rather than his actions), and as his father, General Compson, who had been Sutpen's lone intimate among the Jefferson townspeople, and whom the reader gets to know from his reported voice as much as from his interactions with the Sutpens. Although Mr. Compson understands the magnetic nature of the past and its inhabitants, he cannot explain the legend, not even in his own version, because "something is missing" (101). He has "the words, the symbols, the shapes themselves," but they remain "shadowy inscrutable and serene" (101). When, for example, he spins the tale of Charles Bon and his octoroon, Mr. Compson withdraws his final approval of it because his rational vision that "something is missing" is at odds with his creative impulse. He emphasizes Faulkner's main point: there is no true design for the telling, only the most expedient, practical, or communicative in a given situation.

Mr. Compson's acknowledgment that "something is missing" reminds the reader that *Absalom, Absalom!* is not about Sutpen, Charles, Henry, or Judith; but about Rosa, Mr. Compson, Quentin, and Shreve—about those inhabitants of a modern world (which is growing increasingly more complex) as they reveal and react, by force of habit, inclination, curiosity, or need, to aspects of themselves which appeared long ago, were illuminated, and faded only to be dusted off and held up to the light at the time of an impending personal crisis. At the same time, "something is missing" also suggests the absence of the Negro from the narrators' initial formulations of the past. The Negro's place in the whole pattern is revealed gradually.

The narrators themselves construct the Negro. Independently, they invent their own "Negro" in defining themselves and in expressing the limits of their imaginations, personalities, and humanity. Miss Rosa creates Clytie, Sutpen's slave daughter, and the "wild niggers" who build Sutpen's Hundred. Mr. Compson draws the New Orleans octoroon and her son, Charles Etienne St. Valery Bon. Quentin and Shreve imagine Charles Bon and his mother, Eulalia. They have the most complete authorial control over the Negro because his actual physical presence is the least documented by "facts" from the past. All of their projections operate to enrich the significance of "Negro" as both abstraction and metaphorical reality in *Absalom, Absalom!*

The most readily apparent example of this process is Rosa's construction of the "wild niggers," Sutpen's original band of slaves. She sees them as "his band of wild niggers like beasts half tamed to walk upright like men, in attitudes wild and reposed" (8). This recurring image of the slaves grounds her telling in a recognizable, if distorted, reality which attempts to wrench a personal moral order out of confusion. Because Sutpen is her private demon, she makes the "wild niggers" an extension of Sutpen himself and synonymous with Sutpen's Hundred. The "wild niggers" are her stage props and stage crew, just as they are the actual work horses who clear the virgin land and build Sutpen's plantation.

Beginning with the early segments of Rosa's narrative, the "wild niggers" become an obsessive presence in her mind. She calls them "a herd of wild beasts that he [Sutpen] has hunted down singlehanded because he was stronger in fear than even they were in whatever heathen place he had fled from" (16). She imagines their origins "in the mud" of a "dark swamp" (24) in order to complete her construction of their bestiality. The slaves, according to Rosa, are from a nameless "heathen place," which is a "much older country than Virginia or Carolina but it wasn't a quiet one" (17); her statements link Sutpen to the same place reference. She perceives Sutpen's "wild niggers" as his mirror reflection (somewhat similar to Quentin Compson's view in *The Sound and the Fury* of blacks as an "obverse reflection of the white people" among whom they live). The appearance of the blacks becomes the irrevocable proof of Sutpen's nature ("anyone could look at those negroes of his and tell," 17). They are imaginative projections of Rosa's feelings about Sutpen, about blacks, and about Sutpen's Hundred.

The "wild" slaves as an imagined reality in the novel serve to create psychological atmosphere and mood similar to the function of natural landscape or setting in some nineteenth-century novels (such as the moors in *Wuthering Heights*). For instance, every appearance of Sutpen in Jefferson is colored by Rosa's association of him with his "wild" slaves and land. Her version of the arrival of the Sutpen family for Sunday church services is typical of her perception of Sutpen's union with his slaves:

> This is my vision of my first sight of them which I shall carry to my grave: a glimpse like the forefront of a tornado, of the carriage . . . and on the front seat the face and teeth of the wild negro who was driving, and he [Sutpen], his face exactly like the negro's save for the teeth (this because of the beard doubt-less)—all in a thunder and a fury of wildeyed horses and of galloping and of dust. (23)

The words are aptly chosen, because Rosa is shading a real incident with her own peculiar way of seeing Sutpen.

Mr. Compson's narrative, gathered primarily from his father, General Compson, but also from other members of the community, serves as a corrective to Rosa's presentation of Sutpen and his "niggers." The townspeople and Mr. Compson are by no means egalitarian when it comes to the slaves, yet they do not display Miss Rosa's fanatical view of the blacks. Mr. Compson admits that there is a legend of the wild blacks and that there is some element of "truth" contained in the legend:

> So the legend of the wild men came gradually back to town, brought by the men who would ride out to watch what was going on, who began to tell how Sutpen would take stand beside a game trail with the pistols and send the negroes in to drive the swamp like a pack of hounds; it was they who told how during that first summer and fall the negroes did not even have (or did not use) blankets to sleep in, even before the coon-hunter Akers claimed to have walked one of them out of the absolute mud like a sleeping alligator and screamed just in time. (36)

The view of blacks in this less emotional account is still that of primitive men close to instinctual communication with animals and nature. Mr. Compson suggests, however, that the "wild men" were the mental projections of Sutpen created by the town, as well as Miss Rosa, in its ignorance. Sutpen's slaves, for instance, are not using a heathen tongue, but are West Indians (either from Haiti, as is Sutpen's first wife, or from Martinique, like the architect) speaking a French dialect. Akers and the other townspeople, Rosa included, fill in the shadowy outlines of the real Sutpen slaves with information that appeals to their imaginations.

Other versions balance Miss Rosa's misplaced emphasis, although they, too, represent Sutpen's relationship with his slaves as different from that traditionally depicted between master and slave. For example, General Compson told his son that "while the negroes were working Sutpen never raised his voice at them, that instead he led them, caught them at the psychological instant by example, by some ascendancy of forbearance rather than brute fear" (37). Sutpen, in other versions besides Miss Rosa's, worked intimately with his twenty slaves, all of them "plastered over with mud against the mosquitoes and . . . distinguishable one from another by his beard and eyes alone" (37). The others, too, stress the primitive nature of Sutpen's slaves and actively mythologize them into an integral part of the community legend. But they do not resort to calling them wild beasts; for example, one quite civil reference is to Sutpen's "crew of imported slaves"—though the added comment is that Sutpen's "adopted fellow citizens still looked upon [his slaves] as being a good deal more deadly than any beast" (38). Another reference terms the slaves "human," even while exalting their animal instincts: "human beings who belonged to him body and soul and of whom it was believed (or said) that they could creep up to a bedded buck and cut its throat before it could move" (40).

These views reflect a matter-of-fact depiction of blacks as slaves and whites as masters; they are glimpses of the minds of individuals thoroughly in tune with the dominant social practices. But these other observations of Sutpen's slaves are secondary; Rosa's vision of the "wild niggers" dominates the narrative. Her image of the "wild" slaves emanates from a mind out of joint with reality; it becomes a metaphor that the reader comes to identify, not with the demon Sutpen, but with the dark mysterious force at the center of southern life that, as portrayed in *Absalom, Absalom!* the southerner creates out of an unfailing reserve of self-flagellation and mental anguish.

When Rosa takes fragments of the actual and constructs an extensive, self-satisfying whole, she duplicates in microcosm the process of the novel as a whole. She projects precisely what she has made herself see and what she has come to feel after forty-five years of static rage. Her imaginative process is a more exaggerated version of Quentin's, Shreve's, and Mr. Compson's (as well as of the collective mind of Jefferson, because Rosa's view of Sutpen's slaves is but an exaggeration of the one held less rigidly by the town). In transforming Sutpen's human chattels into an extension of his demon self and into a synonym for his plantation, Rosa reveals the narrow limits of her personality and her humanity. Her picture of the slaves is the most revealing in what it reflects about Rosa herself, her mental condition and conflicting emotions.

Rosa's creation of the "wild niggers" is related to the larger implications of the novel. It brings into the open the hysterical image of blacks which undermines the rational appeal of Charles Bon, Sutpen's elegant mulatto son, who seeks paternal acceptance without regard to race. Because of its intensity and obstinacy, Rosa's distorted vision of the slaves pervades the entire novel and operates as a psychological backdrop for Sutpen's rejection of Bon and his black blood. The struggle between father and son can take on colossal proportions with far-reaching historical and cultural consequences in part because Rosa has so effectively created a forceful, larger-than-life, demonic landscape for the action.

All of the anonymous blacks in the world of *Absalom, Absalom!* represent the paradox of "a soil manured with black blood from two hundred years of oppression and exploitation until it sprang with an incredible paradox of peaceful greenery and crimson flowers" (251). The blacks appear to specify the paradoxical nature of the southern world constituting the novel, and at the same time their presence insinuates that the Negro's "place" is not simply subordinate to whites, but that its dimensions are different, smaller by comparison. Their presence suggests that the Negro is intended, in the proper order of things, to serve the white man. Generally, it is this provincial view of "Negro" growing out of his social functions in the South to which Sutpen adheres in formulating his design and to which the narrators conform in creating the legend.

The major black figures emerge out of conceptions of blacks accommodating themselves to the white world. They evolve out of two rather conventional literary images of blacks; significantly both involve mixed-blood people. One is the free mulatto during the pre- and postwar years who, envisioned as searcher, occupies the tragic "noplace" in southern life; the second is the slave daughter of the master who remains on the family plantation in an ambiguous maternal role as a member and nonmember of the family. In fact, all of the blacks in *Absalom* who are given names and delineated in detail are of mixed blood, or presumed to be by the narrators. Clytie and the Bon men are representative characters. Whereas the Bons are obviously crucial to the resolution of the novel, Clytie reveals the most about Faulkner's art and the Negro in this novel.

Throughout the work, Clytie is the felt black presence that pervades the South. She embodies this presence much more than Charles Bon, the abstraction who is made "nigger" in order to complete the pattern of the legend. She, more than any other character, reveals the ultimately inexplicable nature of human motivation. Both the tension of her existence and the obscurity of her involvement in the lives of others manifest Judith Sutpen's metaphor:

> You get born and you try this and you dont know why only you keep on trying it and you are born at the same time with a lot of other people, all mixed up with them, like trying to, having to, move your arms and legs with strings only the same strings are hitched to all the other arms and legs and the others all trying and they dont know why either except that the strings are all in one another's way. (127)

The process of life, as Judith describes it, means that Clytie is irrevocably connected to other individuals, so that her very existence, not merely her actions, affects and is affected by others.

Clytie is symbolically and literally a fusion of the two worlds of southern life; yet like the other mixed-blood people in the novel, Clytie does not experience the black world as a black person. Nonetheless, like Charles Bon and his son, Charles Etienne St. Valery, Clytie knows what it is to be treated as a "nigger" in the white world. She is, for instance, greeted differently by Sutpen upon his return from the war. Instead of the kiss and touch he gave Judith, Sutpen merely "looked at Clytie and said, 'Ah, Clytie' " (159). And Rosa Coldfield, who recoils from Clytie's "nigger" touch on the day of Charles Bon's death, has from childhood "instinctively" feared her and shunned objects she has touched (140).

Bereft of all that gave meaning to black life, Clytie is denied access to the only two institutions available to blacks—the family and the church. She is deprived of the sustenance of communal identity. Clytie is far from Elnora, the hymn-singing cook-housekeeper of Faulkner's *Flags in the Dust*, who is also the daughter of the white master. In addition, she is unlike Dilsey of *The Sound and the Fury*, who so staunchly endures with the help of the religion of the black community. Clytie is neither hymn-singing nor churchgoing; for her there is no refuge in a private life as a black person. Her lack of affiliation with the black world illuminates Faulkner's development of the black housekeeper-servant in his fiction, for in portraying Clytie he moves away from the character type as it appears in the earlier novels.

Clytie is an attempt at a more innovative, and psychologically modern, character, though she is a less successful characterization than Dilsey. Dilsey is conventionally a more imposing and prominent character; however, Faulkner creates her primarily as a character who obviously and symbolically elucidates and embodies his theme. Despite the innate nobility with which Faulkner endows her, Dilsey is and remains the Compsons' servant who on Easter Sunday emerges phoenix-like, encompassing the extant possibility for human survival with dignity and love. But Clytie is not simply a member of the Sutpen household. She is a member of the family, marked, according to all accounts, with the Sutpen face. She has no connections with individuals who are not Sutpens; her mother, one of Sutpen's original band of slaves, is not even given to her as a memory. Legally chattel before the war and an institution afterward, Clytie is a coffee-colored Sutpen. She is defined mainly in terms of her Sutpen heritage and blood. In terms of traditional place and order, then, she is where she belongs. There are no possibilities suggested for her living apart from Sutpen's Hundred; she has no alternative form of existence.

Clytie's singular position may initially suggest a realistic mode of characterizing blacks; however, the fictional method by which she achieves life, primarily through Rosa Coldfield's imaginative construction of her, is a break with conventional portraits. Clytie's presence, unlike Dilsey's, is not intended to provide ethical certainty or emotional comfort. Instead it evokes the duality of human nature. Whereas Dilsey lacks close personal identification with any member of the Compson family, Clytie is closely identified with both her half sister, Judith, and her father, Sutpen. Described as "at once both more and less Sutpen" (140), she is an extension of the physical selves of Judith and Sutpen, as well as an imaginative projection by the narrators of some dark essence of the Sutpen being. Whatever reality Clytie attains as a character, she attains in the minds of her narrators, but that reality primarily reinforces their central visions. All that readers know of her is filtered through the consciousness of others.

Clytie is preeminently a silent, shadowy presence which, imaginatively delineated, assumes force in the lives of those around her. Her position in the narrative challenges conventional mechanisms contrived for identifying family members and for defining the "central I-Am" of the individual. At the same time, her personal responses to her status as a slave daughter and to her world go unarticulated by words or gestures. What Clytie herself feels remains a mystery, despite the fact that she is one of the participants in the Sutpen legend who survives into the novel's present.

Although Judith and her brother, Henry, are described as "that single personality with two bodies" (9–10), the description is even more fitting when applied to Clytie and Judith. Except for physical coloring, the two could be twins. They appear together initially, and from that first appearance, they are twin, silent, and calm figures of strength. Both frequently are called "inscrutable," "impenetrable," and "serene." As they age, they become more alike and gradually assume the status of living legends in the Jefferson community. Clytie is the shadowy complement of her white sister. In a sense, she is Judith's double, functioning to complete Judith's fragmented self. For example, after Bon's death Judith tells the Compsons that she will not commit suicide because "somebody will have to take care of Clytie" (128). Yet because a Clytie who needs Judith's care is never visible, the reader may speculate that she is instead another part of Judith's own self, which cannot be denied as long as there is some external manifestation of it. Symbolically, Clytie represents both Judith's inner self and the social environment in which Judith functions and exists.

Because Clytie is Judith's complementary part, she follows to conclusion the pattern of action established by Judith and supported by the two of them while Judith lived. She pays for Judith's and Charles Etienne's tombstones, raises Jim Bond, and harbors Henry. Her final action, the burning of the Sutpen mansion, is a desperate attempt to preserve the house and the family from violation by outsiders because the Sutpens have earned that right. As she observes, "Whatever he done, me and Judith and him have paid it out" (370).

Clytie, as black twin to Judith, becomes a subtle statement of the oneness of humankind. The common bonds of temperament, interests, duty, and affection unite the two women in a sisterhood that transcends race. Their relationship is a more sustained and meaningful version of that between Henry and Charles. Because Clytie and Judith relate to each other as "womenfolk" first, then as "daughter" and "sister," they partly escape the racial burden placed on their brothers. Their personal relationship provides a model of sibling cooperation and harmony in the novel, and by extension it suggests the possibility of a different order of social interaction between races in the South.

The limits of Clytie's existence are set not by her slave status but by her identity as a Sutpen, and in that regard she is also Judith's counterpart. The two are locked into a narrow existence; uncomplaining and stoical, they make the best of their lives. They share the "*indomitable woman-blood*" (153) and are as close to survivors as Faulkner comes in *Absalom, Absalom!* They accept a life without joy or frivolity; they assume the burden of existence and accept each other as human beings. Consequently, Clytie and Judith emerge together as the most admirable characters in the novel. Certainly, Faulkner endows them with dignity and endurance, with pity and love—the virtues he esteemed most and identified with his beloved mammy, Caroline Barr, whom Clytie alone of his black women characters resembles.

The relationship between Clytie and Judith is critical to the novel because it achieves a level of communication and kinship across social barriers, but also because it precipitates the destructive cycle of Charles Etienne St. Valery Bon, the son of Charles Bon and a New Orleans octoroon. Charles Etienne's story moves the Sutpen legend into the postwar period and enlarges its social significance. Clytie prevents the boy on his first visit to Sutpen's Hundred from playing with a black youth. Even after Charles Etienne arrives to live on the plantation, he is not allowed to have contact with blacks or whites. By watching him with a "brooding fierce unflagging jealous care" (200), Clytie virtually isolates him from members of either race. It seems that as long as she can keep him on Sutpen's Hundred, Clytie believes that she can protect Charles Etienne from the knowledge that barriers exist between races and that those barriers are socially real. She knows that the plantation is a self-contained world sustained only by Judith and herself, for whom racial distinctions no longer have social meanings. Clytie—not Judith—is the boy's guardian and protector. She becomes "the fierce, brooding woman" (197) who in a "curious blend of savageness and pity, of yearning and hatred" (198) cares for Charles Etienne. Clytie's efforts, nevertheless, lead the boy to a much more painful and premature knowledge: the awareness that the barriers between races and individuals are psychically real. Sutpen's legacy to his rejected black son, Charles Bon, is thus perpetuated in the next generation.

When taken abruptly from the "padded and silken vacuum

cell" (199) of his life in New Orleans, Charles Etienne encounters the "gaunt and barren" (197) world in which Clytie and Judith live. Once he crosses the threshold of Sutpen's Hundred, his "very silken remaining clothes, his delicate shirt and stockings and shoes which still remained to remind him of what he had once been, vanished, fled from arms and body and legs as if they had been woven of chimaeras or of smoke" (197). His silk clothing is symbolic of more than the white world; it represents the hedonistic, cosmopolitan world of New Orleans, "where pigmentation had no more moral value than the silk walls . . . and the rose-colored . . . shades, where the very abstractions which he might have observed—monogamy and fidelity and decorum and gentleness and affection—were as purely rooted in the flesh's offices as the digestive processes" (199). The city with less rigid racial codes and more indulgent mores forms a contrast to the closed world of the plantation and Jefferson. Compared to the delicate, mythical existence Charles Etienne experiences in New Orleans, Sutpen's Hundred (as introduced by Clytie and the denim jumper) is the abrasive "actual world"; Mr. Compson envisions Charles Etienne as

> produced complete . . . in that cloyed and scented maze of shuttered silk as if he were the delicate and perverse spirit symbol, immortal page of the ancient immortal Lilith, entering the actual world not at the age of one second but twelve years, the delicate garments of his pagehood already half concealed beneath that harsh and shapeless denim cut to an iron pattern and sold by the millions—that burlesque of the Sons of Ham. (196)

When Clytie covers Charles Etienne with a coarse denim jumper, she burdens him with a second existence without explanation. She begins the process of alienating the boy and destroying the world he knows to be real. Neither Clytie nor Judith recognizes his loneliness. He is irretrievably an outsider—alien to Sutpen's Hundred and lost to the two women who, in their simplicity, fail to realize that he does not understand (indeed, has no basis for understanding) his new life, the two women themselves, or their awkward protective gestures. Clytie and Judith, for all their strength and endurance, are extremely naive women; they are, like their father and brother, independent country people. Thus, they are unable to see the beginning of Charles Etienne's dividedness. Their naiveté and ignorance compound the boy's problem with identity and place. Both women fail Charles Etienne; he, in turn, fails them and himself. These joint failures emphasize the reciprocal nature of the tragedy resulting from defining human beings in terms of race and caste. The tragedy is social as much as private; it affects whites as well as blacks.

Charles Etienne rejects the white world, which he mistakenly perceives as being peopled by the two stern, shadow women, Judith and Clytie, who seem to need only each other. By their inability to express their feelings for him in terms he can clearly comprehend, his two Sutpen "aunts" propel Charles Etienne into a constant battle with racial barriers, which are mainly presented as social restrictions against open, public displays of interracial activities. (He is reminiscent of Joe Christmas of *Light in August*, who is similarly propelled by a restrictive Puritan disciplinarian into a rootless, embattled life.) Charles Etienne marries a "coal black and ape-like woman" who "existed in that aghast and automaton-like state" (205). He makes his wife, a "black gargoyle" (209), an external projection of his black self. He abuses his wife's humanity, even though Faulkner presents her as physically grotesque and inhuman ("resembling something in a zoo," 209). By his treatment of the helpless woman, he dehumanizes himself and alienates himself from the rest of humanity. After a period of moving through a series of cities and towns as if driven by fury, Charles Etienne returns to Sutpen's Hundred, rents a parcel of land on shares, and lives in an old slave cabin on the place. Nonetheless, he does not penetrate the black world. He remains as alienated from it as he is from his black wife and the Sutpen women.

Clytie's fierce guardianship of Charles Etienne corresponds to mythical allusions evoked by her name, Clytemnestra. According to Mr. Compson, Sutpen "named her himself" (61), though perhaps "he intended to name Clytie, Cassandra, prompted by some pure dramatic economy not only to beget but to designate the presiding augur of his own disaster, and . . . he just got the name wrong through a mistake natural in a man who must have almost taught himself to read" (62). Mr. Compson seems inaccurate here because Clytie is not so much Cassandra, mad prophetess of doom, as she is Clytemnestra, fiercely maternal wife/mother figure of vengeance.

The allusions to the name Clytemnestra seem appropriate, if not precisely so. Clytemnestra is wife/mother, who out of complex motives brings disaster to her children and herself by willfully exacting revenge for her daughter Iphigenia's death. Despite the reference to Clytie's "fierceness," she does not seem to be a personality motivated by a personal fury (such as revenge). However, the mythical Clytemnestra is responsible for Cassandra's death; their two visions of reality and duty fatally conflict. Clytie is related to the mythical Clytemnestra in this sense, because she finally thwarts Rosa's efforts to control the Sutpens by taking charge of Henry. She burns the mansion rather than have Rosa remove Henry and assume responsibility for him. Shortly thereafter, Rosa dies, somehow mortally wounded by her last encounter with Clytie. Clytie's action represents a kind of dual expiation on the part of both races in the South and particularly on the part of the planter class. In burning Sutpen's Hundred with herself and Henry inside, Clytie destroys the two surviving Sutpens, who along with Judith are similar to the mythical Orestes in their attempts to expiate the old crimes, their own sins and those they inherit from their father.

While Mr. Compson speculates that Sutpen intended to name Clytie "Cassandra," he and Quentin actually describe Rosa Coldfield as "Cassandralike." Quentin sees her as having "an air Cassandralike and humorless and profoundly and sternly prophetic out of all proportion to the actual years even of a child who had never been young" (22). And before his explanation of Clytie's name, Mr. Compson speaks of the "Puritan righteousness and outraged female vindictiveness [in which] Miss Rosa's childhood was passed, that aged and ancient and timeless absence of youth which consisted of Cassandralike listening beyond closed doors" (60). Shreve, too, refers to Rosa as "Cassandra" in his description of her peculiar relationship with Sutpen: "instead of a widowed Agamemnon to her Cassandra an ancient stiff-jointed Pyramus to her eager though untried Thisbe" (177).

In linking both Clytie and Rosa to Cassandra, Faulkner reiterates that his characters flow into one another and merge with historical or mythological figures as well. The figurative association of Clytie with Rosa joins the Negro to the white southerner who is the most reactionary about race. Their union is tense because, in Rosa's words, they are *"open, ay honorable, enemies"* (157). Clytie and Rosa, the daughter and the sister-in-law, the slave and the "not-wife," share a relationship with Sutpen that is as tortured as that of either Clytemnestra's or Cassandra's to Agamemnon.

When Rosa and Clytie confront each other on the stairs of Sutpen's Hundred after Charles Bon's murder, they participate in one of the most dramatic, and revealing, scenes in the work.[4] At the moment of their meeting, Rosa sees Clytie as an extension of Sutpen and as her own twin sister because of their joint connection to him: "the two of us joined by that hand and arm which held us like a fierce rigid umbilical cord, twin sistered to a fell darkness which had produced her" (140). Though Rosa, like Charles Etienne, rails against the order of things in her world, she recognizes the complex nature of human interconnectedness (thereby accentuating one of Faulkner's major themes). She describes herself as well as Clytie as "sentient victim" and admits the private, mysterious connection to Sutpen, who is Clytie's biological father and who gives Rosa life (that is, provides her with a raison d'être which in its negative capacity links her even more closely to the negative aspect of Sutpen's indefatigable and undefeated will to duplicate himself). At the same time, Rosa acknowledges the connection between two individuals who share a deeply felt experience: *"we seemed to glare at one another not as two faces but as the two abstract contradictions which we actually were, neither of our voices raised, as though we spoke to one another free of the limitations and restrictions of speech and hearing"* (138). Rosa and Clytie are yoked so that their differences are grossly exaggerated, even though the very intensity of their union destroys ordinary impediments to communication. This yoking of "abstract contradictions" is central to the structural and thematic progress of the novel. For instance, it is one way of approaching Quentin and Shreve as creators, or Henry and Charles as friends.

Rosa's meeting with Clytie is a central scene because it reverberates with all the tensions between blacks and whites, between classes and races that have been used to define the South and to establish the major concerns of the novel. One of the most starkly honest scenes in the Faulkner canon, this meeting probes the psychological and cultural realities of race and kinship. It suggests all of the dramatic meetings which take place in *Absalom* (Sutpen and the "monkey nigger," Charles Bon and Henry, even Shreve and Quentin). Superseded in intensity only by Quentin's encounter with Henry, it is the single extended narration of a confrontation between black and white in a work clearly dependent upon a series of such confrontations for meaning.

Rosa, in her moments of knowing, her "epiphany," encounters Clytie as "Negro" and "woman" but also, paradoxically, as "sister": "*we stood there joined by that volitionless . . . hand, . . . I cried 'And you too? And you too, sister, sister?'* " (140). Prior to this moment, Rosa has neither recognized nor accepted Clytie as Sutpen's daughter, sister to Judith and metaphorically sister to Rosa herself. Still, Clytie is not a person to Rosa. She is "nigger" and a sphinxlike presence invented by Sutpen solely to confound Rosa; she is "*the Sutpen face . . . already there, rocklike and firm . . . waiting there . . . in his own image the cold Cerberus of his private hell*" (136).

Clytie's presence reminds Rosa that she is cut off from significant areas of life, particularly from family participation, just as the Negro, symbolically represented by the "balloon face" and the "monkey nigger," serves to remind Sutpen of his poor white origins. It is not only that Rosa is not a wife, but that finally she is not sister, daughter, aunt, or niece. She is and remains an outsider. Begrudgingly, Rosa recognizes her own inadequacies, Clytie's essential harmony with her world, and their psychological union. But she does so by making Clytie not merely like Sutpen, a demon, but the personification of all that has prevented her full participation in life. Clytie becomes an *"immobile antagonism,"* *"that presence, that familiar coffee-colored face"* (137), which Rosa "sees" as both an object blocking her passage up the stairs and as a force confounding her entire life.

Clytie stands for Sutpen's continuing reality and his insult to the spinster who hurls herself into

> *that inscrutable coffee-colored face, that cold implacable mindless (no, not mindless: anything but mindless, his own clairvoyant will tempered to amoral evil's undeviating absolute by the black willing blood with which he had crossed it) replica of his own which he had created and decreed to preside upon his absence, as you might watch a wild distracted nightbound bird flutter into the brazen and fatal lamp.* (138)

Clytie is the proof (and for the sight-oriented Rosa, the visible therefore incontrovertible proof) of Sutpen's sexual activity, in particular his mating with someone other than a "wife," with someone more animal than human, with the "black willing blood" of one of the original "wild niggers." It is an insult to the spinster that Sutpen, who represented her one opportunity for marriage (here, specifically sex and children), would "grace" even a "nigger" but would deny her. Thus, Sutpen himself, not Clytie, has condemned Miss Rosa to ignorance and blind, futile thrusting. Sutpen is, paradoxically, "clairvoyant," and Clytie is a "brazen and fatal lamp," while Rosa is "a wild distracted nightbound bird." For all their negative capacity drawn by Miss Rosa, Sutpen and Clytie symbolize vision and light for her. On the other hand, Rosa with ironic aptness sees herself as a sightless bird enmeshed in darkness and fluttering blindly into destruction.

Clytie's command, *"Dont you go up there, Rosa"* (138), causes Rosa to assert the authority of her race and the superiority of her position as a white woman in the South: *"Rosa? . . . To me? To my face?"* (139). Yet even while speaking the words, Rosa knows *"it was not the name, the word the fact that she had called me Rosa"* (139); Rosa believes that *"while we stood face to face . . . she did me more grace and respect than anyone else I knew; . . . to her of all who knew me I was no child"* (139). She infers that Clytie recognizes her as "woman," intuits her female urges and sexual drives. Perhaps Clytie alone, with her "brooding awareness and acceptance of the inexplicable unseen, inherited from an older and a purer race" (138), understands Rosa's frustrated sexual energy, understands that Rosa is denied access to marriage and familial intimacy (and in this instance, specifically, denied access as well to the knowledge and experience of life and death she seeks in the upper regions of the Sutpen house).

Nonetheless, Rosa perverts the meeting into a racial confrontation; she is otherwise unable to cope with its implications (that is, Clytie as a Sutpen "belongs" at Sutpen's Hundred and has a natural place in the affairs of the family, whereas Rosa, though white, is relegated to a lower, nonprivileged status). Rosa's tactic reiterates the ultimate tragedy of the Sutpen legend: the son's meeting with the father is reduced to a racial confrontation; kinship, whether physical or spiritual, may be denied when one party is "Negro."

Clytie's hand on Rosa raises the specter of a "nigger" violating racial barriers. Symbolically, the gesture duplicates the larger violation attempted, according to Quentin and Shreve, by Charles Bon, the "nigger" who desires to sleep not with the abstract "white woman," but with the individual "sister" and "daughter" (which Judith personifies). Rosa experiences *"a shocking impact . . . at that black arresting and untimorous hand on* [her] *white woman's flesh"* (139). Her response is automatic: *"Take your hand off me, nigger!"* (140). She retreats into the sanctity of race, and to the safety of racial epithets.

In this moment Rosa exposes the process by which the individual makes "nigger" a scapegoat; it is a microcosm of the larger societal process which the community acts out in *Light in August*, and it is a tableau extending Sutpen's treatment of his son Charles Bon to the conduct of an entire society. Rosa, in attempting to convert Clytie into "nigger" and the physical embodiment of all blackness, reveals her own duality and asserts herself as the flawed component of a flawed society. Clytie is, after all, more Sutpen than black and more Sutpen than woman, primarily as a result of Rosa's own imaginative constructions, which she has made "true" in the progress of the narrative. The two visible realities that Clytie embodies ("Negro" and "woman") are denied and rendered meaningless by her "Sutpenness," which is the true abstraction confronting and confounding Rosa on the stairs. "*Yes,*" Rosa declares, "*I stopped dead—no woman's hand, no negro's hand, but bitter-curb to check and guide the furious and unbending will—I crying not to her, to it; speaking to it through the negro, the woman*" (139–40).

Since Rosa believes that Clytie is most vulnerable because of her race and the social stigma it carries, she can deny her own egalitarian emotions and subvert her own compelling logic:

> There is something in the touch of flesh with flesh which abrogates, cuts sharp and straight across the devious intricate channels of decorous ordering, which enemies as well as lovers know because it makes them both—touch and touch of that which is citadel of the central I-Am's private own: not spirit, soul; the liquorish and ungirdled mind is anyone's to take in any darkened hallway of this earthly tenement. But let flesh touch flesh, and watch the fall of all the eggshell shibboleth of caste and color too. (139)

Rosa's perception is fleeting; her spoken word, "nigger," does not coincide with her internal analysis of the meaning of touch.

Although "touch" seems emblematic of larger possibilities for interracial contact, Clytie's touch is not an ambivalent gesture. Nor is Rosa's response ambiguous; Rosa means to issue her command in terms that carry the weight of social sanction. Rosa's response to Clytie is an overt expression of Sutpen's implicit response to Charles Bon. Sutpen's drama is an internal process not witnessed by the reader, yet the essence of his complex reaction to Bon is mirrored symbolically in the extended development of Rosa's physical and emotional response to Clytie. For all of the characters, touch crystalizes the "eggshell shibboleth of caste and color" and the taboos against interracial union; touch creates, too, the necessity for southern customs, and laws against miscegenation (specifically here because the "secret" of the legend is solved in terms of miscegenation—actual miscegenation for the father, Sutpen, and intended by the son Charles Bon). Nonetheless, southern interracial restrictions, according to one theme of this novel, are not about preventing touch but rather about affirming all of the negative implications of touch when they serve the ends of white society.

Clytie's reactions to this meeting are not provided; she remains as nonverbal as she has been throughout the novel; however, her presence, as a mixed-blood person within the Sutpen family, suggests that either race or kinship must be denied if caste and color are to continue to sustain fixed meanings in a changing world. Clytie's involvement in the lives of other characters forwards the conclusion that in order to avoid self-destruction, and perhaps ultimately social disintegration, bonds of kinship on every level must be honored, even if they exist across racial lines (or most especially when they do, as Faulkner suggests both with the resolution of *Absalom, Absalom!* and with a later novel, *Go Down, Moses*). This idea of kinship, most apparent in the portraits of Clytie and Charles Bon, is, in one sense, an insightful development of the idea of family (both white and black) Faulkner first employs in *Flags in the Dust* and uses more intensively in *The Sound and the Fury;* it partakes, too, of the conception of "blood" and racial definitions from *Light in August.* Blood and family become in *Absalom, Absalom!* human kinship and interconnection—larger abstractions—which Faulkner presents as confused and conflicting, but by means of them he aims toward a more comprehensive way of portraying the divided world of his South. He attempts to probe imaginatively into the causes behind the Sutpen legend, but because neither incest nor fratricide provides him with a means of transcending the inner tensions of his narrative situation, he returns to the Negro. He relies upon conventional beliefs about. "Negro" to solve his narrative dilemma.

In *Absalom, Absalom!* Faulkner seems to have pulled a neat trick. Both Quentin and Shreve are convinced that they have found the "truth" of the Sutpen puzzle in the Negro, technically in their uncovering the secret of Bon's black blood. Almost inevitably their view has been accepted. In a sense their resolution amounts to a discovery of the proverbial "nigger in the woodpile," a not-so-unexpected way for southerners to resolve the complexity of human interactions and motivations. (Shreve is, of course,

Canadian; however, his notions of the South are stereotyped, literary exaggerations.) Both Shreve and Quentin, in conjecturing "Negro" as the key, reflect something basic about their conformity to the ideology of the South. They retrace what Mr. Compson relates as the opinion of the townsmen regarding Sutpen once he became successful:

> There were some among his fellow citizens who believed even yet that there was a nigger in the woodpile somewhere, ranging from the ones who believed that the plantation was just a blind to his actual dark avocation, through the ones who believed that he had found some way to juggle the cotton market itself and so get more per bale for his cotton than honest men could to those who believed apparently that the wild niggers which he had brought there had the power to actually conjure more cotton per acre from the soil than any tame ones had ever done. (72)

The "nigger in the woodpile" to which Mr. Compson refers takes on a literal meaning in the resolution as it is constructed by Shreve and Quentin. The old saw becomes an indispensable part of Faulkner's complex structure and narrative scheme.

IN THEIR RECONSTRUCTION of the final confrontation between Henry Sutpen and Charles Bon, Quentin and Shreve assign Bon the fateful words: "*I'm the nigger that's going to sleep with your sister. Unless you stop me, Henry*" (358). The imagination of the two narrators is frozen into the clichés of southern thinking. Quentin and Shreve do not intuit the terms in which to couch Charles's decisive statement; they know. Shreve's knowledge is a result of his melodramatic vision of the South, Quentin's of his long personal and historical experience of the South.

Shreve deflates the finely tempered rhetorical reality the two have created by calling Bon in his very next reference "the black son of a bitch" (358). Somehow it all becomes very ordinary, so ordinary in fact that Shreve at last is ready to end the night: "Come on. . . . Let's get out of this refrigerator and go to bed"

(359). The Negro is, after all, an expected part of the tissue of southern life. Instead of penetrating something unfathomable about human conduct or life, the two narrators (and Faulkner himself, for all the brilliant shape of the novel) resort to the pedestrian—though it is the pedestrian that has tyrannized conscious and subconscious levels of thought. Perhaps the problem that the Negro represents to the southern white man clouds his perceptions and constricts his imaginative faculties; however, that problem is so enduring and realistic that its power to affect mental processes does not dissipate. Even Shreve's mental capacity to make enlightened conjectures is stimulated as well as circumscribed by the Negro's actual presence in the South. Shreve comes to the legend with an image of the South's depravity, and he concludes with a confirmation of it. The South and the Negro are once again inextricably bound together, though this time it is the result of a piecemeal and tortuous logic.

On one level, that of narrative structure, it is a long way around to a "solution." But on another level, a certain ease is apparent in the way the narrators head with an inevitable, dead reckoning to the Negro, though they themselves try to delay it and prolong the resolution in order to savor or reconstruct all of the elements possible from a logical base. Their fabrications create an illusion of reality; their construct is quite believable. All rational investigations lead to a basic reality: Charles Bon as "nigger."

Nonetheless, the process by which the two young narrators come to Bon as "nigger" suggests an analogy to Rosa Coldfield's poetic analysis of remembering: "That is the substance of remembering—sense, sight, smell, the muscles with which we see and hear and feel—not mind, not thought: there is no such thing as memory: the brain recalls just what the muscles grope for: no more, no less: and its resultant sum is usually incorrect and false and worthy only of the name of dream" (143). The image of the brain's recalling "just what the muscles grope for" is analogous to Shreve and Quentin's simultaneously moving toward Bon's blackness out of separate and distinct conditionings of their muscles. In recreating the past, they are remembering what their experience of life has taught them.

Authority for Bon's black blood, then, is not the point. The point is rather that both for Faulkner in the construction of his novel and for his various narrators in the telling of the tale, meaning hinges upon somehow coming to the "fact" of Bon's being "Negro," when ironically he is the one character the furthest removed (by all narrative accounts) from "Negro" and "nigger" as the novel and society have presented them; even Clytie, whose Sutpenness primarily defines her, remains a "coffee-colored," "dark essence." Mr. Compson's images of Bon as "a young man of a worldly elegance and assurance beyond his years, handsome" (74) and as "watching, contemplating them from behind that barrier of sophistication in comparison with which Henry and Sutpen were troglodytes" (93) function effectively to separate Bon from all social images of Negro as subordinates and servants which Faulkner incorporates into the novel.

What the narrators finally make of Bon as "nigger" is prefigured by Mr. Compson: "Bon with that sardonic and surprised distaste which seems to have been the ordinary manifestation of the impenetrable and shadowy character. Yes, shadowy: a myth, a phantom: something which they engendered and created whole themselves; some effluvium of Sutpen blood and character, as though as a man he did not exist at all" (104). It is only a short step from the conception of Bon that Mr. Compson reports to the two youths' conjecture that Bon is a "nigger." Bon becomes "the abstraction" and "the Negro" created to satisfy the needs of the characters and narrators. His situation, like Clytie's, stresses the force and inevitability of the Negro as a presence, "impenetrable and shadowy," at the center of the South and of Faulkner's creative imagination.

Absalom, Absalom! returns the reader and each of the four narrators to those myths about the southern past (the myth of racial purity is just one) out of an acknowledged helplessness and inability ever really to know or understand the South, and by extension both themselves and the past. The view of miscegenation, or a pathological fear of it, as the primary cause of destruction in *Absalom, Absalom!* ignores the fact that miscegenation is only one piece of the larger race question and only one part of the total pattern of life represented in the novel.

For Quentin and Shreve, it is not slavery alone which accounts for the South's moral deficiency. It is, as well, the white southerner's failure to respond to the black human being; the response instead is to an abstraction—"the Negro" myth. Unfortunately, Quentin's conjecture that Henry kills Bon because of the threat of the Negro points to the individual seeking something outside of himself to hold responsible for his situation. Quentin needs the myth of the Negro in order to escape a personal confrontation of complex moral problems, incest and fratricide. Sutpen, too, is guilty of a similar evasion of self when he fails to ask where he himself went wrong. Whereas Sutpen distorts his understanding of morality to fit the contours of the morally reprehensible, slaveholding South, Quentin rationalizes a morally complex situation by resorting to the scapegoat sanctioned by his society. Ultimately, Quentin in the modern age repeats the mistake of Sutpen in the past. He seeks an external cause which, because of the social composition of the South, is readily available in the Negro.

Regarding the interpretation of Sutpen's story, Faulkner has observed:

> I think no one individual can look at a truth. It blinds you. You look at it and you see one phase of it. Someone else looks at it and sees a slightly awry phase of it. But taken all together, the truth is in what they saw though nobody saw the truth intact. . . . It was, as you say, thirteen ways of looking at a blackbird. But the truth, I would like to think, comes out, that when the reader has read all these thirteen different ways of looking at a blackbird, the reader has his own fourteenth image of that blackbird, which I would like to think is the truth.[5]

What makes *Absalom, Absalom!* ultimately such a fine literary experience is that it succeeds remarkably well in creating the illusion of open-endedness, of expanding possibilities and realms of interpretations.

Although *Absalom* engages the reader in a continuing creative process as detective and interpreter, it retains a hard and fast central core. There is no escaping the conjecture of "the nigger that's going to sleep with your sister," as Shreve has Bon identify himself (358). Faulkner may skillfully execute the illusion of myriad possible interpretations; however, he signals through his omniscient narrator's comment, "probably true enough," a corroboration of precisely what he wishes. And one of these corroborations involves the Negro (the "nigger in the woodpile") at the center, one to whom many narrative clues lead. "Negro" is a central metaphor, albeit a most difficult one to explicate. Representative major black figures in the novel are all as much white as black, and in practically every case, they are more white than black. The visibly "white" product of miscegenation has confounded sight as a test of racial identity. Yet the cognitive image of "Negro," the traditionally conceived and conventionally executed abstraction, provides the prism through which all the black figures are refracted.

The problem suggests Mr. Compson's consideration of Charles Bon among the Sutpens:

> He is the curious one to me. He came into that isolated puritan country household almost like Sutpen himself came into Jefferson: apparently complete, without background or past or childhood—a man a little older than his actual years and enclosed and surrounded by a sort of Scythian glitter . . . yet from the moment when he realized that Sutpen was going to prevent the marriage if he could, he (Bon) seems to have withdrawn into a mere spectator, passive, a little sardonic and completely enigmatic. He seems to hover, shadowy, almost substanceless, a little behind and above all the other straightforward and logical, even though (to him) incomprehensible, ultimatums and affirmations and defiances and challenges and repudiations with an air of sardonic and indolent detachment. (93)

Bon is detached, older than his years, a completely enigmatic spectator. It is a long way from Bon to Sutpen's "monkey nigger." However, Bon's presence, as Mr. Compson describes it, hovering "a little behind and above all the others" (93), duplicates the stance of the balloon-face "monkey nigger":

> You knew that you could hit them [blacks] . . . and they would not hit back or even resist. But you did not want to, because they (the niggers) were not it, not what you wanted to hit; that you knew when you hit them you would just be hitting a child's toy balloon with a face painted on it, a face slick and smooth and distended and about to burst into laughing, so you did not dare strike it because it would merely burst and you would rather let it walk on out of your sight than to have stood there in the loud laughing. (230)

The Negro as a "toy balloon with a face painted on it" represents the helplessness and powerlessness of the existence of poor whites in general and Sutpen in particular. Sutpen's awareness of the futility in taking action against a balloon, which, paradoxically, is concrete yet insubstantial and symbolic in terms of the real world, suggests his attitude toward Charles Bon. Bon, like the balloon face, is an artificial configuration. He is the abstraction that Sutpen refuses to see or acknowledge because Bon's very presence mocks Sutpen, and any action against Bon exposes Sutpen to the possibility of that mockery being extended into the general public or community. Sutpen ignores Bon because he cannot accept Bon's reality. Like the black housekeepers in Sherwood Anderson's *Dark Laughter,* Bon is and remains the anonymous "nigger" ready to burst into laughter at the slightest provocation. Acceptance of Bon would make Sutpen's design an "ironic delusion," while rejection of him foists upon Sutpen and his design an "ironic reality."

This metaphorical presence of the enigmatic "Negro" pervades the entire novel, especially the conclusion. Shreve, for example, presents the metaphor of the "two niggers" to get rid of one

Sutpen: "So it took Charles Bon and his mother to get rid of old Tom, and Charles Bon and the octoroon to get rid of Judith, and Charles Bon and Clytie to get rid of Henry; and Charles Bon's mother and Charles Bon's grandmother got rid of Charles Bon" (377–78). The metaphor suggests the omnipresence and the obstinacy of "the nigger" in the lives of white southerners. Shreve concludes his summary with the theory that "You've got one nigger left. One nigger Sutpen left. Of course you can't catch him and you don't even always see him and you never will be able to use him. But you got him there still. You still hear him at night sometimes. Don't you?" (378).[6] Despite the destructive eliminations basic to Shreve's summary and the legend, the oppressive presence of "the Negro" remains. The illusive, disturbing "nigger," Jim Bond specifically, is a metaphor perhaps for the unknowable, or the contradictions, inherent in southern life and in life generally.

The stubborn "nigger" refuses extinction, and paradoxically, in the sense of Jim Bond being an authentic Sutpen descendant, "the nigger" belongs; he has his place in the physical and mental space of the South. Significantly, because no one—none of the narrators, none of the participants, not even Faulkner's omniscient narrative voice which sometimes interpolates and sometimes intrudes—comes away with an understanding of the Negro as metaphor at work or with an interpretation of the Negro, the herculean efforts (in vision, experience, and telling) remain somewhat mysterious. As long as there is one "nigger" left, southerners (reconstructed or not) and outlanders (sympathetic or not) alike can create myths out of the interaction of "the South" and "the Negro." Faulkner has left the flood gates of Yoknapatawpha open once again.

Literally, Shreve, the outlander who has vicariously experienced it all, revives the process, begins the myth anew, with his fanciful theorizing that the howling idiot and surviving Sutpen haunt the physical place (Sutpen's Hundred) and the psychological space (Quentin's dreams) that make up the South. Shreve concludes with the notion that

in time the Jim Bonds are going to conquer the western hemisphere. Of course, it won't quite be in our time and of course
as they spread toward the poles they will bleach out again like
the rabbits and the birds do, so they won't show up so sharp
against the snow. But it will still be Jim Bond; and so in a few
thousand years, I who regard you will also have sprung from
the loins of African kings. (378)

Shreve continues the process right up to and through the ending.
His image of the Jim Bonds is a fine mythologizing that is not in
the least unfamiliar. The myth of the Negro endures, as rigid and
inflexible as the old one even though it may reflect a diminishing
of the traditional racial hatred and fear.

Shreve pushes the mythology through to another inevitable
conclusion from his analytical perspective. The result is Quentin's
emotional breakdown at the end of *Absalom, Absalom!* which comes
about as a result of the breakdown of his defense mechanism.
Shreve and Quentin conclude their probing of the Sutpen legend,
but Shreve turns the tables and wants to probe Quentin as a
personal representative of the South. "Now I want you to tell me
just one thing more," Shreve states. "Why do you hate the
South?" (378). The reply is instantaneous: " 'I dont hate it,' Quentin said, quickly, at once, immediately; 'I dont hate it; he said. *I
dont hate it* he thought, panting in the cold air, the iron New
England dark; *I dont. I dont! I dont hate it! I dont hate it!*" (Faulkner's
italics; 378). Shreve's analytic question shatters Quentin's forced
composure. Shreve destroys the spell which their introspective
process of constructing a total (that is, harmonious with all
known and conjectured details) fiction has produced. The asking
of the question is as much to blame as any inherent validity the
question might have. The question itself is a violation of a code,
and that violation is even more destructive to Quentin's uneasy
equilibrium than the psychological process of putting together a
compelling whole story from individually biased, fragmented perceptions.

Shreve, concerned all along with the southerner's negative
identity, forges a negative affirmation of Quentin's southernness

by the question and the response to it. Given the moral and psychological dualism intrinsic to southern society, Quentin, paradoxically, is telling the truth, as he knows it. It is no illusion: he does not hate the South. The tendency, of course, is to accept that Shreve has put his finger squarely on Quentin's problem, that Quentin does indeed hate the South. However, Quentin's emotional response can also be attributed, at least partially, to Shreve's violation of a code to which southerners tacitly agree. Shreve, the outlander, forces Quentin to respond to a question that lies outside the boundaries of accepted social interchange. Shreve seeks a union of internal and external realities; for the southerner in this novel, that is an impossibility, and both the Sutpen legend and its reconstruction are confirmations of this "fact."

Both as a participant in a resolution of the Sutpen drama and as a narrator of it, Quentin is an enigmatic figure. Faulkner has put it another way: "It's incidentally the story of Quentin Compson's hatred of the bad qualities in the country he loves."[7] However, Quentin is as mysterious about revealing what it is he hates about his South as he is about what he loves. He does not make emphatic or judgmental statements regarding Sutpen's or the South's morality. Neither does he make specific valuations of slavery and the South's racial dilemma. But what Quentin succeeds in doing as a character is to involve the reader in the large, complex, and shady areas of being, almost because of his inability to provide answers or to identify problems.

Quentin, from the outset, is a ghost because of the past; Henry Sutpen, at the end, is a ghostlike apparition from the past. Together the two remind us of Faulkner's statement that the South is "dead." Henry, once the promise of the South's future, is a death-in-life figure who retains a deathlike grip on Quentin's imaginative and rational faculties. Henry Sutpen, Miss Rosa, Mr. Compson, and the Sutpen legend all mark Quentin for an irreparable, nightmare stasis. He is impotent and unable to resolve the moral dilemma posed by the legend and the southern past, yet he has the ability to involve Shreve actively in it. Similarly, Quentin is alienated from the southern past while at the same time completely absorbed in the South by means of the telling of the tale. In the process of the novel, Quentin condemns, justifies, expiates, and absolves the South from "sin"; nonetheless, the experience of the "sin" remains.

What Quentin goes up the stairs at Sutpen's Hundred to discover is not the same thing that compels Miss Rosa; that is, he does not ascend the stairs, as Rosa does, in order to *see* for certain that Henry is in the house. The purpose for Quentin is to meet his guilt-ridden, death-in-life double, to ascertain the waste of Henry's life, to acknowledge the lost potential of the South's young manhood, and to witness the reckoning of time and futility. Quentin recognizes that Henry embodies all of the "ghosts" of the southern world which haunt Quentin himself. Even though Henry is of an earlier generation, his subjective experiences as a son of the South mirror Quentin's. Henry's suffering makes Quentin self-conscious, and Quentin suffers the more because, while meaningful synthesis is possible for him, it is not necessarily accurate or sufficient for solving his personal dilemma. When the two meet at Sutpen's Hundred, they represent a form of self-confrontation for which the imaginative constructions of the legend throughout the novel have prepared the reader. The horror of self-confrontation in this meeting is Quentin's most illuminating vision. He can no longer experience his world vicariously; the imagination is not enough, because, in this case, it implies a retreat from reality.

Attempting to use this encounter in order to prove empirically that Quentin did or did not learn of Bon's black blood from Henry appears inconsequential ultimately because the heart of the enigma is not the black blood, but the unknown, the mysterious, and the inexplicable written into Henry's wasted life and read on Quentin's "waking and sleeping" face. Henry shows that the pariah is not necessarily the Negro and that there are fugitive southern sons, just as there were fugitive black slaves. The black blood is a device, a red herring in the sense that it suggests a false significance to the meeting between the two sons of the South, the old and the new, who are linked in a death grip from which neither will emerge to tell, in specific terms, the "truth" of his existence and his experience because neither can—given both human frailty and the inexplicable in individual motives.

Henry's guilt and Quentin's fear (of life's possibilities for him) join in presenting a powerful image of the dark at the core of southern life and the southern imagination as Faulkner demonstrates. The image has power because it is a unique turn of the tradition; the Negro in the South (either slave or free) usually stands for the dark that has overshadowed and blighted the South, and Faulkner himself sometimes uses this notion. However, in *Absalom, Absalom!* it is, as the ending suggests, the southerner himself, his own mind—conscience (Henry) and imagination (Quentin)—that encompasses and creates the dark. The Negro, whether Clytie, Charles Bon, or Jim Bond in type, becomes in comparison a rather benign force. There is, then, in the ending a marginal pulling away from the myths of southern existence, although the retreat is not strongly verbalized. Faulkner relies upon an emotional experience (as he does in resolving *The Sound and the Fury*) to imply an abandoning of a traditional position: Look at what the black man has done to me; look at what the black man has made me do. Even though the new position is more of a felt experience than a statement, it seems to be: See what I have done to myself. This recognition, which Faulkner can present only obliquely, is one that Quentin cannot thoroughly absorb.

Whether external elements are real or imagined, the individual has to come to terms with them because they are aspects of himself. If the individual does not, he is doomed. Whether dream or waking reality, the "Nevermore of peace. Nevermore of peace. Nevermore Nevermore Nevermore" (373) which punctuates Quentin's thoughts after he reveals his meeting with Henry echoes neither "Negro" nor "nigger" but the powerful namelessness, the metaphysical "dark" that has wasted Henry's life and promises to waste Quentin's as well. It is Faulkner's ability to portray, not the meaning of that dark in the human heart, but so surely its multifaceted existence there that contributes to the power and intensity of *Absalom, Absalom!*

Notes

1. William Faulkner, *Absalom, Absalom!* (1936; New York: Random House, 1964), 151–52. All parenthetical references are to this edition.

2. A possible source for Wash Jones is a character by the same name, Washington Jones, which is shortened to Wash Jones, in "Ananias," a short story by Joel Chandler Harris. I do not wish to emphasize the coincidence of the name; however, the situation is suggestive. Wash Jones, a lower-class white, is the one-time overseer of Colonel Benjamin Flewellen's plantation who becomes rich after the war and is the colonel's chief creditor. Jones is a commission merchant who forecloses the mortgage on the Flewellen plantation and thereby becomes the owner. See Joel Chandler Harris, "Ananias," in Harris, *Balaam and His Master* (Cambridge: Riverside, 1891), 113–48.

3. Joel Chandler Harris, "Free Joe and the Rest of the World," in Harris, *Free Joe and Other Georgian Sketches* (New York: Scribner's, 1887), 1. Harris's fiction resonates throughout *Absalom, Absalom!*

4. One measure of the importance of the encounter between Rosa and Clytie is the care that Faulkner took in revising the scene. According to Gerald Langford, there were four stages of revision apparent in Faulkner's presentation of the meeting between the two women. The manuscript shows that much of Faulkner's rewriting of the scene involves emphasizing the dramatic impact of the confrontation. Specifically, Faulkner added to the section in such a way as to extend the significance of the touch of Clytie's coffee-colored hand on Rosa's white flesh. See Langford, *Faulkner's Revision of "Absalom, Absalom!": A Collation of the Manuscript and the Published Book* (Austin: University of Texas Press, 1971), 29–31.

5. Frederick L. Gwynn and Joseph L. Blotner, eds., *Faulkner in the University* (New York: Vintage, 1959), 273–74.

6. According to Langford, "The most significant revision in Chapter IX is the added emphasis given to Jim Bond in the closing pages of the book" (*Faulkner's Revision of "Absalom, Absalom!"* 40). Faulkner added the image of Bond's howling to the manuscript, but the impact of the addition does not seem to be "the heritage of man's long inhumanity to man," as Langford suggests (41), but rather an enduring concern with the presence of the Negro as a symbol of the tensions in the southerner's existence. See, for instance, Langford's reproduction of the manuscript and book revisions (360–61).

7. Gwynn and Blotner, eds., *Faulkner in the University*, 71.

Absalom, Absalom! and the House Divided

ERIC SUNDQUIST

✦　✦　✦

T HE "FLAW" IN THOMAS SUTPEN'S grand "design" is, of course, his first son's supposed black blood. Abandoning his wife and son in Haiti, Sutpen carries his dynastic scheme to frontier Mississippi, only to have that repressed son return as his second son's best friend and, apparently, his daughter's fiancé. Sutpen does not (according to Quentin, according to his father, according to his grandfather) call it "retribution, no sins of the fathers come home to roost," but just a "mistake," one that inescapably impedes his vision of "fine grandsons and great-grandsons springing as far as the eye could reach" and leaves him immobilized in attempting to fathom its meaning. He can either recognize Charles Bon or not recognize him, he says, "either destroy my design with my own hand" or, letting the affair take its own course, "see my design complete itself quite normally and naturally and successfully to the public eye, yet to my own in such a fashion as to be a mockery and a betrayal."[1]

There is no doubt that the paradoxically lost, but defiantly maintained, innocence of the South has numerous motives and outcroppings, many of them practically necessary and others anxiously fantastic. One might trace them, for example, to the "flaw" W. J. Cash detects in antebellum pretensions to aristocracy, which were "not an emanation from the proper substance of the men who wore it, but only a fine garment put on from the outside."[2] For Cash, the planters could not have been properly aristocratic because they were often violent and acquisitive, and their origins in frontier vulgarity were too recent and obvious. But, we might ask, as Eugene Genovese has, "What aristocracy ever arose from any other kind of men?"[3] The economic and political aspects of those two points of view are important; but in the case of Thomas Sutpen, who would appear to support either contention, the major flaw in his aristocratic design overwhelms his vulgarity and renders visibly specious the veneer of innocent grandeur upon which most every design for slavery depended and to which the South, at least through Faulkner's career and life, tenaciously clung. In any event, as Cash later notes, the most vocal pretensions to aristocracy were retrospective. The defensive posture of the South after the war and into the next century created, among other peculiarities, the strange situation in which, "while the actuality of aristocracy was drawing away toward the limbo of aborted and unrealized things," the claim of its possession as an "indefeasible heritage" was "reasserted with a kind of frenzied intensity."[4]

Because not only the South but the entire nation may be said to have lost its innocence in the Civil War, its most fratricidal conflict, that flaw is larger than Sutpen himself can reveal. Both North and South appealed to the revolutionary fathers throughout the war, just as they had prior to it in arguments over the place of slavery in the Constitution and the founding fathers' grand design for America itself; it is therefore not at all fortuitous that Sutpen's first mistake occurs on an island that, in Faulkner's description, might be a mythic replica of American history itself, "a theater for violence and injustice and bloodshed amid all the satanic lusts of human greed and cruelty," a country located

halfway between the dark inscrutable continent from which the black blood, the black bones and flesh and thinking and remembering and hopes and desires, was ravished by violence, and the cold land to which it was doomed, the civilized land and people which had expelled some of its own blood and thinking and desires that had become too crass to be faced and borne any longer, and set it homeless and desperate on the lonely ocean—a little lost island in a latitude which would require ten thousand years of equatorial heritage to bear its climate, [its] soil manured with black blood from two hundred years of oppression and exploitation.[5]

As in the telescoped history of slavery in the Americas that Melville presents in *Benito Cereno*, Faulkner's description of Haiti indicates that, though the crisis was long in coming, the flaw was there all along. To this extent, Sutpen's crisis of innocence, as well as the flaw that engenders it, is the nation's. That *Absalom, Absalom!* was even written is perhaps the best evidence that the flaw was deep.

It is nonetheless striking how close the Civil War came to circumventing the question of slavery, to postponing it, as Lincoln hoped to do, until a later date. One factor in Lincoln's attitude, though certainly not the only one, may be found in his continually having to defend himself against charges of fostering (in crueler moments, of practicing or being the product of) miscegenation. Almost as often as he spoke against the Dred Scott decision, he was called upon, or felt compelled, to make this defense. "There is a natural disgust in the minds of nearly all white people at the idea of an indiscriminate amalgamation of the white and black races," Lincoln remarked in an important 1857 speech that echoed Jefferson's beliefs. As usual, the charges had come from Stephen Douglas, who argued (as Lincoln summarized it) that those who contended that the Declaration of Independence included Negroes did so "only because they want to vote, and eat, and sleep, and marry with Negroes!" Here, as he would throughout the 1858 debates with Douglas, Lincoln protested the "counterfeit logic which concludes that, because I do not want a black woman for a slave I must necessarily want her for a wife." He adds that he too is horrified ("Agreed for once—a thousand times agreed") by "the mixing of blood by the white and black races" and goes on to note that, because nearly all of the mulattoes in the United States "have sprung from black slaves and white masters," a "separation of the races is the only perfect preventive of amalgamation."[6]

Lincoln's most famous speech on the House Divided, delivered the following year, would make no clear mention of the miscegenation issue; by then he was Douglas's official opponent for the Senate, and it may be that he thought it best to leave tacit his defense of one of the Republican party's thornier issues. In the 1857 speech, however, Dred Scott's family itself is rallied as "an illustration only" of Lincoln's basic position. Had the court's decision gone the other way, Lincoln pointed out:

> the chances of these black girls ever mixing their blood with that of white people would have been diminished at least to the extent that it could not have been without their consent. But judge Douglas is delighted to have them decided to be slaves, and not human enough to have a hearing, even if they were free, and thus left subject to the forced concubinage of their masters, and liable to become the mothers of mulattoes in spite of themselves: the very state of case that produces nine-tenths of all the mulattoes—all the mixing of blood in the nation.

Given this situation, separation of the races—"if ever effected at all, [it] must be effected by colonization," Lincoln remarked—is the only ultimate answer. But because "an immediate separation is impossible, the next best thing is to keep them apart where they are not already together. If white and black people never get together in Kansas," for example, "they will never mix blood in Kansas. That is at least one self-evident truth."[7]

The New Testament image of the House Divided that Lincoln invoked the following year in his most famous speech on slavery not only prefigured the fratricidal conflict he maintained would not be necessary but also, as George B. Forgie has demonstrated, included for Lincoln his own fraternal rivalry with Douglas, who in Lincoln's view had been engineering an attack on the House of the Founding Fathers ever since the Kansas-Nebraska Act in

1854.[8] It would be two years before Lincoln would defeat the rival brother and then enter the White House resolved to save the Union by restoring the vision of the founding fathers, a vision that in his opinion held slavery repugnant and implicitly called for its *eventual* elimination, but one whose ambiguity, of course, had never ceased to provide evidence for either (or any) point of view. Although "a husband and wife may be divorced," Lincoln said in his first inaugural address (4 March 1861), we "cannot remove our respective sections from one another, nor build an impassable barrier between them." Instead, we must take our time, let passions cool, until "the mystic chords of memory, stretching from every battlefield and patriot grave to every living heart," are "again touched, as surely they will be, by the better angels of our nature." A little over a month later, Fort Sumter fell, and Lincoln called forth an army to protect the nation—as he would later phrase it in appointing McClellan to command the army—from "parricidal rebellion."[9] The crisis Lincoln feared had come—not exactly as, and much faster than, he had expected.

The tendency toward legalizing slavery in all states—the inevitable result, as Lincoln saw it, of the Kansas-Nebraska Act and the Dred Scott decision—had been exacerbated rather than lessened in recent years. Lincoln's remarks on the occasion of his House Divided speech in 1858 held this possibility at a point of perilous balance, which in retrospect would seem to articulate as well a crisis and division stretching beyond that of sectional conflict alone:

> In my opinion, [slavery agitation] will not cease until a crisis shall have been reached and passed. "A house divided against itself cannot stand." I believe this government cannot endure permanently half slave and half free. I do not expect the union to be dissolved—I do not expect the house to fall—but I do expect it will cease to be divided. It will become all one thing, or all the other.

Lincoln saw the tendency toward extending slavery as a conspiracy—or, as he put it, a "design," a "concert of action among its

chief architects."[10] Lincoln's theory of a conspiracy has been much
debated, but whether or not there was such a design, Lincoln's
theory virtually brought it into being. Like the figure of the House
Divided itself, and like the fraternal conflict with Douglas it promoted, the conspiracy theory fed into the increasingly melodramatic structure of the national debate over slavery.

The further Christological significance of Lincoln's assassination on Good Friday 1865 at the time obscured the fact that the
resonant House Divided speech had *not* predicted, much less ad-
vocated, war and that it expressed Lincoln's essential belief that
preserving the Union *did not* require the abolition of slavery. He
did not expect "the Union to be dissolved . . . the house to fall,"
but he did expect it would "cease to be divided" into "half slave
and half free"—not immediately, but some time. Lincoln's avoid-
ance of the miscegenation charge in the House Divided speech is
significant, and it does not seem misleading to suggest that it is
conscious and intentional, that its introduction would have rendered more problematic than ever Lincoln's desire to postpone
the question of abolition.

His opinion about the conspiratorial design on behalf of an
extension of slavery must necessarily be seen to contain a fear
that miscegenation—up until then largely restricted to the slaveholding South, he said—would also spread. Yet by the same to-
ken, how could slavery eventually be abolished without creating
potentially more rampant, if less inhumane, forms of amalgamation? As Lincoln's 1857 speech indicated, he thought the second
less likely and in any event preferable in the long run to the first;
but he also thought its complete prevention, by separation of the
races, the best and most natural solution of all. That solution
was colonization in Haiti, among other places; he died without
finding a better one. The House divided between North and South
concealed a further division between white and black, one that
was paradoxically evident in their literal, physical union and one
that, far from being dissolved by a reunion of the warring sections
and an abolition of slavery, could only be made more promi-
nently explosive. Insofar as the Emancipation Proclamation was
more a military and technically political decision than an

embracing act of human liberation, it is probably to the advantage of Lincoln's mythic career that he did not live to struggle with the further crisis it precipitated. In short, his own design for restoring the Union, not to say his original design for preserving it, was flawed.

I AM SUGGESTING, of course, that there is an analogy between Abraham Lincoln and Thomas Sutpen, each of whom labors heroically to build or preserve a magnificent "house" symbolic of his national and personal dream, and both of whom, at about the same time, face a crisis in the house and try desperately to postpone it. In each case, the Civil War itself forces a resolution of the crisis—though not in either case without violent consequences. It is not by any means an analogy in which they or their designs are exactly duplicated but, rather, one in which they are mirror images in the sense that a mirror image reverses the figure to which it corresponds. To the extent that Lincoln and Sutpen both derive their visions of perpetuated design from that of the founding fathers—the Declaration of Independence and the Constitution—their careers and public pronouncements (Lincoln's speeches and Sutpen's rehearsed story) embody the essential American dream and its fundamental "mistake." In remarkable counterpoint to his prominent statements of white supremacy, Lincoln's troubled devotion to equality is everywhere evident in his speeches, and his rise from humble origins to heroic magnificence, like Sutpen's rise, dramatizes the dream denied to an entire race of Americans for close to a century after the signing of those documents—a dream redeemed into a promise by Lincoln and others but broken and betrayed, for nearly another century, by those judiciously read in the thought of the fathers and devoted to perpetuating their visionary design.

We do not, I think, have to torture Lincoln's position too much to make it resemble Sutpen's dilemma over the recognition of his "black" son, Charles Bon: if Lincoln had let the abolition of slavery take its own eventual course, his restoration of the Union would indeed, to some observers then and perhaps to all in retrospect, have been "a mockery and a betrayal." By abolishing slavery "with [his] own hand," he necessarily destroyed the design—for saving the Union without interfering with slavery where it already existed—that he had insisted on time and again. Lincoln was ready to assume the role of the founding fathers and preserve their design (ambiguous though it was on this issue), but he was often—and by necessity—as paternalistic as most of his contemporaries, slaveholders included, in his attitudes toward blacks. (It is not for nothing that many liberated slaves unavoidably and gratefully saw him in the role not just of Moses or Christ but more simply of a father.) Likewise, Thomas Sutpen is determined to continue to enhance the southern design of slaveholding paternalism, but he is not ready to accept a "Negro" son into that design. (It is not for nothing in this case either that Bon wants not a piece of that design but simply his father's recognition of him as a son.) As Quentin and his father, and *his* father, put it, "Sutpen's trouble was innocence."[11]

Such innocence is obviously tormenting. The frenzy of *Absalom, Absalom!* reveals this again and again—and then again. If we are still in doubt, let us add C. Vann Woodward's observation that, though it resembled other American dreams of opulence, the dream of the South has seldom been so convincing. Because the South for half of its history "lived intimately with a great social evil and [for] the other half with its aftermath," its preoccupation is "with guilt, not with innocence, with the reality of evil, not with the dream of perfection." If it "plunged into catastrophe" to escape "the torments of its own conscience," however, the escape was not very successful.[12] Yet, in its still peculiar fashion, it was: how else explain the long procession of grandiloquent myths? As Faulkner saw quite clearly, the razor's edge dividing repressed guilt and ostentatious innocence was painfully sharp. It still divided the mind as it had once divided the nation. In the case of *Absalom, Absalom!* it divides nearly everything in view—every pair of characters and every pair of narrators, every possible resolution of Charles Bon's tragedy and Quentin Compson's reliving of it, every physical and psychological body, every one of its many real and mythic houses (of Sutpen, of Compson, of David, of Oedipus, of Atreus, and the House Divided), every marriage in fact and fantasy, blood and memory—everything, even the form of the novel itself.

The correlative pressure of such division is *union*—the reforged and redeemed innocence that includes but overcomes guilt, the resurrected, undead might-have-been, the *"world filled with living marriage"* that Miss Rosa Coldfield, for example, inhabits one *"summer of wistaria"* in 1860.[13] There is no way to overestimate the stupendous, tortuous effort Faulkner makes in *Absalom, Absalom!* to force into crisis and overcome the tragic divisions upon which his novel is built; the repeated metaphor of that effort, and its perfect formal analogy, is marriage and its implied recognitions and responsibilities. It operates throughout the book in ways we must take into account, but it derives its power quite simply from expressing, at its deepest, potentially most tragic and threatening level, one central issue that the Civil War would in retrospect seem to be about and the issue *Absalom, Absalom!* is so outrageously about: amalgamation—or rather, miscegenation. It is worth making this distinction, for *miscegenation* first came into being as a term in 1863, almost on the heels of the Emancipation Proclamation. *Amalgamation* meant simply a mixing, but *miscegenation* quite clearly meant interracial *sexual* mixing, and the term therefore quickly acquired a contagious and derisive force, one that expressed the nation's most visceral fears, paradoxical or not, about emancipation.

As we have seen, Lincoln's 1857 defense against charges that the Republican party encouraged miscegenation took the logical form of pointing out that his not wishing to own a black woman did not entail his wishing to marry one. Clearly, miscegenation was not the only point of conflict between the sections, and the charges against Lincoln were not taken overly seriously by anyone in the North; indeed, they largely subsided until emancipation became probable and, finally, actual. In late December 1863, they exploded again in the form of an anonymous pamphlet entitled "Miscegenation: The Theory of the Blending of the Races, Applied to the American White Man and Negro."[14] The proslavery authors coined the term *miscegenation* (from *miscere*, to mix, and *genus*, race) and represented the pamphlet as the work of an abolitionist, in hopes of discrediting the Republican party in the upcoming elections. Only miscegenation, the pamphlet claimed, could ensure the progress and prosperity of the country; the war would guarantee not only physical freedom for blacks but also sexual freedom for both races, particularly in the South, where organized interracial breeding would be carried out on a massive scale and white women would at last be free to give expression to their secret passions. Eventually the pamphlet was recognized as a hoax, but not before it unleashed a barrage of attacks and a strong response from J. H. Van Evrie, whose "Subjenation: The Theory of the Normal Relation of the Races" exactly imitated the style and format of "Miscegenation" but argued violently against its doctrines. As the 1864 campaign progressed, the charges against the Republicans and Lincoln grew more hysterical. One pamphleteer claimed, for example, that the Republicans were plotting to kill or castrate all southern white men and apportion their women for the use of "Black Ourang-Outangs." Others spoke of Lincoln's "Miscegenation Proclamation" or depicted him in political cartoons and prints as the sponsor of miscegenation, while one leaflet offered a "Black Republican Prayer," which parodied the Lord's Prayer and called upon "the spirit of amalgamation" to shine forth and flourish, "that we may become a regenerated nation of half-breeds, and mongrels" and "live in bonds of fraternal love, union, and equality with the Almighty Nigger, henceforward, now and forever. Amen."

Such charges, again, were not taken seriously by a very large number of people in the North, but they became widely, if not universally, credible in the South—if only at a profound emotional and rhetorical level. In the case of Van Evrie, the refutation of the ameliorating theory of miscegenation was a passion; he had already written *Negroes and Negro "Slavery"* (1861), and, when the book was reissued in 1868 as *White Supremacy and Negro Subordination*, its claims seemed more vehement and relevant than ever. It has to be noted, however, that since Van Evrie argued against *all* miscegenation, throughout the world and in the slaveholding South, as well as against what he thought to be the most serious menace posed by emancipation, he is in important respects emblematic of the schizophrenic position of the South in particular and the nation in general. In the "awful perversion of the instincts of reproduction" that we see around us daily in the South, Van Evrie wrote, God's design is transformed into "the most loathsome and most hideous of social miseries." Abolition will only further this degeneration; once it is accomplished, we will be left for years "to struggle with the load of sin and disease thus brought upon ourselves by our crimes against reason and the ordinances of the Eternal" and will require a span of time that "cannot be estimated with any certainty" in order finally "to recover from the foul and horrible contamination of admixture with the blood of the negro." Like his Jim Crow counterpart Charles Carroll, Van Evrie held mulattoes responsible for nearly all crimes and racial disorder, and he attacked the "strange and disgusting delusion," the "diseased sentimentality" of the North, which casts "an air of romance" over mongrel women while the terrible miseries of "their own white sisters falling every hour from the ranks of pure womanhood" are totally disregarded.[15]

Because he anticipated, among other things, the hysterical defense of southern womanhood that would become and remain the touchstone of white racism, it is no wonder that Van Evrie's book seemed more to the point after the war than it had upon initial publication. That anticipation is significant, however, for it serves to enact the mechanism of repression that the war revealed—a mechanism that had certainly been at work in the antebellum South all along but became necessarily more and more extravagant in its aftermath. Such repression inevitably entangled an outcry against threatened sexual violence by blacks and a vehement denial of similar violence by whites (or, if not its denial, its fanatically righteous justification), a denial that Van Evrie's own protests could not reduce and one, as we will see, that took a logical and tragic form. Even *Gone with the Wind* (1936), that rarified epic fantasia of the Jim Crow South, would manage to suggest that the many "ignominies and dangers" brought upon the South by Reconstruction "were as nothing compared with the peril of white women." Such a particular fear amid a more general anarchy leads Scarlett O'Hara to feel for the first time "a kinship with the people around her."[16] Because it held the invading Yankees most responsible for miscegenation in the South, Mitchell's novel of hot-blooded gynealotry and patriotic fervor could, of course, make little allusion to the requisite counterpoint of this hysteria, the absolute perversion of "kinship" that Mary Chesnut recorded in her notorious diary entry of 1861:

> We live surrounded by prostitutes. An abandoned woman is sent out of any decent house elsewhere. Who thinks any worse of a negro or a mulatto woman for being a thing we can't name? God forgive us, but ours is a *monstrous* system and wrong and iniquity. Perhaps the rest of the world is as bad—this only I see. Like the patriarchs of old our men live all in one house with their wives and their concubines, and the mulattoes one sees in every family exactly resemble the white children—and every lady tells you who is the father of all the mulatto children in everybody's household, but those in her own she seems to think drop from the clouds, or pretends to think so.[17]

Chesnut might certainly have endorsed Van Evrie's contention that "*mulattoism is to the South what prostitution is to the North*," but she could have agreed only in figurative terms with his insistence that, just as in cases of prostitution and incest, so in the case of mulattoism, nature opposes this "monstrous violation of the physical integrity of the races," this " 'original sin,' as it may well be termed," by physiologically punishing the children it produces "to the third and fourth generations for the sins of the fathers."[18]

Van Evrie's theory of degeneration depended on detecting a "similarity of species" between the *mulatto* and the *mule* (they have the same etymology), one that results in a "diminishing vitality," a "tendency to disease and disorganization," and an eventual sterility among the "mongrel" element, and therefore ensures that it will never be "of sufficient amount to threaten the safety or even disturb the peace of Southern society."[19] This rather striking conclusion is unsurprising only when it is recognized to contain (or sublimate) one threat by dismissing another. When the book was first published before the war, the theory of degeneration (with its biblical sanction of punishment unto the fourth generation) was a scathing critique of slaveholding miscegenation; after the war, it could only appear to express as well an ironic rationalization of the counterthreat that abolition seemed to entail. Van Evrie was not whistling in the dark, however, for at a social and psychological level the punishment of the third and fourth generations (of *all* generations) was real indeed—so real that Faulkner himself would seek recourse in the figure of physiological degeneration in order to describe the dilemma of Jim Bond, the fourth-generation descendant in *Absalom, Absalom!* of his family's "original sin," whose unintelligible howling unites the novel's disparate voices and engulfs their frantic attempts to salvage the Sutpen dynasty in a single anguished cry. As Shreve says to Quentin Compson on the last page of the book, there is still "one nigger Sutpen left. Of course you can't catch him and you don't even always see him and you never will be able to use him. But you've got him there still."[20]

This is the conclusion of the novel, however, and to reach it Faulkner had first to create a design and, it seems, destroy it with his own hand. To see clearly how he did so, we must see clearly how central the facts and metaphors of marriage are in *Absalom, Absalom!* Van Evrie was certainly not alone in thinking that marriage among slaves, because they are governed by "capricious affections" and characterized by a "feeble moral nature," would be "obviously unnatural, monstrous, and wicked."[21] By situating his observations on this subject within the context of a romantic tribute to the sacred institution of white marriage, Van Evrie once more made painfully explicit the reason that miscegenation was the gravest threat to slavery in the South (and would seem the even graver result of abolition). It made a mockery of white marriage in a particular and terrifying way—by making the races indistinguishable (in theory and sometimes eventually in fact) and by making them, therefore, *equal.* The South was destroying its own design by sinning against God's design. The precarious balance between these points of view—between slavery itself as sin and miscegenation alone as sin—is one that would drive both the South and the nation into fantastic forms of refutation and denial for the next hundred years, forms as utterly deranged and precious (and immensely popular) as *Gone with the Wind*, and as penetrating and tragic (and widely ignored) as *Absalom, Absalom!*

That these two books—both obsessed with marriage and family to the point of obscuring the political crisis of civil war to which they refer—could appear in the same year at first seems almost irrational.[22] Mitchell's novel, of course, sold millions of copies and became America's favorite movie; Faulkner's novel was greeted with perplexity, disbelief, and outrage. The one made clear to some observers how strange Jim Crow's career was, while the other measured the length and complexity of that career by exposing the enervating intimacies within the grand design that made it possible. Both in their complementary ways continued to measure the physical and emotional entanglements between white and black in the South, the one by denying the sins of the fathers altogether, the other by expressing their intimate, intolerable actuality. Yet it is only when we see how much of *Gone with the Wind* Faulkner had, as it were, internalized in *Absalom, Absalom!* that its full significance is made clear.

Scarlett O'Hara descends not only from countless white heroines in the novels of Thomas Dixon, Thomas Nelson Page, and others, but she is also much the antecedent of the sister Quentin Compson could never truly possess, the one Faulkner could never clearly portray. The one impossible marriage to which *Absalom, Absalom!* refers continually is the one that divides the house of Compson and the house of Sutpen alike, brings the two into momentary union before tearing them apart, and creates the extraordinary psychological and stylistic turbulence in Faulkner's reimagining of Quentin's dilemma. It also, we shall see, raises from the detritus of eccentric observation to the dignity of acute psychological truth a passage from Mississippian Henry Hughes's *Treatise on Sociology* (1854), whose seeming burlesque of syllogistic argument is a perfect index of the tormenting issue of miscegenation:

Hybridism is heinous. Impurity of races is against the law of nature. Mulattoes are monsters. The law of nature is the law of God. The same law which forbids consanguineous amalgamation forbids ethnical amalgamation. Both are incestuous. Amalgamation is incest.[23]

Although she does not finally dominate the novel, Rosa Cold-field's obsessive rehearsals for Quentin of Sutpen's failed dynasty, the murder of Bon, and her own tortured courtship by the "ogre" generate the atmosphere of spent dreams and feverishly maintained innocence in and against which subsequent versions of the tragedy are played out. The novel's magnificent opening scene between Rosa and Quentin is itself a kind of courtship, a ritual immersion of Quentin into the Gothic convulsions of Rosa's fading by hyperdistilled erotic memories. The turning rhythms of Faulkner's prose here, as elsewhere, create a strained communion in which Quentin and Rosa, breathing and memory, body and house and voice, are fused in a sensation of calm that is poised nevertheless on the extreme edge of violence.

The extraordinary balance between nostalgia and rage, in which the solid present—the dust, the screens, the heated air, the twice-bloomed wisteria—breaks down into the resurrected ghost of past grandeur, the stillborn lust of Rosa's "impotent yet indomitable frustration," creates an eroticism not simply of the flesh but of memory, creates of Rosa herself the demon she accuses Sutpen of being and (as Mr. Compson later expresses it) an "instrument of retribution" rising "bloodless and without dimension from the sacrificial stone of the marriage-bed." The exact purpose of that retribution is made no clearer to us than Rosa is able to make it to herself; and it is not clearly retribution at all, for as she tells Quentin of Sutpen's proposal that they breed on trial before getting married, "*I forgave him. . . . Why shouldn't I? I had nothing to forgive.*" Rosa's balked courtship and marriage to Sutpen do, as Shreve will suggest, leave her "irrevocably husbanded" to an "abstract carcass of outrage and revenge"[24]—but not in her version of the courtship, which is less a smoldering desire for revenge than an excessively melodramatic lament over the denial of desire itself. Rosa is neither wife nor mother; in one respect she is for Faulkner emblematic of those war widows who were never brides at all, the many undefeated for whom the war took not only their land, their slaves, their golden dream but also the men they would never have. In the nervously exposed contours of her passion, Rosa also betrays, as the novel restrains her sister, Ellen, and her niece, Judith, from doing, a further aspect of the crisis of union the war would release into the hysteria of racism for a century to come.

Rosa's "demonizing," as nearly every reader of *Absalom, Absalom!* has characterized it, is certainly conspicuous, but it becomes significant only when it is seen within the context of her now brittle but still tender passion and grief for her first "nothusband," *"Charles Bon, Charles Good, Charles Husband-soon-to-be."* The *"shadow-realm of make-believe"* in which her passion lives, the *"fairy-tale"* she creates for herself and the young man she never sees, even in death, brings Rosa closer to incest than her later courtship by Sutpen will, and it brings her close to an act of miscegenation she does not recognize as such. Or so it seems. There is no direct evidence in the novel that Rosa ever knows Bon is a "Negro," but then there is no direct evidence that Quentin does either, and his peculiar testimony is assumed to be conclusive, at least to the extent that nearly all readers of the novel take it for granted. He finds out the truth about Bon when he visits Sutpen's Hundred with Rosa—not, apparently, from Henry but from Clytie. As Shreve puts it: "She didn't tell you in so many words because she was still keeping that secret for the sake of the man who had been her father too. . . . she didn't tell you, it just came out of the terror and the fear after she turned you loose and caught the Aunt Rosa's arm and the Aunt Rosa turned and struck her hand away."[25]

The 1909 scene repeats the 1865 scene Rosa has already described to Quentin, in which Clytie attempts to stop her from mounting the stairs to Judith's room after Bon is murdered. It is worth reproducing a portion of this scene, for it is the heart of Rosa's chapter and brings into focus the conflicting passions and stunned recognitions of consanguinity that compel the entire novel. Approaching the stairs to see at last the dead Bon she would never see, Rosa is stopped first by the *"immobile antagonism"* of Clytie's face, by her body, which seems to *"project upward something*

. . . *inherited from an older and a purer race than mine*" and shapes in the air between them "*that bedroom long-closed and musty, that sheetless bed*" and its "*pale and bloody corpse.*" When her commands to Rosa fail to stop her, Clytie grasps her arm:

> *Then she touched me, and then I did stop dead. . . . my entire being seemed to run at blind full tilt into something monstrous and immobile, with a shocking impact too soon and too quick to be mere amazement and outrage at that black arresting and untimorous hand on my white woman's flesh. Because there is something in the touch of flesh with flesh which abrogates, cuts sharp and straight across the devious intricate channels of decorous ordering, which enemies as well as lovers know because it makes them both. . . . We just stood there—I motionless in the attitude and action of running, she rigid in that furious immobility, the two of us joined by that hand and arm which held us, like a fierce rigid umbilical cord, twin sistered to the fell darkness which had produced her. . . . And then suddenly it was not outrage that I wailed for, out of which I had instinctively cried; it was not terror: it was some cumulative non-reach of despair itself. . . . I cried—perhaps not aloud, not with words (and not to Judith, mind: perhaps I knew already, on the instant I entered the house and saw that face which was at once both more and less than Sutpen, perhaps I knew even then what I could not, would not, must not believe)—I cried "And you too? And you too, sister, sister?"*

Like so many passages in the novel, this one (if not at first, certainly in retrospect) intimates the secret of Bon's blood, but it does so in a fashion charged with ambiguous power. Rosa's shocked exclamation, "you too, sister, sister?" suggests not only that Clytie is clearly Judith's sister (Sutpen's daughter) and not only that Clytie, like Rosa, may be vicariously in love with Bon, but also that those possibilities reveal two further ones that constitute, in Faulkner's imagination if not her own, precisely what Rosa "could not, would not, must not believe" and what the novel holds in passionate suspense: that Bon is Clytie's "brother" and that Bon is "black." The scene does not spell out this recognition, but it certainly suggests it more pointedly than does Quentin's climactic visit to Sutpen's Hundred forty-five years later. When the three of them—Rosa, Judith, and Clytie, "*as though*

we were one being, interchangeable"—await Sutpen's return after the
war, Rosa speaks of Clytie as one who embodies the war's *"perverse
and inscrutable paradox: free, yet incapable of freedom who had never once called
herself a slave"* and, moreover, *"who in the very pigmentation of her flesh
represented that debacle which had brought Judith and me to what we were."*[26]
In between this assertion of Clytie's tragedy and the earlier scene
that so clarified the "debacle" she represents, Rosa speaks passionately, with the rapture of fantasized violation and husbanding,
of the *"world filled with living marriage"* that only imagination can
create.

Rosa's failed courtships, one in imagination and one in fact,
have often and quite rightly been read as the rhetorical high-
points of Faulkner's novel, but the psychological complexities of
her expressed passion—complexities that the novel both reveals
and buries at the same time—have for good reason resisted elaboration. In particular, the issue of miscegenation has been largely
ignored because it is assumed that Rosa suspects nothing of Bon's
parentage. Because it is the strategy of *Absalom, Absalom!* to intimate
but suppress its critical information until the very end, and even
then to reveal it only in the dramatic, self-reflexive mask of tacit
recognition, the true torment of Rosa's courtship by Sutpen may
be explicable only if we assume—as the scene between Rosa and
Clytie suggests—that Rosa herself, perhaps vicariously, understands the full dimensions of Bon's tragedy as well as Sutpen's.
The debacle represented by Clytie's "pigmentation" is purposely
ambiguous: it is the debacle of slavery and the war itself that
makes Judith and Rosa widows without having been brides, but
it is also the debacle of miscegenation, which the novel so continually engages as the curse and sin that brings Sutpen's design,
like that of the South itself, to collapse. It is the debacle that
makes Clytie neither slave nor free (neither before nor after the
war) and makes Charles Bon neither slave nor son and brother.
Like the motive for Bon's murder, the psychological tragedy
Rosa's failed dream represents must be seen to exist in the inter-
stices of the novel's action and its assumptions about the crisis of
consanguinity; for if it seems to gather together and swallow up
the grief Ellen and Judith never express, and therefore to transfer

into the atmosphere of volatile fantasy the one passion in actuality Faulkner seems unable or unwilling to articulate, it does so with a particular emotional urgency.

Although the language of Rosa's recreated courtship, its burgeoning moment of passion held forever on the brink of fulfillment, contains as clear an expression of the recognized truth about Bon as we may wish, there is no reason to insist on its actuality. What matters, rather, is that Faulkner, in creating this powerful scene, should invest so much deliberate energy in drawing the fated Bon toward recognition at all, a recognition the novel intimates again and again but that its events can actualize only in brutal denial. What else does Bon want but recognition—by his sister, his brother, his father? And why should not Rosa, the fever of her vicarious life driving her toward that recognition, see now in Clytie's darkened face what we are to imagine Quentin sees a half century later? Faulkner does not present that recognition clearly in either instance; his language is thoroughly charged with it, however, charged with a recognition wasted and betrayed year after year, beyond Quentin's death and well into Faulkner's life, but charged as well, Rosa's ecstatic memories tell us, with a recognition more vital and lasting—and threatening—than we may wish. In this book filled with shadows blurring into visions, with unliving marriage and passion consummated in death, it is entirely appropriate that this scene bring us to the verge of a recognition we are unwilling to make, that it vitalizes the scene, the act, the moment that never *will be* in the certain tragic fullness of what *might have been.*

Southern gynealotry and, in this instance, the fanatic undefeat of the maidens and spinsters whose "nothusbands" never came home, include and themselves express an acute psychological division that makes dramatically immediate the other forms of divided sensibility *Absalom, Absalom!* explores. The "monstrous" antagonism that Rosa confronts in the form of Clytie is nothing less than that which Mary Chesnut found "monstrous" about slavery—its sexual crimes and not simply their physical violence but even more so, perhaps, the emotional violence that miscegenation entailed. That violence enclosed both black and white, parents and children, husbands and wives in a cage of paradoxical feelings. To the extent that "sexual intimacy strikingly symbolized a union he wished to avoid," Winthrop Jordan writes, the slaveholder could indeed deny the fruits of his passion by not recognizing them. Because they confused the essential distinction between the races, mulattoes threatened to "undermine the logic of the racial slavery upon which his society was based," and by classifying them as Negroes, the slaveholder-father "was in effect denying that intermixture had occurred at all."[27] But that inevitably put his wife, and southern white women in general, in a peculiar position, for it heightened the mythic melodrama of gallantry and courtesy that almost every account, fictional or not, makes characteristic of the slaveholding South and that Faulkner rendered with exceptional emotional complexity in the characters of Clytie and Rosa.

The *"unravished nuptial"* in which Rosa lives along with Judith (and, it seems, Clytie), the *"one constant and perpetual instant when the arras-veil before what-is-to-be"* awaits *"the lightest naked thrust,"* the *"cocoon-casket marriage-bed of youth and grief"* she lies down in once and forever in 1860, the long relived and remembered *"might-have-been which is more than truth"*[28]—these singular moments of a marriage that was never to be acquire their energizing power from the fact that, leaving aside altogether the question of Rosa's knowledge of Bon's blood, we have to read them as revealing a desire for Bon that the novel itself must express, even if it can do so only indirectly or unconsciously. Exactly because these moments are offered up in the realm of remembered fantasy, Rosa's Gothic eroticism contains a virulent nostalgia and willful innocence that betray the dark underside of slaveholding marriages: that white women often lived in the face of a monstrous affront and—more alarming indeed—may well have had passions of their own. The children of miscegenation not only threatened to blur the distinctions that made slavery possible, but the unions that produced them threatened to distort sexual relations and marriage itself, for black and white alike, into peculiar and tragic forms.

In the year before the war, Rosa says, *"Ellen talked to me of trousseau (and it my trousseau), of all the dreamy panoply of surrender which was my surrender*"; when the news of Lincoln's election and the fall of Sumter comes, Rosa is sewing "for her own vicarious bridal" the garments that she "would never wear and never remove for a man whom she was not even to see," and she is still sewing when Mississippi secedes and the regiment commanded by Sutpen and Sartoris appears in town beneath regimental colors "sewed together out of silk dresses."[29] The superimposing of these actions is a symbolic expression of their relentless entanglement in *Absalom, Absalom!* Still sewing those marital garments in memory, and still unable to put them on or take them off forty-five years later—later still, when Faulkner writes the book we read—Rosa lives in a world of tortured innocence that is conceivable only because it is, in this case more than ever, the product of a superannuated guilt. That guilt is not necessarily Rosa's, but it is Faulkner's (as author), and it is the South's. The fevered moment of union she lives in still, distended by the ruinous divisions that bring it into being, is haunting in its extremity: it is a moment in which she cannot, will not, will never "surrender." For reasons absolutely dependent upon the tragic realities of miscegenation, Rosa's marriage to Bon that never was is a crucial part of the failure of Sutpen's design—crucial because it illuminates the mockery of Sutpen's actual marriages to Eulalia Bon and Ellen Coldfield and the one he proposes to Rosa.

No tragedy is greater than Bon's or Clytie's or that of their mothers, but Rosa's brings them into perspective, not only by uniting them but also by diffusing their shadows through and into the intimate heart of the slaveholding South and its unsurrendering memories. The greater passions Rosa and Faulkner express in her extraordinary disembodied meditation on the world of lost love are nearly unaccountable unless we take seriously the unsettling dimensions of sexual union to which they refer, dimensions in which sexuality became split between love and lust, and in which familial and affectionate relations of every kind could be torn from their natural paths of development and turned into grotesque reflections of the institution they supported. One can measure the achievement of *Absalom, Absalom!* no more clearly than by noting with what inspired passion, and without capitulating either to sentimentality or to bitterness, it works against the violent limitations such a situation placed on human love.

Faulkner's novel can express that love only by remarkable in-direction—most significantly, as we will see, in the recreations of Quentin and Shreve, but most passionately (and therefore most indirectly) in the pressures that culminate in Rosa's unravished nuptial, the mock marriage that in its reciprocal affirmation and denial of love most ably characterizes the central emotional trag-edies of slavery. As Rosa sews her trousseau, the conflict that will suspend all actions and decisions for four years begins. The mur-der and the design it will at once present and destroy are held in suspense while the South seeks, in magnificent fashion, to deny its union with the nation, and the North seeks, in fashions devised by Lincoln, to restore union without abolishing slavery. Neither plan will work; the price for both the South and the North is the story Faulkner will still tell more than a half century later when, dividing his novel in half, he shifts its burden from Rosa Coldfield, widow, to Quentin Compson, suicide, one of the char-acters he "had to get out of the attic to tell the story of Sutpen."[30]

When Wilbur Cash comes to speak of contemporary southern writers in *The Mind of the South*, he notes that they are, Faulkner included, "romantics of the appalling" who only hate the South "with the exasperated hate of a lover who cannot persuade the object of his affections to his desire," much as "Narcissus, growing at length analytical, might have suddenly begun to hate his image reflected in a pool."[31] The Quentin Compson who claims raptur-ously at the conclusion of *Absalom, Absalom!* that he does not hate the South certainly falls under Cash's definition, and there is every reason to see the later book as a lengthy, analytic explo-ration of the narcissistic hatred of himself and his heritage that Quentin expresses, but Faulkner cannot fully explain, in *The Sound and the Fury*. In the first book, Faulkner had clearly shown his house to be divided, but he had not made entirely clear the psycholog-ical complexities of that division and the Gothic collapse of sen-sibilities it could produce. At that point, the horror remained essentially unnameable; at best it was focused in a term that had immediate emotional and formal significance but little psychological depth—*incest*. It is now difficult, if not impossible, to read *The Sound and the Fury* outside the context of *Absalom, Absalom!* but it is worth bearing in mind the purposeful ambiguity of that context, despite its more literal phrasing of the horror—miscegenation.

The attempts readers have made from time to time to divorce the two books, to claim none but coincidental connections in either formal or psychological terms, can only seem more incredible than ever after John Irwin's splendid reading to the contrary.[32] Irwin's elucidation of the mirroring, antagonistic psychological relationships among *Absalom, Absalom!*'s principal actors and narrators, involved as they are in a dramatic reconstruction of events that may have taken place in the form they devise but cannot be said undoubtedly to have done so, makes conspicuous their necessary interchangeability, that is, it makes them "family." The energizing power of Sutpen's design and its collapse drives into union with him and his family all of those who try to "tell" his story—Rosa, Mr. Compson, Quentin, and Shreve. As though imbued with "gaunt and tireless driving" by "sheer association with him" and enclosed in the "aura of unregeneration" his "invoked ghost" continues to create, they engage vicariously in Sutpen's own "amazed recapitulation" of his design and participate once again in estimating its tragic flaw. What Mr. Compson speaks of as Rosa Coldfield's "vicarious bridal," as well as the "vicarious image" of himself in Bon with which he claims Henry Sutpen has seduced his own sister, describes the pervasive narcissism of the novel's relationships.[33] Such narcissism, as Irwin argues, makes every character the potential or implied double of others and brings them all into positions of intimate emotional involvement in which what is only vicarious, only *imagined*, takes on a psychological immediacy and tangibility that overrides and engulfs what might have been actual.

Faulkner's own tortured effort to measure Sutpen's design through "a rhetoric strained almost to the breaking point by an agony of identification"[34] is the medium of that vicarious involvement, a medium that fully conforms to the pressures it seeks out and fabricates by dissolving the barriers between fact and fantasy, fathers and sons, brothers and sisters, brother and brother, white and black. As in the contradictory case of Quentin's incestuous (that is, "impure") obsession with Caddy's "purity" in *The Sound and the Fury*, one might speak of that mediation, forced into action by the greater cultural strain it seeks to identify, as a formal realization that the imposed structures of containment that make moral action meaningful and powerful do so only in reaction to implied violations of those limiting structures. Only the approach toward, and transgression of, such limits fixes their meaning, just as the desire, in Quentin's case, to commit incest is exactly what defines it; it becomes incest when the taboo remains in place, even in violation, or more significantly when the *act* cannot be actualized at all but only expressed as *desire*, that is, as an imaginary or vicarious possibility. Because it nearly repeats his remarks to Quentin in *The Sound and the Fury*, Mr. Compson's description of Henry Sutpen's discovery of "the pure and perfect incest"—"the brother realizing that the sister's virginity must be destroyed in order to have existed at all, taking that virginity in the person of the brother-in-law"[35]—represents both his understanding of those limits and his inability to explain the Sutpen tragedy. His explanation here makes Henry into Quentin as Mr. Compson understands him; but because it apparently occurs before he has received the crucial information that Quentin's visit to Sutpen's Hundred with Rosa reveals, Mr. Compson's version cannot account for the more tragic extenuation of the limits to which incestuous desire responds in this instance. That further stricture of limitation, which is paradoxically more fixed and more resolutely dissolved both in fact and in the entangling reciprocities of the novel's own imaginative design, is miscegenation.

In this chapter, as elsewhere in the novel, Faulkner's narrative covertly reveals what it strives to hold in suspense, for Mr. Compson goes on to speak of Bon's "effluvium of Sutpen blood and character" even as he elaborates a theory for the murder based on the "morganatic ceremony" between Bon and his octoroon mistress. As he himself recognizes at this point, however, such a theory "just does not explain." "You re-read" the story of the

Sutpen family, "the paper old and falling to pieces, the writing faded, almost undecipherable," he remarks, "you bring them together again and again and nothing happens." Even so, Mr. Compson's dwelling on the "ceremony" between Bon and his "wife" provides a significant context for the unraveling of Bon's tragedy eventually undertaken by Quentin and Shreve, for it is at the climax of his recapitulation of Bon's gradual exposure of Henry to the peculiar sexual conventions of New Orleans that the ultimate barrier of the novel is preliminarily revealed. Unable to convince Henry that the mulatto mistresses of New Orleans are neither whores nor wives but part of a doomed race who are perhaps "the only truly chaste women, not to say virgins, in America," Bon plays his "trump" card: "Have you forgotten that this woman, this child are niggers? You, Henry Sutpen of Sutpen's Hundred in Mississippi? You, talking of marriage, a wedding, here?"[36]

The barrier of Bon's marriage to the octoroon is ultimately overwhelmed by the barrier of incest and, later still, the barrier of miscegenation. But as the etymology of incest (*in* + *castus*) suggests, it is the superimposition of these barriers, which are themselves opposed, mirroring figures, that expresses the tragic depth of *Absalom, Absalom!* by making exceedingly "monstrous" the love Quentin and Shreve try desperately to understand by creating. They do so in a series of compelling inventions that, as they progress, more and more deviate from the simpler but less conclusive explanations of the tragedy offered by Rosa and Mr. Compson virtually in order to create a barrier that can be, that *must be* passed in imaginative violation and union. The novel's extreme exertions of kinship—notably among Henry and Bon, Quentin and Shreve, "not two of them but four, the two who breathed not individuals now yet something both more and less than twins"—struggle to rehearse once again the disintegration of Sutpen's design by accepting its flaw as irreducible but redeeming the passions that force it to tragic culmination. Nowhere is this more evident than in the narrative scene that follows Shreve's reconstruction of the relationship between Bon and Henry at college, Bon recognizing his brother, and Henry asserting that, if he had a brother, he "would want him to be just like you."[37] The scene grows out of the novel's most precarious invention, the New Orleans lawyer engaged by Eulalia Bon to blackmail Sutpen (first with the threat of bigamy, then with the threat of incest), and as such it presents the gravest crisis, the potentially most damaging flaw in Faulkner's own design.

Because it is the burden of Quentin and Shreve to save from wasted effort the previous struggles of Rosa and Mr. Compson to bring Sutpen's story into coherent focus, the lawyer's role, knitting together a series of unlikely incidents, is necessarily perilous and seemingly fortuitous. But the crisis this produces in Faulkner's own design perfectly matches, and by analogy forces to an agonizing pitch, the reciprocal relationships of Bon and Henry, Shreve and Quentin. More than anything, perhaps, it grows out of the novel's expressed need to suggest, to intimate, to wrest from doubt while leaving all doubts in place a motive for Bon's actions that is more than simple revenge. "And now," Shreve says, "we're going to talk about love":

> But he didn't need to say that either, any more than he had needed to specify which he meant by he, since neither of them had been thinking about anything else; all that had gone before just so much that had to be overpassed and none else present to overpass it but them. . . . it did not matter to either of them which one did the talking, since it was not the talking alone which did it, performed and accomplished the overpassing, but some happy marriage of speaking and hearing wherein each before the demand, the requirement, forgave condoned and forgot the faulting of the other—faultings both in the creating of this shade whom they discussed (rather, existed in) and in the hearing and sifting and discarding the false and conserving what seemed true, or fit the preconceived—in order to overpass to love, where there might be paradox and inconsistency but nothing fault nor false.[38]

The "marriage of speaking and hearing," so gracefully elaborated in the probing rhythms of Quentin's and Shreve's shared rehearsal of the Sutpen story, constitutes the reaching and passing of the novel's greatest emotional and imaginative crisis. The act of "overpassing" expresses the danger of this crisis and its manifest resolution, for the love between Bon and Judith, and most particularly the love between Bon and Henry, that Shreve and Quentin go on to design, itself extended in their own fraternal intimacy, is one that must overpass momentarily, and hold in passionate suspense for the duration of the Civil War, the single barrier that will at last lead to fratricide. In order to achieve this union, the novel's own design must engage in a risk equal to that of Bon and Henry, must pass over possibilities and likelihoods that run counter to that forged union; most significantly, it must continue to suppress the very information (which Quentin has possessed ever since the events that occur between chapters five and three—but are not revealed until the last pages of the novel—and which Shreve too now possesses) that makes the "overpass to love" dramatically necessary: that Bon is Henry's brother and a "Negro."

Quentin and Shreve are probably correct in thinking that to Henry the "ceremony" between Bon and the octoroon would have been irrelevant, "only something else about Bon to be, not envied but aped if that had been possible."[39] So far as the novel is capable of revealing it, the incest as well would have the same repulsive attraction; for as Quentin and Shreve reconstruct it, even incest can be overpassed by love. The one thing Henry cannot pass over is Sutpen's own "trump," that Bon is "black." Instead, he kills his brother. It is worth emphasizing the brutal immediacy of this act, for the novel strives heroically to delay it, obscure it, render it unfathomable or mysterious, hide it from view—and yet makes murderously apparent the overriding reason for it. The entanglement between Bon's "passing" as white and the "overpass to love" between Henry and Bon it first makes necessary and then impossible is a thoroughly tormenting one; it circumscribes the crisis of blood that would be the very crisis of the South now and for the next hundred years. Henry kills Bon approximately a month after the end of the war, some three weeks after Lincoln's assassination, and one day before Lincoln's burial following the ritual journey home of his coffin. The crisis of union that Lincoln presaged had been "reached and passed" but, as suggested earlier, at the cost of a further crisis with which Lincoln was not clearly prepared to deal. In *Absalom, Absalom!* the one crisis holds the other in abeyance for four years and then resolves it, destroying in a further, nearly unnameable act of fratricide the momentary union that has been achieved.

From the point of view of the South, of course, the restoration of the Union was obviously no victory. One can lay the two crises upon each other only to the extent of recognizing that the retrospective acts of imagination Quentin and Shreve engage in to restore a union between brothers, even to the point of condoning incest, must inevitably lead—as the events of both the novel and history dictate—to a last crisis in which brothers are, more than ever, not brothers at all; in which freedom either makes continued affection between master and slave largely impossible or, as was more usually the case, exposes that affection as an utter fabrication; and in which the actualities of kinship that miscegenation produced appear more intolerable than ever. Leslie Fiedler is certainly right to point out that *Absalom, Absalom!* is remarkable in the genre of American Gothic fiction "for having first joined to the theme of slavery and black revenge, which is the essential sociological theme of the American tale of terror, that of incest, which is its essential erotic theme."[40] That union is indeed a remarkable one, but we need to note as well that the one barrier that Faulkner's novel cannot pass, even as it tries in desperation to repair Sutpen's design with its own, is both fused with and yet absolutely opposed to the other. Miscegenation and incest, here in fiction as elsewhere in fact, create a drama of intimate merger and extreme alienation that both doubles and divides husband and wife, father and son, brother and brother. More to the point, however, the potential miscegenation between Bon and Judith cancels out the potential incest. No one fact more characterizes the schizophrenic nature of slaveholding miscegenation. In killing for the first, Henry denies the latter: Bon is not his brother but, as he himself puts it to Henry, *"the nigger that's going to sleep with your sister."*[41]

These potential sins cannot, of course, be so neatly separated—no more so here than in the history of slavery, where "sons" were and were not sons and "brothers" were and were not brothers, and where the successive mingling of masters and slaves, white and black, therefore could not possibly be the incest it unavoidably might be in fact. One need only think ahead to the rival McCaslin lines of descent in *Go Down, Moses* to understand how accurate Henry Hughes's seemingly irrational exclamation that "amalgamation is incest" might be. The paradoxical tragedy and promise of such mixing only becomes evident, however, in the aftermath of the war—ten years, twenty years, fifty years later—in, say, 1909 or 1910 when Quentin Compson probes the Sutpen tragedy and kills himself, or in 1936 when William Faulkner writes a novel about incest and miscegenation. Slavery controlled miscegenation and whatever incest accompanied it by denying that they had any meaning, by denying, in effect, that any limits had actually been violated. Emancipation not only released a convulsive hysteria about potential miscegenation in the form of black violence against white, then, it may also be said to have destroyed the mechanisms of control that were a barrier to incest and to have made possible, if not entirely likely, a further mixing, a "monstrous" violation of blood in which, because both black and white strains could be hidden from view, miscegenation and incest could indeed occur at once.

Although it is not the most explicit part of his argument, Irwin's reading of Quentin's dilemma continually suggests that it grows out of a possibility he only comes to understand (and we only recognize retrospectively) in *Absalom, Absalom!*—that his frantic obsession with Caddy's purity, as well as his inability to ensure it or preserve it for himself, are motivated by the contagious threat of miscegenation. For Quentin, incest ensures not only emotional and moral purity but also purity of blood; what the Sutpen tragedy reveals to him, however, is that incest *may not* ensure such genealogical purity, or that even if it does, it can do so only by mocking reference to a dream long dead and long since turned nightmare. The reunion of the House Divided dissolved the barrier between North and South, between free and slave, and gradually defined a new social and political self for blacks; but by making acts of miscegenation legitimately (if not yet legally) meaningful, it necessarily introduced a new barrier, a suddenly unthinkable and more frightening form of "impurity" that whites in particular thought there was good reason to fear. As courts, legislatures, and the history of American race relations would prove for years to come, the miscegenation taboo was as strong as, even stronger than, the incest taboo—strong enough, at times, to justify the utmost violence. In this respect, *Absalom, Absalom!* can perhaps be seen only to "explain" *The Sound and the Fury* by means of *Light in August*, the novel in which Faulkner can first be said to have extended his major theme and brought to fruition his explorations of novelistic form.

As Faulkner reread the story of Quentin Compson in the light of the Sutpen tragedy, he was searching out Quentin's own tragedy; he was reaching back toward the ecstasy of composition that had eluded him ever since *The Sound and the Fury*; and he was struggling, along with all of the narrators of *Absalom, Absalom!*, to set in place a lost dream whose precise nature is that it has already collapsed. He was "reading by repercussion" his own work and the tragedy, the original sin, that set it in motion, knowing full well, as Rosa once again puts it, that *"there is no all, no finish; it is not the blow we suffer from but the tedious repercussive anti-climax of it, the rubbishy aftermath to clear away from off the very threshold of despair."*[42]

Rosa's assertion here appears in the context of the "echoed shot" that was all she ever heard of Bon's murder and the closed door of Judith's bedroom she could not enter. It is the same door that Quentin, throughout the novel, cannot pass through, and it is the door Faulkner himself refuses to enter, perhaps because for him, as for Quentin, it hides the ultimate intimacy of incest, whether between Quentin and Caddy or between Bon and Judith. In this respect, the most important mysteries, the crucial points of obscured or undelivered information in *Absalom, Absalom!* as in *The Sound and the Fury*, revolve around moments of unfulfilled and nearly unnameable love and around Quentin's Oedipal battle with his father to fulfill and articulate that love. If one were to assert that there is a formal relationship between the two books that is

itself incestuous or marital, one might measure the powerful ecstasy that Faulkner's reworking of Quentin's dilemma sought,
successfully or not, to recapture. We do not need to do so, however, in order to see that the two novels' formal relationship, like
those of the characters involved, is one of merged intimacy and
antagonism, and that the crisis of family identity each involves
depends upon the exact crisis that incest and miscegenation bring
into being: a crisis of blood in which sons are not sons and brothers are not brothers, and in which the distinctions between them
that must be maintained, however fantastically, are also the ones
that keep the lost dream in place long after it has collapsed.

As Faulkner later remarked, and as the multiple allusions to
Aeschylus, Sophocles, and Euripides make clear, it is "the old
Greek concept of tragedy" that destroys Sutpen. "He wanted a
son which symbolized [his] ideal, and he got too many sons—his
sons destroyed one another and then him. He was left with—
the only son he had left was a Negro."[43] Faulkner's explication is
a little hazy, but the crisis of Sutpen's cultural order, which is
also that of the South at large, is clearly one that results from
an effacement of necessary racial and familial differences. Such a
"destruction of differences is particularly spectacular," René Girard notes, "when the hierarchical distance between the characters, the amount of respect due from one to the other, is great—
between father and son, for instance." When the conflict is prolonged over the course of time or the course of generations, "the
resemblance between the combatants grows even stronger until
each presents a mirror image of the other," and at extremity,
"the whole cultural structure seems on the verge of collapse."
The potentially most disruptive and paradoxical form of such
conflict and disintegration appears in the reciprocal violence of
twins or brothers, who in their very nature contain such discord
and, when that discord is actualized, represent the violent crisis
of reciprocity in its utmost configuration. Precisely because "sym-
metry and identity are represented in extraordinarily explicit
terms" in the case of twins or brothers, Girard adds, this formal
mirroring, in its singular state of nondifferentiation, "ultimately
becomes the very exemplar of difference, a classic monstrosity

that plays a vital role in sacred ritual." At a further reach of the crisis is the threat posed by incest, which "leads to formless duplications, sinister repetitions, a dark mixture of unnameable things."[44]

The bearing of Girard's theory upon the doubling and "twinning" of characters and narrators in *Absalom, Absalom!* is readily apparent. And though he does not discuss it, the last remark I have quoted suggests an even more critical extenuation of the reciprocal crisis—that which appears in the admixture of blood and identity when incest is involved with, and ultimately paired with, miscegenation. It is exactly the nature of the crisis that leads the South into Civil War (and the entire nation into a prolonged act of fratricide) that it grows out of a "monstrous" system in which, at the simplest level, slaves both were and were not human beings, and in which, at a more significant level for our purposes, sexual violence could issue in a state of simultaneous differentiation and nondifferentiation between father and son or brother and brother. (One should add that the same crisis prevails and, as we have seen, is furthered in the paradoxical relationships among husbands, wives, mothers, and daughters.) The slave father whose "son" was not his son and particularly the slave son who had, therefore, no father at all stand in the most painful roles in this reciprocal tragedy. To the extent that Charles Bon embodies the dilemma of the latter with a particularly violent and ironic power, what Genovese points out about the potential emotional dilemma of the slave is exceedingly relevant here. The pressured relationship between master and slave could create a situation in which the master seemed at times to embody not only cruelty and injustice but also strength and virtue, and therefore could create in the slave a "longing for the master, understood as absolute other." But once this "act of love" is frustrated, as it usually was, it "collapses into hatred, and generates, at least potentially, great violence."[45] *Absalom, Absalom!* includes this dimension of the crisis but engages its most volatile configuration by representing as well the other, more reprehensible aspect of the parental conflict—that between the white father and the son who is and is *not* his son.

It is this mirroring conflict—"mirroring," in that brother and brother, son and son, are completely alienated yet nearly interchangeable—that Faulkner drives to a hallucinating pitch in the fraternal entanglements among Henry, Bon, Quentin, and Shreve, the first two resembling each other and their father, the second two resembling each other and mutually assuming, as their recreation of the tragedy progresses, a voice that sounds just like Mr. Compson's. The attempts many readers have made to separate the voices into distinct genres (the Gothic, the Greek tragedy, the romantic, and so on) are certainly warranted, but only because such attempts reflect an inevitable anxiety that the voices, effacing necessary narrative distinctions just as the action of the novel effaces cultural distinctions, *will* begin to be indistinguishable. As the crisis of the book is prolonged and held in abeyance in parallel with the suspension of the Sutpen crisis over the course of the Civil War, each of the storytellers and actors wears the "mask" of Greek tragedy to which Mr. Compson alludes early on, "interchangeable not only from scene to scene, but from actor to actor and behind which events and occasions [take] place without chronology or sequence"; and they do indeed, to borrow a prophetic passage from *The Sound and the Fury,* seem to talk all at once, "their voices insistent and contradictory and impatient, making of unreality a possibility, then a probability, then an incontrovertible fact, as people will when their desires become words."[46] As in Poe's tales of incest and Melville's *Pierre*, the distinctions between narrators (or authors) and characters dissolve in a frenzy of nondifferentiation in which identity collapses along with almost every vestige of plot, chronology, and order.

Yet this collapse, like that of Sutpen's design, does not quite take place—and for good reason. At a narrative level, we are left with enough clues, enough fragile threads of evidence to reconstruct the novel's design; and at the level of action, where the two designs merge and separate, we are met with a violent reassertion of order and chronology. That violence is Henry's murder of Bon, which, despite its tragic consequences for all involved, saves Sutpen's design in theory by vigorously asserting distinctions that have threatened to become obliterated. It does so in a peculiar way, however, for as we noted earlier, the murder has extremely ambiguous motivations, ones that extend the reciprocal crisis to a more complex level. In murdering Bon not as the "brother" but as the "nigger" who is going to sleep with his sister, Henry in effect asserts that Bon is not his brother and not his father's son (that is, he "overpasses" the incest): if he had killed him as "brother" rather than as "nigger" (had overpassed the miscegenation), he would have had to recognize the legitimacy of a paternity his allegiance to his father, and to the South, finally will not permit. If Henry had not killed Bon at all (or if Bon had killed Henry), the crisis of reciprocity—what "might have been"— would have become unbearable: the design would have become a "mockery and a betrayal" (as Sutpen puts it), and incest and miscegenation would have become more than ever the "monstrous double" whose existence the southern slaveholding design must deny.

The scintillating merger of characters and voices that *Absalom, Absalom!* creates as it drives toward its climax thus reflects, but at the same time stands in opposition to, the narrative form of *Light in August*. The earlier novel depends upon suggesting dramatic entanglements that cannot take place and upon alienating the story of Joe Christmas, in both formal and actual terms, from those that surround it. The story that revolves around Charles Bon, however, does indeed sacrifice him, and just as violently; but it does so only after thoroughly fusing his story with those of the characters who struggle to accept him as "brother," who recognize, as it were, that his blood is their blood and that his tragedy is undeniably theirs as well. The crisis of novelistic form in both *Light in August* and *Absalom, Absalom!*—the one creating extremities of separation and alienation, the other creating extremities of merger and imitation—matches the crisis of blood, in the second instance making intimately visible the contours of the tragedy that would propel the South and the nation with which it had ostensibly been reunited into the further tragedy of Jim Crow. At that point both the design of the South and the design of the country, after provisional separation, seemed to come together again.

Faulkner's own design comes together as well, for *Absalom, Absalom!* incorporates aspects of all of his previous fiction and reveals both the origins of Joe Christmas's tragedy and the obscure motives for Quentin's. As they merge in the intimacies of kinship, the voices of the novel perhaps most resemble—"just like father's"—that of Sutpen, which, though he is long dead, is strangely clarified by their re-creations. The clarity of Sutpen's voice as he tries with calm desperation to fathom his "mistake" reveals to Quentin and to Shreve everything Quentin's own father cannot and at last—at long last, in the novel's final recollection—brings Quentin face to face with the self he will kill six months later as he confronts the act of fratricide that the novel can reveal only in a dramatically sharpened, self-reflexive form:

> And you are——?
> Henry Sutpen.
> And you have been here——?
> Four years.
> And you came home——?
> To die. Yes.
> To die?
> Yes. To die.
> And you have been here——?
> Four years.
> And you are——?
> Henry Sutpen.

The urgently restrained moment of union between Quentin and Henry brings into perspective the other moments of perilous and violent communion that define the novel's own flawed design: the "touch of flesh with flesh" that unites and divides Rosa and Clytie; the vicarious intimacy that Quentin and Shreve create for Henry as he contemplates Bon ("I used to think that I would hate the man . . . whose every move and action and speech would say to me, I have seen and touched parts of your sister's body that you will never see and touch"); the exchanged warning and cry of outraged fraternity that accompanies the vengeance of

Wash Jones ("Stand back Wash. Don't you touch me." ... "I'm going to tech you, Kernel"); and most of all the extraordinary passion that infuses Quentin's and Shreve's recreation of Bon, Sutpen, and Henry on the battlefield in the spring of 1865, Bon seeking only to "*touch flesh*" with his father, Sutpen refusing, and Henry forced in the utmost agony of intimacy to face the crisis for him. The language of the encounter between Henry and Quentin, withholding virtually everything that burgeons within it, mirrors the crisis joining 1865 to 1909 and entwining their respectively fated chronologies—Henry at last revealed as the murderer of his own "brother" and Quentin, now more than ever, as Rosa says of Henry, "almost a fratricide."[47]

The Sutpen house, as Judith archly puts it on the occasion when she hands over Bon's letter to Quentin's grandmother, is "like a bed already too full" and its story like that of "five or six people all trying to make a rug on the same loom."[48] The novel's endless repetition and repercussion of images and actions certainly bears this out—to such an extent that any full account of the layering patterns is forbidding. They all lead toward and fall away from that which cannot be expressed: first, the bedroom of his sister in which the dead Bon lies, and second, the bedroom in which the dying Henry lies. Those beds, in figure and in fact, hide to the end the secret they appear to reveal, the secret that the whole burden of Faulkner's novel rests upon. The "overpass to love" that Quentin and Shreve create in order to force the fraternal rivalry between Henry and Bon to its ultimate crisis fails, as it must, to prevent the act of fratricide, but it succeeds, to the only extent that it can, in preserving at a point of precarious union the love that must paradoxically be expressed and denied in an act of violence. The novel's refusal to reveal fully its ultimate secret is in perfect keeping with the perilous, indirect admissions of paternity and fraternity that the scenes between Sutpen and Henry, and between Henry and Bon, on the eve of the collapse of the South can reveal: for how else express the agony of Bon, Henry, and Sutpen alike, how else intimate the "monstrous" thing at the heart of the defeat that the South now faces? The passion consumed in that moment of wasted intimacy is as close as they, and Faulkner, can come to discovering the reason "why God let us lose the War."

The "overreach of despair" that Rosa's touching of flesh with Clytie produces, and the "overpass to love" that Quentin and Shreve require to culminate their own involvement in the Sutpen tragedy, are themselves mirroring images that merge and divide Faulkner's characters and his country with all of the virulent contagion that actual or imagined mixing of blood can create.

In the end, that contagion spreads to a bedroom in Cambridge, Massachusetts, in 1910. Donald Kartiganer is certainly correct to point out that the last chapter of *Absalom, Absalom!* represents a "painful disintegration of [the] communion"[49] created between Quentin and Shreve in their reimagining of Bon's own anguish, for it is essential at this level, as at every other, that the momentarily created union, the passionate fraternity, give way to violent ambivalence—Quentin frantically denying that he hates the South and Shreve taunting him about the Jim Bonds who are going to take over the world, so that "in a few thousand years, I who regard you will also have sprung from the loins of African kings."[50] The brutal antagonism of Bon's son, Valery, so reminiscent of Joe Christmas, and the howling idiot produced by his marriage to an animalistic black woman, are impossible to overpass, but they must be seen to represent not only Faulkner's deepest fears and prejudice, but also his most painful and sympathetic understanding of the South that he, like Quentin, claimed not to hate. They are the remaining fragments of Sutpen's nightmarish design, and as such they continue to express the long trauma that outlived the design. "As a social factor," George Washington Cable observed, the slave was "purely zero," no better than "the brute at the other end of his plow-line." The mingling of white blood with black made little difference: "One, two, four, eight, multiplied upon or divided into zero, still gave zero for the result."[51] Jim Bond is a concentrated emblem of the sins of the fathers to the same extent that *Absalom, Absalom!* is, as Faulkner would later say, a "condensed and concentrated" version of the "general racial system in the South."[52] Nothing could more severely betray Faulkner's own ambivalence or make any clearer that his novel has virtually nothing to say about the horrors of slavery as a labor system, but rather it revolves around the flaw that, far from abrogating those other horrors, only made them more prominent. The heroic stature of Sutpen and his willed "innocence" are no more denied by his sons than are David's by Absalom and Amnon; and in the biblical account, David's cry— the novel's title—is prompted not by Absalom's murder of Amnon, who has raped their sister, but by the later death of Absalom, the son who has risen up in rebellion against his father. It might well have been Lincoln's cry, and it might, seventy-five years later, have been Faulkner's. Like the fall of David's house, the fall of the South seemed more and more to Faulkner, in myth and in fact, an extended fulfillment of prophecy or, more exactly, a lasting curse for original sins. By the time he wrote *Absalom, Absalom!* the House Divided had long been restored in name, on paper, but the South and the fictions it lived by, and the nation and the policies it tacitly or legally endorsed, were as nearly divided as ever. In his next major novel, *Go Down, Moses*, Faulkner would compose a serial history of the South that contained from one end to the other the long, halting progress of the design for freedom that was constructed, collapsed, and reconstructed again over that period and then beyond it. In several stories that went into the novel in revised form, the character who finally became Ike McCaslin was first represented as—who else?—Quentin Compson. He was still not dead.

Notes

1. William Faulkner, *Absalom, Absalom!* (1936; reprint, New York: Vintage-Random, 1972), pp. 267, 271, 274.

2. W. J. Cash, *The Mind of the South* (1941; reprint, Vintage-Random, 1960), p. 71.

3. Eugene D. Genovese, *The World the Slaveholders Made: Two Essays in Interpretation* (1969; reprint, New York: Vintage-Random, 1971), p. 140. As Genovese goes on to point out, Cash "identifies as aristocracies only those classes exhibiting the grace and *noblesse oblige* of fourth- or fifth-

generation gentlemen. There is some advantage to this viewpoint, which Cash uses to devastating effect against attempts to romanticize the antebellum planters, but for the most part it represents a secondary line of criticism. All ruling classes have been, by definition, acquisitive, and therefore their origins have been violent and ugly; the first and second generations have naturally borne the marks of their origin, and in a frontier country so may have later generations. The juxtaposition of elegance and vulgarity existed in [southern slaveholding] society as a whole and could easily have been reflected within any given family" (p. 141). See also C. Vann Woodward, "The Southern Ethic in a Puritan World," in his *American Counterpoint: Slavery and Racism in the North-South Dialogue* (Boston: Little, Brown, 1971), pp. 13–46. For extended considerations of Sutpen as a typical planter, see Melvin Backman, *Faulkner: The Major Years* (Bloomington: Indiana University Press, 1977), pp. 88–112; Cleanth Brooks, *William Faulkner: Toward Yoknapatawpha and Beyond* (New Haven, Conn.: Yale University Press, 1978), pp. 283–300; and particularly the fine discussion by Carolyn Porter, *Seeing and Being: The Plight of the Participant Observer in Emerson, James, Adams, and Faulkner* (Middletown, Conn.: Wesleyan University Press, 1981), pp. 207–40.

4. Cash, *The Mind of the South*, p. 127.

5. Faulkner, *Absalom, Absalom!* pp. 250–51.

6. Philip Van Doren Stern, ed., *The Life and Writings of Abraham Lincoln* (New York: Modern Library, 1940), pp. 421–22, 425. An excellent account of ambivalent abolitionist views of the South as an arena of sexual dissipation may be found in Ronald G. Walters, *The Antislavery Appeal: American Abolitionism after 1830* (Baltimore, Md.: Johns Hopkins University Press, 1976), pp. 70–87; cf. George M. Fredrickson, *The Black Image in the White Mind: The Debate on Afro-American Character and Destiny, 1817–1914* (New York: Harper & Row, 1971), pp. 97–129. Lincoln's own ambivalence even made it possible years later for Thomas Dixon, ironically enough, to represent him in *The Clansman* (1905) as the true friend of the defeated South: "I have urged the colonisation of the negroes, and I shall continue until it is accomplished. My emancipation proclamation was linked with this plan.... I can conceive of no greater calamity than the assimilation of the Negro into our social and political life as our equal. A mulatto citizenship would be too dear a price to pay even for emancipation.... It was the fear of the black tragedy behind emancipation that led the South into the insanity of secession. We can never attain the ideal Union our fathers dreamed, with millions of an alien, inferior race among us,

whose assimilation is neither possible nor desirable. The Nation cannot now exist half white and half black, any more than it could exist half slave and half free" (pp. 46–47). The further irony, of course, is that Dixon's Lincoln is not far from the real one.

7. Stern, ed., *Life and Writings of Abraham Lincoln,* pp. 425–27.

8. George B. Forgie, *Patricide in the House Divided: A Psychological Interpretation of Lincoln and His Age* (New York: Norton, 1979), pp. 123–58, 243–81. Forgie's general argument that the American Revolution issued in fraternal rivalries between individuals and groups that were both devoted to and recoiled from the paternal authority of the founding fathers is continually relevant at different levels to the familial-social conflicts engaged by *Absalom, Absalom!*

9. Stern, ed., *Life and Writings of Abraham Lincoln,* pp. 654, 657, 684.

10. Ibid., pp. 429, 439. For a detailed reading of the House Divided speech, see Don E. Fehrenbacher, *Prelude to Greatness: Lincoln in the 1850s* (Stanford, Calif.: Stanford University Press, 1962), pp. 70–95.

11. Faulkner, *Absalom, Absalom!* p. 220.

12. C. Vann Woodward, *The Burden of Southern History,* rev. ed. (Baton Rouge: Louisiana State University Press, 1968), pp. 20–21.

13. Faulkner, *Absalom, Absalom!* p. 145.

14. On miscegenation and the aspects of the 1864 campaign that follow, see Forrest G. Wood, *Black Scar: The Racist Response to Emancipation and Reconstruction* (Berkeley and Los Angeles: University of California Press, 1970), pp. 53–79 and plates 1–5.

15. J. H. Van Evrie, *White Supremacy and Negro Subordination* (New York: Van Evrie, Horton, 1868), pp. 151, 157, 167.

16. Margaret Mitchell, *Gone with the Wind* (1936; reprint, New York: Avon, 1973), pp. 647, 640.

17. C. Vann Woodward, ed., *Mary Chesnut's Civil War* (New Haven, Conn.: Yale University Press, 1981), p. 29.

18. Van Evrie, *White Supremacy and Negro Subordination,* pp. 152, 201.

19. Ibid., pp. 144–45, 153–55. For Sherwood Anderson's assertion that Faulkner himself once claimed miscegenation would lead, in human beings as in mules, to sterility, see Joseph Blotner, *Faulkner: A Biography,* 2 vols. (New York: Random House, 1974), 1:498–99. There is less doubt, however, that Faulkner considered miscegenation part of the South's doom and curse for its sins.

20. Faulkner, *Absalom, Absalom!* p. 378.

21. Van Evrie, *White Supremacy and Negro Subordination,* pp. 233–44.

22. For an interesting account of the critical and popular receptions of both novels, see James W. Mathews, "The Civil War of 1936: *Gone with the Wind* and *Absalom, Absalom!*" *Georgia Review* 21, no. 4 (Winter 1967): 462–69.

23. Henry Hughes, *Treatise on Sociology: Theoretical and Practical* (Philadelphia: Lippincott, Grambo, 1854), p. 31.

24. Faulkner, *Absalom, Absalom!* pp. 7, 61, 171, 180.

25. Ibid., pp. 146–48, 350. It is not entirely clear whether Rosa's monologue (chapter five) is delivered in the afternoon, and thus continues from chapter one, or at night when she and Quentin ride out to Sutpen's Hundred. In any event, it is clear that Quentin's conversations with his father are divided by the visit to Sutpen's Hundred (and his purported discovery of the crucial information about Bon) and that the chronology of the first five chapters is thus, more or less, one, two, four, five, three. With respect to the later chapters, it should also be recalled, from *The Sound and the Fury,* that Quentin goes home at Christmas 1909 and for Caddy's wedding in April 1910. Among the numerous investigations of the novel's narrative confusions, the most useful are the two by Cleanth Brooks, *William Faulkner: The Yoknapatawpha Country* (New Haven, Conn.: Yale University Press, 1963), pp. 295–324, 429–41, and *William Faulkner: Toward Yoknapatawpha and Beyond,* pp. 301–28.

26. Faulkner, *Absalom, Absalom!* pp. 137–40, 155–56.

27. Winthrop Jordan, *White over Black: American Attitudes toward the Negro, 1550–1812* (1968; reprint, New York: Norton, 1977), 178, 149.

28. Ibid., pp. 145, 142, 136, 143.

29. Ibid., pp. 149, 77, 80.

30. Gwynn and Blotner, eds., *Faulkner in the University*, p. 73.

31. Cash, *Mind of the South,* pp. 386–87.

32. Irwin's interpretation of the relationship between the two novels and their characters is essentially an Oedipal one; rather than make my debt to him cumbersome by constant reference, let me quote at length several passages that seem to contain the crucial points of his reading:

That Quentin identifies with both Henry, the brother as protector, and with Bon, the brother as seducer, is not extraordinary, for in Quentin's narrative they are not so much two separate figures as two aspects of the same figure. Quentin projects onto the characters of Bon and Henry opposing elements in his own personality—Bon represents Quentin's unconsciously motivated desire

for his sister Candace, while Henry represents the conscious repression or punishment of that desire.

The brother avenger and the brother seducer are substitutes for
the father and the son in the Oedipal triangle.... Thus, when
Henry kills Bon he is the father-surrogate killing the son, but
since Henry, like Bon, is also in love with their sister Judith, he
is as well the younger brother (son) killing the older brother who
symbolizes the father, the father who is the rival for the mother
and who punishes incest between brother and sister, son and
mother.

Since the relationship between the brother avenger and the
brother seducer is a substitute for the father-son relationship in
the Oedipal triangle, it is not surprising that when Quentin and
Shreve identify with Henry and Bon, the narration turns into a
father-son dialogue.... This basic interchangeability of the roles
of father and son is present in both the [fantasy of a reversal of
generations] and the incest complex, and it is internalized in the
father-son relationship of the roles of the superego and the ego
within the self.

See John Irwin, *Doubling and Incest, Repetition and Revenge: A Speculative Reading
of Faulkner* (Baltimore, Md.: Johns Hopkins University Press, 1975), pp. 28,
118, 77. A treatment of this theme that expands upon Irwin's account
may be found in Richard H. King, *A Southern Renaissance: The Cultural Awakening of the American South, 1930–1955* (New York: Oxford University Press,
1980), pp. 112–29.

33. Faulkner, *Absalom, Absalom!* pp. 36, 13, 263, 77, 107.

34. Hyatt H. Waggoner, *William Faulkner: From Jefferson to the World* (Lexington: University of Kentucky Press, 1959), p. 150.

35. Faulkner, *Absalom, Absalom!* p. 96.

36. Ibid., pp. 104, 100–101, 117–18. On the New Orleans *plaçage,* see
John W. Blassingame, *Black New Orleans, 1860–1880* (Chicago: University
of Chicago Press, 1973), pp. 17–20, 210–19.

37. Faulkner, *Absalom, Absalom!* pp. 294, 316.

38. Ibid., p. 316. For an important and innovative reading of this
scene and the marriage figure as it defines the articulation of desire and
consecration throughout Faulkner's narrative, see John T. Matthews,
"The Marriage of Speaking and Hearing in *Absalom, Absalom!*" *ELH* 47, no.
3 (Fall 1980): 575–94.

39. Faulkner, *Absalom, Absalom!* p. 336. Given the "monstrous" nature of miscegenation, deriving to such an extent from prevailing views of the Negro as simian "beast," the pun on "ape" is ironically to the point.

40. Leslie Fiedler, *Love and Death in the American Novel,* rev. ed. (New York: Dell, 1966), p. 414.

41. Faulkner, *Absalom, Absalom!* p. 358.

42. James B. Meriwether, ed., "William Faulkner: An Introduction for *The Sound and the Fury,*" *Southern Review,* n.s., 8 (October 1972), p. 709; Faulkner, *Absalom, Absalom!* p. 150.

43. Gwynn and Blotner, eds., *Faulkner in the University,* p. 35. Although the Oedipus cycle and *Agamemnon* contain readily obvious analogues to Faulkner's drama, a full explication of revenge and reciprocal action, and particularly the motifs of incest and twinship, require reference to the rest of the Oresteian trilogy *(The Choepheri* and *The Eumenides)* and to Euripides' *Iphigenia in Tauris.*

44. René Girard, *Violence and the Sacred,* trans. Patrick Gregory (Baltimore, Md.: Johns Hopkins University Press, 1977), pp. 47, 49, 64, 75; cf. pp. 50–67, 159–63.

45. Genovese, *World the Slaveholders Made,* pp. 6–7. For a further elaboration of this ambivalence and the crisis it can produce, see Stanley M. Elkins, *Slavery: A Problem in American Institutional and Intellectual Life,* 3d ed. (Chicago, Ill.: University of Chicago Press, 1976), pp. 115–33.

46. Faulkner, *Absalom, Absalom!* p. 62; *The Sound and the Fury* (New York: Vintage-Random, 1956), p. 145.

47. Faulkner, *Absalom, Absalom!* pp. 373, 139, 328, 286, 348, 15.

48. Ibid., pp. 127–28, 348.

49. Donald M. Kartiganer, *The Fragile Thread: The Meaning of Form in Faulkner's Novels* (Amherst: University of Massachusetts Press, 1979), p. 103.

50. Faulkner, *Absalom, Absalom!* p. 378. Shreve appears to have read *Pudd'nhead Wilson.*

51. George Washington Cable, *The Silent South* (New York: Scribner's, 1885), p. 6.

52. Gwynn and Blotner, eds., *Faulkner in the University,* p. 94.

The Silencing of Rosa Coldfield

MINROSE GWIN

◆ ◆ ◆

> The question underlying madness *writes*, and
> writes itself. And if we are unable to locate it,
> read it, except where it already has escaped . . .
> it is not because the question relative to madness
> does not question, but because it questions *some-*
> *where else*: somewhere at that point of silence
> where it is no longer we who speak, but where,
> in our absence, we are *spoken*.
> —Shoshana Felman, *Writing and Madness*

> You see, I was that sun, or thought I was who
> did believe there was that spark, that crumb in
> madness which is divine, though madness knows
> no word itself for terror or for pity.
> —Rosa Coldfield, in William Faulkner's
> *Absalom, Absalom!*

I. Rosa's Mad Text

WE CANNOT SAY MADNESS; madness instead says us.
For to interrogate madness—to ask it what it is—is to
affirm reason, and thereby to defer the question of madness in
the very process of articulating it. Rosa Coldfield shows us just
how slippery that very question is—and how dangerous—particularly for the woman whose narrative desire to speak the madness
of patriarchy, to say what it is, may lead her to become the
spoken. In short, to become herself mad. On the other hand, as
Shoshana Felman points out, madness, in its very inexplicability,

makes literature what it is "by virtue of the dynamic *resistance to interpretation* in the literary thing" (*Writing and Madness* 254).

What is most mysterious and provocative about *Absalom, Absalom!* is how it insists on its own madness as a text and so generates its poetics out of madness's resistance to interpretation. This is a tricky trick, for such a text's meaning must always depend on its not meaning. Its madness is a silence which floats away whenever language moves to say it. In *Absalom, Absalom!* Rosa Coldfield is the avatar of madness. She speaks the madness of her culture, but at times she too becomes that madness. This is not surprising if we think of Rosa's story as the repressed hysterical (to say both is redundant) narrative of patriarchy, as the feminine symptom of what patriarchy has silenced in order to construct its systems.

In rereading Freud's analysis of the famous hysteric Dora, Jacques Lacan observes in hysteria a lower threshold and a more transparent screen between the unconscious and the conscious (*Feminine Sexuality* 73). This lowering of the threshold between the conscious and the unconscious and its association with women link Rosa's story to what we may call the hysterical text, its narrative of repressed desire which converses in the space between the conscious and the unconscious and thus, as one sees also in *The Sound and the Fury*, exists beyond the symbolic order of language.[1] The hysterical text is thereby the figuration of all that the symbolic order must repress in order to speak. Rosa Coldfield's articulations of female desire, her "summer of wistaria," and her mad text, which engages the space between consciousness and unconsciousness, are precisely what Thomas Sutpen must deny in order to maintain the "innocence" that privileges rationality by repressing desire. Like the hysteric, who has always been associated with female deviance,[2] Rosa marks the uncanny return of repressed desire. And this desire, figured in *Absalom, Absalom!* as Rosa and her insistent voice, fuels the madness of this narrative and becomes that about it which is resistant to interpretation, which goes in all directions at once, which makes everything more, and less, than it seems. As Mary Jacobus suggests, to read toward a text's strangeness, that which is unknowable and mysterious about a text, is not to repress the gendering of hysteria as female but rather to exploit it. "Hysterical reading" that is powerfully connected to a text's unconscious, just as Dora's hysteria was a powerful expression of her culture's repression of women, can uncover and unleash its own internal differences and divisions (which certainly *Absalom, Absalom!* contains in abundance) (Jacobus 233).

Like Caddy Compson in *The Sound and the Fury*, but more insistently than Caddy, Rosa insists on the possibility of female desire and female symbolization within what Hélène Cixous has called "the realm of the proper"—that is, within a patriarchal culture which turns on the male fear of deprivation of power ("Castration or Decapitation?" 50). Sutpen's actions throughout the book are obviously motivated by such a fear, set in motion by his rejection as a boy at the front door of a plantation. Sutpen's "innocence" is indeed based upon the economy of "the realm of the proper," which is founded on a system of returns through which power is given away only on the condition that it be returned (Cixous, "Castration or Decapitation?" 50). Sutpen's is a precise system of measures, much, as we are told through three levels of male Compson discourse, like the ingredients of a cake or pie: what you put in, you get out. At the same time, though, Rosa reveals her own complicity in the realm of the proper. Even though her outpouring may be perceived, as it is by Mr. Compson, as a "breathing indictment . . . of the entire male principle" (46), she nonetheless speaks the seductive power of that principle.

In beginning to converse with Rosa and her hysterical narrative of white patriarchy, I envision her as being, as she is literally, *inside* (later, I will envision her *outside*) what Mr. Compson calls the "dim grim tight little house" of the father. Decades after his death Goodhue Coldfield retains the power of the Word. It is he who has named the "dim hot airless room" which still encases his daughter as an old woman, within which she speaks the madness of the Father's House. There is indeed "something" in this tomb-like house, and it is Rosa herself. Contained within her own dead father's house, her old woman's body hysterically rigid in the "black which did not even rustle," Miss Rosa, as Quentin first sees her, is the image of castration and impotence. To the white male gaze, which attempts to objectify and distance her in various ways through the book, Rosa's "female old flesh long embattled in virginity" configures lack. From "the too tall chair in which she resembled a crucified child," she embodies a frontal view of phallic absence, "the faint triangle of lace at wrists and throat" forming a repetitive pattern of blankness. As the male gaze is confronted with Rosa's white triangle, which, at once, speaks man's castration and woman's infantilization, an uncanny bisexual text of impotence is written across Rosa's body. She becomes the site of discourse between men's fears of expropriation, of castration, and women's loss of access to their own desires. In this sense, the blankness of Rosa's body, as an icon which elicits fear, can be compared to Charles Bon's, which is made threatening through its racial ambiguity.

Yet Rosa's body seems also to tell how one woman's loss of her sexuality actually results from one man's fear, from patriarchy's movement to cover its own lack, or the possibility of lack, by appropriating, like Sutpen with his slaves who are black and wives who are assumed white, that which it constructs as vacancy: women and women's bodies. Through a cycle of anxiety and expropriation, then, white patriarchy encodes and empowers itself. So, as Rosa's "unmoving triangle of dim lace" speaks her own loss, it also conveys to Quentin the threat of male castration as that fear which fuels the economy of the realm of the proper. In this regard, at least, Mr. Compson is more accurate than he knows when he constructs Rosa (her younger self) as "not only a living and walking reproach to her father, but a breathing indictment ubiquitous and even transferable of the entire male principle" (46).

Yet, in this initial encounter with Rosa, which seems crowded with male presences (Quentin, soon to be a suicide; the ever-present watcher and listener Mr. Compson; even Sutpen himself are all textures within this first chapter), that same woman's voice valorizes male power as well. For it is Miss Rosa who speaks Sutpen's phallic potency and the power of his symbolic authority, as surely as she makes evident his rapacity and inhumanity—as surely as her lace triangle mirrors his own castration. "Making" and "unmaking" the father, Rosa thus reads the mad male text ambiguously; as she herself knows so well (and this is what her story is about), she has herself been seduced by the godlike Father whose power can "overrun suddenly the hundred square miles of tranquil and astonished earth and drag house and formal gardens violently out of the soundless Nothing and clap them down like cards upon a table . . . creating the Sutpen's Hundred, the *Be Sutpen's Hundred* like the oldentime *Be Light*" (4). Rosa's creation of the difference within the masculine is indeed so compelling that Quentin himself is split by it. He, like Rosa, is seduced and yet repelled by Sutpen. Her story creates "two separate Quentins now talking to one another in the long silence of notpeople, in notlanguage," talking of the Father (Sutpen) who raped the land and begot children, as Rosa says, "*without gentleness*" (4–5), and yet who exerted masculine privilege and power in a culture maddened by its own desire for such.

This seductive power of the Father, that which makes his madness cut a dashing figure across the red clay hills of northern Mississippi much like Faulkner's own grandfather the Old Colonel, is Rosa's creation and her question. It is the question which generates the novel, which writes itself in endless repetition off this book's last pages echoed as it is in Quentin's anguished cry, "*I dont hate it! I dont hate it!*" (303). This is "the question underlying madness" which Felman says cannot be asked, for language is not capable of asking it, and yet the question Rosa, like Faulkner, insists on raising in a series of multiple and proliferating texts of "madness" which exist, like literature, in their active resistance to interpretation. So the question underlying madness proliferates across the narrative landscape on which Rosa set Sutpen to ride so seductively and so treacherously. And he rides on, disappearing in a cloud of dust before we can discern his shape.

II. Rosa's Madness

Perhaps history is not to be found in our mirrors, but in our repudiations: perhaps the other is ourselves.—James Baldwin, "Everybody's Protest Novel"

As the mad texts of *Absalom, Absalom!* begin to take life and fluctuate with their own rhythms, we may find ourselves, with Quentin, turning away from Sutpen's receding form to float back even further in the past, to what Rosa calls her culture's "fell darkness." That darkness, in all of its complex associations, links expectations of what black and white men and women should be to the terror of racial encounters and the urgency of cultural guilt. In *Absalom*, as in several other Faulkner novels such as *Light in August, Go Down, Moses*, and *Intruder in the Dust*, madness writes itself in the intensity of what one might call *racial events*—those charged expressive moments when racism speaks its own text of madness, when it says itself as mad, as stubbornly resistant to interpretation or explanation. These racial events, their mad texts, seem inescapably generated by gender-inflected discourses which spiral out to engage the relationships of race and gender under white patriarchy.

One of the most intense racial events in the Faulkner canon is Rosa's memory of herself and Clytie Sutpen on the stairs of Sutpen's Hundred; Clytie blocks her way as Rosa rushes up the stairs to find Judith and the corpse of Charles. When young Rosa destroys the alterity and generative power of Clytie's touch and address ("Dont you go up there, Rosa") with her demand ("Take your hand off me, nigger!"), she as a white woman embraces the realm of the proper, which similarly has denied *her* humanity.[3] Knowing that Clytie's address "did [her] more grace and respect than anyone else" and called her to human and female kinship, Rosa nonetheless rejects her violently, thereby invalidating herself as a subject, as the *Rosa* of Clytie's defining voice.

This denial of Clytie, and the concomitant show of alliance with white patriarchy, is precisely what leads the young Rosa to position herself as object within the realm of the proper. That positioning—and its seductions of power—results in her eventual seduction by the father. Yet, in that frozen moment on the stairs, those shells that we think of as encasing identity mysteriously dissolve: whiteness becomes blackness, for both are signs which suddenly shift and merge within the intensity of the moment. Rosa writes the moment across the female body: "*But let flesh touch with flesh, and watch the fall of all the eggshell shibboleth of caste and color too*" (111). As John Irwin suggests, the confrontation of the Other, "the self with a difference," is a painful, often terrifying act, a loss of control over the repressed "dark self" whom one would deny at almost any cost (92). Once that confrontation occurs and those barriers dissolve, however, there is no retreating from the connections forged. So, as Rosa is the uncanniness within the Father's House, Clytie is the uncanniness within Rosa, that which she has repressed in order to remain sheltered by the Father, whose madness she will continue, paradoxically, to embrace and decry for the rest of her life.

Just as Miss Rosa's white triangle constitutes to Quentin's male gaze the castration he fears, Clytie on the stairs of the Father's House embodies Rosa's complicity in the cultural text which she will come to speak as madness. What the encounter between Clytie and Rosa reveals is that the question underlying the madness of racism is as elusive as Felman says. Racism/madness becomes an intensely personal event in which one human being denies the humanity of another, yet in that act of denial paradoxically splits her own subjectivity, enacts her own loss of humanity and power.

Both Irwin and Lee Jenkins have remarked on the connection within the white male unconscious between repressed fear of castration and blackness (another intertext between gender and race) and the referential burden the black individual bears as a projection of "the repressed impulses" of white male fear (Jenkins 14). In another context I have suggested that, historically in the slave-holding South, cross-racial female relationships within a cultural matrix demanding moral superiority from white women and sexual availability from black women enact a volatile admixture of anxiety, terror, and sexual jealousy—one which informs Rosa and Clytie's early encounter.[4] Rereading this crucial encounter, this moment of flesh on flesh, I envision Clytie on the stairs with Rosa's hysterical text written across her body. Thadious Davis points to the fact that the speakers of *Absalom, Absalom!* invent themselves out of their varying concept of "Negro" (189). Here, though, Rosa seems to write Clytie's black female body as the very site of Rosa's own erasure as a subject, and so as the very sign of the question of cultural madness.

In Rosa's remembering, Clytie's touch dissolves ego boundaries and allows free play between subject and object:

> *Because there is something in the touch of flesh with flesh which abrogates, cuts sharp and straight across the devious intricate channels of decorous ordering, which enemies as well as lovers know because it makes them both—touch and touch of that which is the citadel of the central I-Am's private own: not spirit, soul; the liquorish and ungirdled mind is anyone's to take in any darkened hallway of this earthly tenement. But let flesh touch with flesh, and watch the fall of all the eggshell shibboleth of caste and color too.* (111–12)

Why then does the young Rosa destroy that space of acknowledgment by denying its bearer, the biracial woman who, as Rosa herself remembers, "*did me more grace and respect than anyone else I knew?*" (11). What is most terrifying here is the double loss. Clytie is lost to Rosa (though not to herself, it would seem), and through her denial of Clytie, Rosa is lost to herself. Rosa's tragedy at nineteen is that she could not read what Barbara Johnson has called the difference *within* the cultural text, that which makes it speak against itself; in this case she could not read the possibility of cross-racial female relationships which would dismantle white patriarchal constructs of racial interaction in the slaveholding South. As an old woman, Rosa speaks from a female space which disrupts culture; yet she cannot help but speak her culture as well, with its voices of racial and sexual repressiveness. As she undermines the Father's systems and plays creatively with the language of desire and loss, she remains, in some sense at least, frozen on those stairs, her body, like the hysteric's, "a theater for forgotten scenes" (Clément 5).

The bisexual space between Faulkner and Rosa, then, may be less than we think; for he, like this woman of his own creation, tells us that history can never be over, that "was" can never be "was," and that cultural madness writes itself . . . incessantly.

III. Seduction and Reading

But it was not love: I do not claim that; I hold no brief for myself, I do not excuse it. I could have said that he had needed, used me; why should I rebel now, because he would use me more? But I did not say it; I could say this time, I do not know, and I would tell the truth. Because I do not know.—Rosa Coldfield

Rosa came to Sutpen, she says, *"like a whistled dog"* (28). Forty-three years later she still struggles with the question underlying her own madness, her own uninterpretable willingness to negate her own identity and become *"whatever it was he wanted of me—not my being, my presence: just my existence, what it was that Rosa Coldfield or any young female no blood kin to him represented in whatever it was he wanted"* (134). Between Rosa's insistent, maddening questions about her seduction and our (hysterical?) readings of those questions, the question underlying madness creates its own resistance to interpretation, and, not insignificantly, in the process, questions the interpretability of Faulkner's text (and our own) through our questioning of Rosa's question. The question underlying madness thus writes itself. It belongs to no one—not Sutpen, not Rosa, not the cultural "them" to and for whom Rosa speaks. It becomes instead what Felman calls a "reading effect," which may transfer itself to its readers by seducing us with its rhetoric (*Writing and Madness* 30–31).

In a peculiar and mysterious way, *Absalom, Absalom!* reads us. This is particularly true in Rosa's mad text of chapter five, which seduces us into pondering what is unrepresentable about writing and textuality as surely as Sutpen seduced her into that treacherous space of absence. We become, then, as Felman has suggested more generally, "unconscious textual *actor[s]* caught without knowing it in the lines of force of the text's *pure rhetoric*" (31).

Just as considering Rosa as a traditional character influenced by culture leads us to ponder the madness of racism, Rosa's evocative rhetoric leads us toward *Absalom*'s deconstructive energies, those forces which allow the book to make itself by unmaking itself, to enact its own castration but to rename castration as pleasure. Speaking from the inside of madness, as the hysteric whose discourse is the text of the unconscious, Rosa as a rhetor unmakes and remakes herself out of her own sense of loss and mourning.

And we as readers may find ourselves, like Rosa, performing the rhetoric of the text, which is, in *Absalom*'s case, a rhetoric of madness. Rosa—her rhetorical reproduction of identity always created by her own fluctuation between selfhood and self-erasure—speaks the unrepresentable rhythms of her own fullness and emptiness, those *"things for which three words are three too many, and three thousand words that many words too less"* (134). This is, as Felman might point out, the rhetoric of the mad text, whose reading is a "slippage . . . *between* the excessive fullness and the excessive emptiness of meaning" (254). *Absalom, Absalom!* is a text in whose fluctuations and forces we seek and find pleasure, whose openings and gaps may lead us to the Faulkner who is seduced by his own text and who sometimes disappears into its femininity. And so, having entered a bisexual space connecting female character and male author, we may find it, and them, reading us . . . reading.

Rosa's rhetoric, it has been pointed out again and again, is generated by her unwillingness to let go of loss. She instead lives it. Critical thought about Faulkner has concerned itself with the pervasiveness of loss in his works and the ways in which loss initiates narrative desire—tracing and retracing in language those spaces created by absence.[5] John T. Matthews has shown us, moreover, that this tracing does not reconstruct that which has been lost, but instead constitutes a fluid and creative play of differences which, in their very creativity and playfulness, dissolve the possibility of reconstruction or retrieval of the lost one or thing. Loss thereby triggers narrative desire, which in turn is both absorbed and regenerated in its own playful explorations of the infinite and mysterious spaces left by absence. As we know, these processes, as they become themselves by differing from themselves, signify both the constitutive and deconstructive qualities of a text.

Yet, what most obsesses Rosa and what generates her overwhelming desire to tell is not the loss of Sutpen but the loss of herself as teller. What she struggles to do in chapter five and in her whole narrative is to restore herself to her text of desire and fullness and her text to herself, to recreate herself as the female subject who creates language. What makes her story so powerful and so beautiful—so madly seductive—is that, like the disjunctive narrative of the hysteric, it follows the laws of its own desires and constitutes itself out of their free play. Rosa's need is to reconstruct in language that desire, that sense of embodiment. Clothed in the old stale female flesh which constitutes her absence to the male desiring gaze, Miss Rosa Coldfield speaks her sexuality, not just in the past, but in the present. In this way she turns absence back into presence, reclaiming her body and her text.

Readers have marked the intensity of Rosa's description of her youthful *"world of living marriage."*[6] Yet what may be most moving about Rosa's sexual text is its own present tense: her *"summer of wistaria"* is perennial, insistent, as she is, on *"root and urge."* Sutpen created Rosa as an absence to be filled; Quentin describes her body as "lonely thwarted old female flesh" (9). Rosa, to the contrary, imagines herself as *"warped chrysalis of what blind perfect seed: for who shall say what gnarled forgotten root might not bloom yet with some globed concentrate more globed and concentrate and heady-perfect because the neglected root was planted warped and lay not dead but merely slept forgot?"* (116). Sutpen's interest in Rosa was in the emptiness she constituted: her womb.[7] Rosa instead constructs the womb as part of her subjectivity, as a *place*—rather than a space—of interiority, through which she as a girl viewed external reality, lurking *"unapprehended as though shod with the very damp and velvet silence of the womb"* (116).

The questions underlying the madness of Rosa's text are, then, not so much the questions of what makes it impossible to interpret the historical text of the father (Sutpen's text: who he was, why he did what he did, and so on) but

—How can one be seduced into losing one's own text?

—How can one's own text can be rewritten out of its own

loss, or miswriting, that is, how can subjectivity be erased and then reconstructed out of its own erasure?

—How can rhetoric itself generate that reconstruction?

—How does such rhetoric, as it writes the libidinal economy of the female body, create a bisexual space between male author and female character?

—How may *that* space and its tensions seduce us as readers in a mysterious and uninterpretable way?

What is so resistant to analysis, so *mad* then, about chapter five is that its seduction creates both pain and pleasure, absence and presence, destruction and construction. Rosa's seduction by Sutpen destroyed her life yet creates her text as something so beautiful and powerful that it may seduce its readers (Quentin? us?) to embrace its rhetoric, and perhaps even its madness.

How and where, exactly, is this madness written? As Rosa asks "*Why? Why? and Why?*" (135) she allowed herself to be seduced, madness with all its gaps and stoppages of meaning writes itself across her and reaches out to mark us as readers. Sutpen, Rosa says, was "*mad, yet not so mad,*" for madness "*has faster rules*" (134). With their seductive rhetoric, those "faster rules" reweave Rosa's original and conventional definition of madness as insanity into a new fabric in which madness becomes indecipherable, unreadable. In Rosa's memory, then, madness writes its own text across Sutpen's words of insult, the "*blank naked and outrageous words,*" and across young Rosa herself, who indeed was "*that sun, or thought I was who did believe there was that spark, that crumb in madness which is divine, though madness know no word itself for terror or for pity*" (135).

I have been trying to show how madness creates and recreates itself in *Absalom*. If one follows Rosa's text carefully at this point, the ongoing rhetorical progress of madness emerges. Rosa is here remembering the moment of her seduction, how "*that ogre . . . held out its hand and said 'Come' as you might say it to a dog, and I came*" (135). Yet she has, she says, slain the ogre in her mind and made him into a mortal villain who is both pitiful and mad. She has told herself through the years:

Why should not madness be its own victim also? or, Why may it be not even madness but solitary despair titan conflict with the lonely and foredoomed and indomitable iron spirit; but no ogre, because it was dead, vanished, consumed somewhere in flame and sulphur-reek perhaps among the lonely craggy peaks of my childhood's solitary remembering—or forgetting; I was that sun, who believed that he (after that evening in Judith's room) was not oblivious of me but only unconscious and receptive like the swamp-freed pilgrim feeling earth and tasting sun and light again and aware of neither but only of darkness' and morass' lack—who did believe there was that magic in unkin blood which we call by the pallid name of love that would be, might be sun for him (though I the youngest, weakest) where Judith and Clytie both would cast no shadow; yes, I the youngest there yet potently without measured or measurable age since I alone of them could say, "O furious mad old man, I hold no substance that will fit your dream but I can give you airy space and scope for your delirium." (135)

I quote this passage so extensively because I believe it constitutes a rhetorical space in which madness actually moves about in rhetoric from one character to another. It writes itself as the Sutpen who seduces Rosa. Then it moves to write itself as the Rosa who seduces herself into reifying his phallic dream and who thus becomes the absence, the "airy space" which that dream desires to fill, while at the very same time continuing, mistakenly, to construct herself as *presence*, as "that sun" whose being is the quintessential presence, central to all earthy life.

What Rosa "writes," then, in addition to female sexuality, is an intertext between female presence and female absence. And this intertext carries the chilling implication that, as a cultural presence, a woman can seduce herself into thinking that objectivity is subjectivity—that she is "that sun" when she is actually nothing more than "airy space." This seduced woman is therefore mad, for she has become the opposite of what she thinks she is; her text becomes uninterpretable, even to herself. Madness thus writes itself in an expansive and troubling way, for it reveals what one fears and what one is seduced by—and they are the same.

So, as Miss Rosa Coldfield speaks her sexuality as that text which she still must write, madness writes its own intertext of the female subject/object. A woman thus generates the libidinal energies of the novel, and its/her hysterical narrative splatters madness everywhere at once and nowhere in particular. Yet madness writes itself in other spaces, and these are recoverable only through their rhetoric, Rosa's rhetoric of madness, which moves somewhere below the level of consciousness all the while gazing over the brink of rhetoric at the unrepresentable. To the feminist reader Rosa's rhetoric may seem to gaze also at a state of female subjectivity which is frighteningly incongruent with its own self-construction, which is not what it thinks it is. The question underlying madness thus writes itself across Rosa's "*Why? Why? and Why?*" as it explodes out of the mouth of an old and difficult southern lady . . . who is called a ghost, but is anything but.

For the symbolic order—the realm of the proper—to assert itself over the unrepresentable, it must silence the difference.

It must shut the old lady up.

IV. Shutting Rosa Up

Because he was not articulated in this world. He was a walking shadow. He was the light-blinded bat-like image of his own torment cast by the fierce demoniac lantern up from beneath the earth's crust and hence in retrograde, reverse: from abysmal and chaotic dark to eternal and abysmal dark completing his descending (do you mark the gradation?) ellipsis, clinging, trying to cling with vain unsubstantial hands to what he hoped would hold him, save him, arrest him——Ellen (do you mark them?) myself, then last of all fatherless daughter of Wash Jones' only child who, so I heard once, died in a Memphis brothel——to find severence (even if not rest and peace) at least in the stroke of a rusty scythe.——Rosa Coldfield

Rosa Coldfield's mad text has made Sutpen; at the end of chapter five, it unmakes him. Clinging to first one "fatherless daughter," Ellen, and then another, Rosa, and then a third, Milly Jones, this Sutpen of Rosa's unmaking fades into a castrated shadow of a man, cut off from the object of his desire—his masculine replication in a son. If we consider how "character" may be constituted, diminished, and dissolved in narrative, we may see how Rosa's text, as much as Wash Jones's scythe, slays the ogre, as surely as she conjured him initially, with his "French architect" and "wild slaves," out of a whirl of northern Mississippi dust. Her mad text thus *seems* to wind itself toward some sense of closure, albeit an illusory one, for it enacts the death of the Father: the demise of Sutpen and his realm of the proper.

Yet Rosa's silencing of Sutpen is one of *Absalom, Absalom!*'s many illusions; in the end, she herself is shut up, shut down, and shut out by men. The last half of *Absalom, Absalom!* is dominated by male voices. These voices encode the sexual politics of patriarchy by silencing women as speaking subjects within its narrative of mastery. These male voices seize the narrative, and they speak with authority. In allowing them to speak at full pitch—and one must, for they do—and surviving the sheer weight of the communal patriarchal voice which silences Rosa Coldfield, I can perhaps *hope* to hear finally the mad voice of Faulkner's own text. This voice speaks out of its own uninterpretable ability to recreate woman as speaker. The woman so created (I do not know her name) speaks out of a silence that men have created but which men cannot control. She speaks out of the spaces of rhetoric which are somewhere else, between and beyond language.

I am beginning at the point of Rosa's text quoted in the epigraph to this section so as to pay attention to *Absalom*'s narrative sequence between chapters five and six. Again, the hysteric instructs us. Like Rosa's narrative, the story the hysteric tells in analysis usually wanders, yet its wanderings instruct the listener/reader "about the crucial role of sequence, at once foreseen and unforeseeable." The hysterical narrative, in literature and psychoanalysis, thus "derives its meaning from the temporal order which constitutes it; narrative exists in the time of its telling rather than the order of its events" (Jacobus 218). This idea seems essential to any understanding of *Absalom*, but particularly crucial to our reading of the text between these two chapters. This seems to be a space in which binary opposition does generate and regenerate itself along the lines of sexual difference. As such, this textual fault line of bisexual stress may be read as one of many such sites

of the production of *Absalom's* madness, its mysterious and cease-
less disruptions of meaning, its stubborn resistance to analysis. If
we continue to approach the hysterical text as language's nego-
tiation of an unrepresentable space in discourse, we may begin to
experience the back-and-forthness, the tautness of this discursive
space in which female and male voices do battle.

Rosa Coldfield has her differences *within*, and they generate her
own text's madness, *its* incredible resistance to interpretation. She
has been "seduced" as sexual object, as displayed in her acquies-
cence to Sutpen, and as ideological subject, as we see in her denial
of Clytie's humanity. Now, as chapter five ends and chapter six
begins, the focus of the novel moves from Rosa's own internal
contradictions to the external binarism of sexual difference. Yet,
as Barbara Johnson has noted, binary opposition is never crisp but
always deconstructing itself (x–xi). The difference *between* is always
collapsing into the difference within. This latter part of *Absalom,
Absalom!* enacts this collapse, again and again.

To begin: as Rosa recounts Sutpen's death, she is completing
her hysterical narrative, at least so it should seem to Quentin.
This, of course, is the point in the psychoanalytic process at which
"reminiscence loses its grip on the present and life [supposedly]
can begin again": the hysteric is "cured"; she should no longer
suffer from the painful, and consequently repressed, scenes of her
own history (Jacobus 219, 216).

What happens next, though, is strangely provoking. Quentin
the listener ceases to listen! He, like Freud in Dora's case, constructs his own narrative, hence his recreation of the scene of
Judith Sutpen, with her raised wedding dress, confronting Henry
after he has killed Charles Bon. Is this creation simply the result
of Quentin's obsession with the Judith-Henry confrontation and
its implication of brother-sister incest? It is difficult to know. Twice
we are told that Quentin "was not even listening" to this, the
last gasp of Rosa's long history (140). Is Quentin's problem perhaps more closely related to the fact that he simply cannot bring
himself to participate in Rosa's killing of the masculine in her
text, in her actual speaking of the castration her triangle of lace
constitutes to his male gaze? For whatever reason, he does not

participate imaginatively in the "unmaking" of Sutpen's phallic power, for, as in his conflicted response to the Sutpen story, such power is what he both desires and detests.

Yet Miss Rosa will not allow Quentin to write his own male narrative for long. She insists that he confront the failure of that "something" in the patriarchal house. She will not be shut up:

> "There's something in that house."
> "In that house? It's Clytie. Dont she——."
> "No. Something living in it. Hidden in it. It has been out there for four years, living hidden in that house." (140)

So ends the fifth chapter of *Absalom*. At the beginning of chapter six, Mr. Compson, who throughout the book attempts to diminish the importance of Rosa's text, takes control of the narrative and announces her death in his letter. In the same sense that she rhetorically "killed" Sutpen, Mr. Compson kills her. This is a "killing" seconded by Quentin's and Shreve's subsequent comments. Quentin, explaining his father's letter to Shreve and denying his own kinship to Rosa, kills her before her time. He names her as "neither aunt cousin nor uncle, Rosa. Miss Rosa. Miss Rosa Coldfield, an old lady that died young of outrage in 1866 one summer" (142). To which Shreve responds, "You mean she was no kin to you, no kin to you at all, that there was actually one Southern Bayard or Guinevere who was no kin to you? then what did she die for?" (142). Here, then, is the denied kinship to the female/feminine, the repressed and feared female sexuality (why else the name Guinevere?), again, the speaking of the death of a woman.

Yet Rosa/Guinevere rises out of the complicitous male narratives of her death—out of her early death in Quentin's consciousness, out of Shreve's misnaming (in which he persists throughout the book), out of the folds of Mr. Compson's sardonic letter proclaiming her death—to force Quentin to confront the "something in that house." Like Caddy Compson, whose voice emerges and reemerges out of the male discourse it is buried within, Rosa is reborn to move through "the moonless September dust" of Quentin's mind. Dressed in black, clutching her umbrella, "the implacable doll-sized old woman" rides the smothering dust cloud to lead him to the dark house and its "something," which is, not surprisingly, a double of himself—a man, a man cut off and dying (142–43).

Let me restate the sequence of what we may construe as this space between chapters five and six: (1) woman's text "kills" man; (2) men's texts kill woman; (3) woman will not stay dead. She is reborn and eventually leads man to "the something" in the patriarchal house, which, it seems to me, is the vision of his own madness. A reader of the hysterical text that is *Absalom, Absalom!* may be instructed by the chronology of this brief narrative space. What I have not paid much attention to until this point in my reading is what Johnson has called "difference *between* entities," specifically the bisexual space between the novel's male and female characters. In Cixous's vision of artistic bisexuality, the bisexual space of "in-between" consciousness is one in which female and male elements are exacerbated through interaction with each other, hence the permanent state of tension in thinking and writing generated in an ongoing exchange between the two. What one finds illustrated by the narrative sequence just outlined, however, is another text of bisexual interaction. Rather than an exchange, it is an intense struggle for narrative authority. On the one hand, Rosa's woman's voice, like the voice of the hysteric, resists and refracts the cultural text of patriarchy. On the other, the male voices of *Absalom, Absalom!* seem engaged in a constant struggle to distance and disavow women's bodies and stories.

Rosa tells the men of *Absalom, Absalom!* that they are all castrated, that they lack power, wholeness, being, that their narratives lack authority. Yet she also reconstructs lack as pleasure, as the very beginning of desire, play, production: as text. Quentin, his father, and Shreve fear Rosa's text, its mad defiant resistance to interpretation, its flow beyond structure. They, like Sutpen, want to empower themselves both to control and to interpret experience. They want to erect their own master narrative, their Sutpen's Hundred, and so encode the authority of their own mutual story. Like Freud, they must erase the hysterical text which reads them too well. Had they been asked, they might indeed have agreed with Freud and asked Dora: Is Herr K. really so bad after all? Is Rosa's ogre really such an ogre? Are not Dora's and Rosa's hysterical texts themselves aberrant? Is not the presence of madness (coded female) simply the proof of sanity and rationality (coded male), rather than that which questions the very bases on which the notions of sanity and rationality are constructed?

Since Rosa, at this point at least, threatens and disrupts southern white patriarchy, it is no surprise that the novel's males are often ambushing her text, marginalizing and diminishing it.[8] My purpose here is to inquire not only where Faulkner figures in this textual war of the sexes, this difference *between*, but also, how binary difference in this book can be seen as functioning in unpredictable ways. As Johnson asks, what "subversions" of the binary difference of gender are "logically prior to it and necessary in its very construction"? (xi). From within Quentin's imagination at the end of the novel, Rosa's helpless silenced woman's body can write itself only as obscenity in (my) feminist consciousness. How then do we read Faulkner's stance toward the shutting up (in, out, down) of Rosa Coldfield? After all, Rosa is indeed the threshold into the male text, and her sense of herself as lost and lacking is its productivity. Rosa's desire for what she does not have has by now become the text's pleasure, and perhaps ours as well.

To retrace if not answer these questions, I will first turn to Mr. Compson's male gaze and consider how it pins down the feminine.[9] Like Nietzsche, Mr. Compson appreciates and insists upon the construction of distance, which allows the male gaze to configure its own representation of woman: she is (and must be) "an effect at a distance" (Derrida, *Spurs*, 47). Within such a construction, Mr. Compson's text freezes the feminine and activates the masculine. Consider how he constructs these women's images: Ellen, the dissolving butterfly, "the substanceless shell, the shade impervious to any alteration of dissolution because of its very weightlessness: no body to be buried: just the shape, the recollection" (100); Judith, "the blank shape, the empty vessel" of her brother's male texts (95), the "bucolic maiden" who read Bon's letters without understanding them (102); the nameless octoroon, "a woman with a face like a tragic magnolia, the eternal female, the eternal Who-suffers" (91); and seventeen-year-old Rosa Coldfield, the "Southern Lady" who feeds upon others of her own blood "like a vampire . . . with that serene and idle splendor of flowers abrogating to herself" (68). Mr. Compson's gaze is as innovative as it is deadly. It fixes that which he perceives as feminine as a butterfly pinned to a paper, flapping feebly, eventually becoming still, flat . . . thoroughly analyzable.

In writing about Italo Calvino's *Invisible Cities*, Teresa de Lauretis discusses how the city of Zobeide, depicted therein, was built by men of various nations out of an identical ongoing dream in which they pursued a naked woman who, running through the dark streets of an unknown city, always escaped them. The men came together and constructed a city with spaces and walls different from the ones dreamed, so that the fugitive woman of the dream could not escape. The city itself, de Lauretis writes, "tells the story of male desire by performing the absence of woman and by producing woman as text, as pure representation" (12–13). This is the same narrative process that Mr. Compson initiates when he answers Quentin's first question about Rosa Coldfield ("But why tell me about it?" 12) with the statement that southern women are ghosts. Shreve and Quentin together take up this male story and participate in the complicitous male struggle for narrative authority over Rosa's story. This is the difference *between* that generates *Absalom, Absalom!*

Yet, as I have suggested, there is a difference *within* the difference *between*. Up until now we have read some of that internal tension in Rosa's mad text. Now, as we read the struggles of the male texts to silence women's stories of cultural madness, we will attempt to discover where the men of this book falter, where they gape and sputter, where they cannot pin women down or keep them at a distance.

For illustration let us look again at how Mr. Compson constructs Rosa as a girl. Placed in "that grim tight little house with the father," nurtured by the "outraged female vindictiveness" of the aunt, the young Rosa of Mr. Compson's creation lurks and eavesdrops outside closed doors in the "mausoleum" inhabited by father and aunt (47). As a girl she sits at the table with Sutpen and his family, her small body "with its air of curious and paradoxical awkwardness like a costume borrowed at the last moment and of necessity for a masquerade which she did not want to attend" (51). Mr. Compson writes a text in which young Rosa is silent. He derides her "schoolgirl's poetry about the also-dead" (65). She is the watcher, the listener—always outside, always on the other side of the closed door or across the way. Yet the difference *within* her silence, as it is created by Mr. Compson, is its (and her) uncanny, and empowering, ability to listen beyond language. This Rosa, as she sits across from Sutpen, has extrasensory powers of perception "as though she actually had some intimation gained from that rapport with the fluid cradle of events (time) which she had acquired or cultivated by listening beyond closed doors not to what she heard there, but by becoming supine and receptive, incapable of either discrimination or opinion or incredulity, listening to the prefever's temperature of disaster" (51–52). This Rosa is frozen in silence, but her silence bespeaks an ability to listen, like Cassandra, beyond the teleologies of time and space to what has yet to happen.

Of course, no one wanted to hear what Cassandra knew. De Lauretis points out that we may not be surprised at depictions of history in which women are absent as subjects. Calvino's absent woman "is thus an accurate representation of the paradoxical status of women in Western discourse: while culture originates from woman and is founded on the dream of her captivity, women are all but absent from history and cultural process" (13). Mr. Compson constructs women who are absent to their own historical voices. For the most part, they are seen, gazed upon, but, like Cassandra, avoided when they have something to say. These silent women constitute striking visual presences in his text, with their strange postures: young Rosa sewing "tediously and without skill" (61), Judith's "impenetrable and serene face" (99) (it is only Quentin's grandmother's story, emerging through Mr. Compson's, that permits Judith to speak), the voluptuous octoroon with her tragic magnolia face, Ellen the butterfly pinned to the patriarchal board.

Yet, even within the tight grim house of Mr. Compson's narrative, the feminine oozes and flows up and out of containment, much as Caddy Compson emerges over and over out of her brothers' voices. Gail Mortimer points out that Faulkner's female characters have an "affinity for flowing, touching, doing, and being" (*Faulkner's Rhetoric of Loss* 90); and that Faulkner's association of woman with water expresses his "anxiety about the eruption of her placid surface into something threatening annihilation"— an anxiety which leads him to picture woman as a vase or urn, "an emblem of desire and a work of art" ("The Smooth, Suave Shape of Desire" 151). Certainly within Mr. Compson's consciousness (which distinguishes itself from Faulkner's in many ways), the flow of female sexuality, like encroaching lava, is both seductive and ominous. Mr. Compson's description of Judith's sexual development seems to become, in itself, a kind of liquid solution of femininity which both threatens and beckons, that which Alice Jardine would call the feminine space over which narrative (in this case, the patriarchal voice) has lost control and which threatens to overflow its bounds at any moment (something Faulkner's text does actually do in *If I Forget Thee, Jerusalem*). In this sense, Mr. Compson's relation to women and femininity is a reflection of Sutpen's to African Americans and blackness. Judith, Mr. Compson tells his son, has arrived at

> that state where, though still visible, young girls appear as though seen through glass and where even the voice cannot reach them; where they exist . . . in a pearly lambence without shadows and themselves partaking of it; in nebulous suspension held, strange and unpredictable, even their very shapes fluid and delicate and without substance; not in themselves floating and seeking but merely waiting, parasitic and potent and serene, drawing to themselves without effort the post-genitive upon and about which to shape, flow into back, breast; bosom, flank, thigh. (52–53)

Here, and in others of his descriptions, Mr. Compson "makes" woman/object in the same way he describes the thousand white men of New Orleans who "made" the female octoroons, who constructed them as pure representations of male desire ("made them, created and produced them") in order to access and appropriate "a female principle" which those men constructed as being implicit in black female sexuality and as constituting what Mr. Compson calls (with relish) the "strange and ancient curious pleasures of the flesh" (92). As Mr. Compson tells his son, these women were bred for pleasure and sold for a price, "accepted or declined through a system more formal than any that white girls are sold under since they are more valuable as commodities than white girls, raised and trained to fulfill a woman's sole end and purpose: to love, to be beautiful, to divert" (93). Female sexuality—the sexual and reproductive functions of octoroons as well as white and black women—is thus bounded and bargained for; it is the multiple commodity which fuels the economy of the realm of the proper. And Mr. Compson's slightly ironic tone at this particular point is more than obviated by his obvious pleasure in his subject matter.

It is difficult to know how to assess Mr. Compson's own "making" of women and its relation to Faulkner's. Mr. Compson writes a masculinist text which challenges Rosa's story for narrative authority. He distances her text and diminishes her. She is a ghost, a vampire, a girl with dangling legs, which never grew. Yet his self-consciousness about the cultural representation of gender, his sardonic awareness of his own statements about women in general, gives pause. Even as he tries to pin down the feminine, he also senses, as Nietzsche, Derrida, and Freud did, his own inability to do so. "Woman," even as Mr. Compson freezes her with the male gaze, continues to carry the potential for overflowing the male text and becoming Miss Rosa Coldfield, who just will not shut up, who talks and talks.

And *that* Miss Rosa, the one who refuses to be dead, seeps subversively through the rational and controlled surface of Mr. Compson's talk, which persists nonetheless in putting women in their proper places, according to their relative commodification as "ladies or whores or slaves." Although he speaks of what men do to women and, by his self-consciousness, distances himself somewhat from the cultural values he is explaining (and transferring) to Quentin, we sense his participation in the masculine "we" that he describes as creating women as commodities.

Mr. Compson thus comes to reify patriarchal narratives of mastery, in which female desires such as Rosa's, or perhaps Judith's or the octoroon's (the difference within his text—that which he is pulled toward yet repelled by), are objectified and pinned down. Mr. Compson's male gaze does what Sutpen's did: it sees woman in terms of pure representation, as the vehicle of male desire. Like Sutpen, Mr. Compson only wants Rosa to shut up, to be true to his own configurations of her as the child with dangling legs, as the lurker behind doors, as the southern lady vampire, as woman on the outside. But "this other-than-themselves,"[10] this Rosa Coldfield, won't stay in *or* out of the Father's House; she will not shut up and she will not stay put. The male gaze seeks to pin her down and keep her still. It seeks to silence Rosa's articulations of difference, which themselves link race and gender to the hauntings of dehumanization and commodification seen in the ghostly face of Clytie Sutpen surrounded by flames. Its failure to do so ultimately results in the fall of the Father's House, that "gray huge rotting deserted house" that Sutpen built (153).

The perimeters of Mr. Compson's gaze extend further than we think. His voice reverberates through the chill New England air of Quentin and Shreve's dimly lit room. Shreve is right when he says to Quentin, "Dont say it's just me that sounds like your old man" (210). For, as Quentin himself realizes, his father's way of seeing and his father's voice contain *"the old ineradicable rhythm"* to which they both move. Walter Brylowski finds that these rhythms constitute a shared mythic consciousness which may be connected to Rosa's mythologizing of Sutpen (123–24). I want to argue that Quentin and Shreve participate in, and come to construct, a shared *male* consciousness. Irwin reads these male relationships as highly competitive and structured upon the Oedipal model of father-son struggles for dominance (122). Certainly this is true of Sutpen and Charles Bon and, less obviously perhaps, of Mr. Compson and Quentin. Yet what may strike us as much more important are these men's shared narratives of mastery, handed down by men to men, sometimes all the way from Sutpen himself to grandfather to father to Quentin and Shreve, the latter four saying and resaying the story back and forth to one another. This is a community of male telling. *"Yes,"* Quentin thinks, *"we are both Father. Or maybe Father and I are both Shreve, maybe it took Father and me both to make Shreve or Shreve and me both to make Father or maybe Thomas Sutpen to make all of us"* (210).[11]

In the final third of the book particularly, these male voices merge and mingle as if they were multiples of one voice. Mr. Compson's presence is everywhere. His voice, his gaze layer Quentin's story of Grandfather's story of Sutpen's story. We may, in fact, think of Quentin's father's talk as an ongoing narrative act that runs under the whole last section of the book, sometimes emerging to speak in its own voice but mostly speaking through other male voices. This shared discourse reifies itself again and again until it arrives at the pure language of the Father. This is, I find, the point in the text which records Sutpen's bald statement of patriarchal quest, related through Grandfather Compson's/Mr. Compson's/Quentin's voice(s):

> You see, I had a design in my mind. Whether it was a good or bad design is beside the point; the question is, Where did I make the mistake in it. . . . I had a design. To accomplish it I should require money, a house, a plantation, slaves, a family— incidentally of course a wife. I set out to acquire these, asking no favor of any man. (212)

I am not arguing that all of the male speakers in *Absalom, Absalom!* approve of what Sutpen did. Nevertheless, as male subjects constituted by a cultural order that privileges men, they engage in a common discourse, in a form of "man talk" that enables Sutpen's voice to emerge loud and clear to speak white patriarchy's narrative of mastery; in this sense they reify patriarchy's authority at the same time they construct their own. My-riam Díaz-Diocaretz has discussed how women in some of Faulkner's stories and novels become *"repeatable* text[s]" created by Faulkner's strategic consciousness in combination with the voice of "cultural belief" (258). Her argument has particular application to *Absalom.* Despite their judgments on the blatancy of Sutpen's phallic order, Grandfather Compson, Mr. Compson, Quentin, and Shreve all seem to articulate the "cultural belief" of white patriarchy—belief which legitimizes itself by placing certain others (women, blacks) outside the symbolic order and thus diffusing their potential to disrupt that order while at the same time positing the female body, however raced or classed, as a commodity of exchange. In the mutuality of these male conversations, Faulkner indeed teaches us about the ongoing quality of the grand narrative of white patriarchy—how it passes itself along; how, like Mr. Compson's voice and gaze, it can be always moving under the surface of how certain men talk to one another, and particularly of how they join together in a symbolic order which configures woman as Other; how the exclusion of the feminine actually becomes the necessary element for the masculine to order itself and its interactions.

In considering what is necessary to legitimize cultural narratives, Jean François Lyotard suggests that people actualize such narratives "not only by recounting them, but also by listening to them and recounting *themselves through them;* in other words, by putting them into 'play' in their institutions—thus by assigning themselves the posts of narratee and diegesis as well as the post of narrator." Through this process, narratives of culture "thus define what has the right to be said and done in the culture in question" (23). Matthews has remarked on how "marriages of speaking and hearing" in *Absalom, Absalom!* show "that the truth of a narrative arises from the way it is created and shared, and not strictly from its content" (151). Within the male interchanges we are exploring here, a cultural narrative of power, which is gendered, raced, and classed, legitimizes itself as a process of listening to and recounting stories which do not tell about or do not listen to the culture's own voices of difference. And in *Absalom, Absalom!* those voices, as I have said, are figured as feminine. (Charles Bon's femininity is much more obvious than his blackness.) In the latter part of the book, this "man talk" empowers Thomas Sutpen to speak by shutting Rosa Coldfield up.

This gendering of cultural difference figures itself as a process of devaluation. ("It wasn't a son. It was a girl.") This devaluation is most obvious in Sutpen's systematic usage of women for various, albeit thwarted purposes—Bon's mixed-race mother, the slave women on his plantation, Ellen, and Rosa—but it shapes all of the male texts of *Absalom*. Rosa is its primary target, for she is the hysteric who erases the boundaries between the conscious and the unconscious and so shows the father to himself in disconcerting ways. As a result, much of the tension in Quentin and Shreve's talking seems to be generated out of two gendered spaces: one which contains their continual struggle to legitimize their (Mr. Compson's, Sutpen's, Grandfather's) own cultural narrative by silencing Rosa's/woman's; and the other, that space in which the feminine text writes what patriarchy does not know and does not want to know across the man talk of the dormitory room (which is filled with homosocial/homosexual currents that must remain below the level of consciousness).

Shreve consistently distances and diminishes the authority of Rosa's narrative by misnaming her. Despite Quentin's attempts to correct him, he calls her, at various times, "this old dame" (143); "the old gal, this Aunt Rosa" (175); "the old dame, the Aunt Rosa" (143, 258, 279); "the old Aunt Rosa" (260). In chapter eight he explodes into a Mr. Compson–like misogynistic tirade of male entrapment, as he envisions Charles Bon leaving the octoroon without saying goodbye, and for good reason:

> Because you cant beat them: you just flee (and thank God you can flee, can escape from that massy five-foot-thick maggot-cheesy solidarity which overlays the earth, in which men and women in couples are ranked and racked like ninepins; thanks to whatever Gods for that masculine hipless tapering peg

which fits light and glib to move where the cartridge-
chambered hips of women hold them fast);—not goodbye: all
right. (249–50)

Appropriating Mr. Compson's male gaze, Shreve goes on to speak
of women (Judith in particular) as a cup of sherbet which men
can either pass up, or suddenly desire and take. Yet, at the same
time, Shreve seems oddly fascinated by Rosa's own fascination
with what is at the very margins of meaning. He asks Quentin,
"What was it the old dame, the Aunt Rosa, told you about how
there are some things that just have to be whether they are or
not, have to be a damn sight more than some other things that
maybe are and it dont matter a damn whether they are or not?"
(258). Again, in the final chapter, he associates Rosa with what
we might call "the essential unknowable": like madness, the essential unknowable is consistently uninterpretable, yet its (her)
very resistance to meaning is paradoxically and mysteriously crucial to meaning. To Quentin, he says:

> "Yes. You dont know. You dont even know about the old
> dame, the Aunt Rosa."
> "Miss Rosa," Quentin said.
> "All right. You dont even know about her. Except that she
> refused at the last to be a ghost." (289)

Shreve seems, then, to find Rosa's mad text of castration, of *not*
knowing to be fascinating, terrifying, and seductive.[12] He leans
ambivalently toward, then away from, her and it.

Quentin's fear of losing control, his desperation to cover up
his inadequacies (I am thinking of *The Sound and the Fury* as well as
Absalom, Absalom!), dictates finally that he allow his father's voice
of mastery to take hold of his own (Quentin's) consciousness and
speak its (his) discourse of empowerment. Finally, with his father's
voice ringing in his head as it did on his final day of life in *The
Sound and the Fury*, Quentin shuts Rosa up for good. Let us plunge
into a strange bisexual space of Quentin's and his father's shared
narrative. In the sixth chapter, Mr. Compson, speaking through

his son's memory, says, "They lead beautiful lives—women. Lives not only divorced from, but irrevocably excommunicated from, all reality" (156). Quentin's father then goes into his story about his aunt whose main worry was that she would be buried in the wrong dress, and so on. How do we read within this space of the male text in which woman is both freed from fear of death, the ultimate castration, at the same time she is denied full participation in life? "Woman" is not alive; thus she need not fear death. This narrative sequence, constructed between Quentin and his father, denies women as subjects in history.

Again within his son's memory, Mr. Compson offers his description of the octoroon visiting Bon's grave, a "magnolia-faced woman a little plumper now" but still the sexual object of the male gaze, wearing, Mr. Compson says with relish, a "soft, flowing gown designed not to infer bereavement or widowhood but to dress some interlude of slumbrous and fatal insatiation, of passionate and inexorable hunger of the flesh" (157). This description of the octoroon is followed by Mr. Compson's depictions of Clytie and Judith as Charles Etienne's jailers (162) and of the animalistic qualities of Charles Etienne's "ape-like" and "kenneled" wife (167). There is a fear of woman's subjectivity, her potential to *mean*, which runs at the bottom of all of these descriptions, carried on by Quentin's participation in his father's mythologizing of "woman" as absence and of women's lives as a charade of what living really is.

The fact that Quentin knows his father's/Shreve's narratives before hearing them should not be surprising. For what Mr. Compson articulates is the systemic devaluation of women, African Americans, and poor whites in southern culture, a devaluation which is intimately related to the way difference, herein figured as feminine, is placed outside the realm of those essential interactions that legitimize cultural narratives of mastery. What Quentin's father says does not, as Quentin knows, tell him anything new, but strikes *"word by word, the resonant strings of remembering"* (172). Quentin's father places women either outside the realm of those essential interactions which create and reify cultural narrative, or he articulates "woman" as a sign in social discourse, further encoding the narrative of mastery so baldly stated by Sutpen and handed down through three generations of Compson males. This devaluative mythologizing of difference as feminine reaches a crescendo in three male voices which merge in Quentin's text of woman as absence, articulated in thought as a response to his father's and Shreve's complicitous narratives. Hearing Shreve retelling Judith's death, conjuring Rosa inscribing Judith's tombstone, Quentin thinks:

> *I didn't need to listen then but I had to hear it and now I am having to hear it all over again because he sounds just like Father: Beautiful lives—women do. In very breathing they draw meat and drink from some beautiful attenuation of unreality in which the shades and shapes of facts—of birth and bereavement, of suffering and bewilderment and despair—move with the substanceless decorum of lawn party charades, perfect in gesture and without significance or any ability to hurt. Miss Rosa ordered that one.* (171)

This, finally, is how woman is shut up. She is (note the passive voice) stripped of substance. She is placed on the periphery of culture. Her narrative is judged illegitimate, unreadable, hysterical. In this way, systems of mastery assert themselves by placing their own difference within *outside* themselves. Like the "balloon-faced nigger" at the front door of the plantation house, like Sutpen, like three generations of male Compsons, like a Canadian Harvard man, like Rosa herself in her confrontation with Clytie on the stairs of Sutpen's Hundred, they prescribe and validate their own systems of order by keeping difference out.

What Rosa Coldfield wants is to get in. What she wants Quentin to know is what it feels like to be out, how that kind of pain must be articulated. But he cannot converse with her loss and her desire, not really, because it speaks his own too clearly, because it writes the hysterical text of repressed fear, because it says the terrible pleasure of writing such a text. His imagination silences her in front of the big house. It makes her a "light thin furious creature making no sound at all now, struggling with silent and bitter fury, clawing and scratching and biting at the two men who held her" (301).[13] And his father's letter, read in

Shreve's voice, buries her, with the sardonic hope that she will be reborn in an afterlife which allows *"the privilege of being outraged and amazed and of not forgiving"* (301).

What happens when difference becomes the subject? When it writes upon *us* the terror of its madness, its resistance to interpretation? As I feel this madness, this resistance, in Faulkner's uninterpretable text, what seems most true is perhaps what has been obvious about this book all along. And that is its very real terror. This terror occupies every corner of *Absalom, Absalom!*—from the initial crying out of the title itself to the anguish of Quentin's final words. It is everywhere at once, yet at the end of the book it becomes larger and denser. It imbues Shreve's description of the horror of sameness in a way which recalls Melville's descriptions of whiteness. *Absalom, Absalom!* shows the terror of disallowing difference, of creating cultural narratives which insist on mastery as a goal, which say no to all but one story—which, in Shreve's words, "bleach[es] out" the world. When Quentin says he does not hate the South, he speaks an ironic truth; for what he has done is kill that part of it (and of himself) he hates, that bisexual space in the text between himself and an angry old woman. In doing so, however, he has killed his own difference within. Locked in a chain of constituted codes of sameness, he himself becomes culturally constituted by those codes and so loses that quality of subjectivity which can speak the unrepresentable mad text of Rosa Coldfield.

Yet what is so astonishing, and so brilliant, about *Absalom, Absalom!* is that, paradoxically, while Quentin allows himself to be encoded by one master narrative of culture, while he denies bisexuality, difference, madness, and woman, his own text—like Rosa who denies Clytie—speaks against him. He says, *"I dont. I dont! I dont hate it! I dont hate it!"* (303). But what he also says is the cost of writing the narrative of mastery. That cost is the silencing of Rosa Coldfield, who speaks difference from the position of subject and so who writes upon Quentin, and upon us as readers, what it is to be pure representation, to be constituted as absence. In this way *Absalom, Absalom!* inscribes its own difference. In Rosa's talking, Quentin's hearing, and the tension between their two narratives, it writes the gaps and ruptures within white patriarchy. This tension in turn creates a bisexual space in the novel, which, like the hysteric, emerges to write its own mad text of alterity. *That* text, Faulkner's text, curls around upon us in a mysterious yet highly political way to affirm its own madness by affirming the difference it configures as feminine.

Notes

1. Philip M. Weinstein believes that Rosa's "voice verges on a state of feeling all too easily associated with the female: hysteria" and that her "utterance courts hysteria because it is so inattentive to its audience as a *participant*, so unaware of its status as *narrative*" (92). As I explain in note 2, I am using the term *hysteria* and its associations with women in a much more positive sense. More generally, in a 1986 article, "Meditations on the Other: Faulkner's Rendering of Women," Weinstein writes that Faulkner's female characters occupy the position of Other in relation to the narrative voice of the fiction. As I see it, the problem with positing woman as Other in Faulkner's texts is that it leaves little avenue for exploration of either the feminine energies of those texts or the female characters themselves, since such a stance denies female subjectivity before exploring the possibility of its existence. I take an approach to Rosa which in some ways is similar to that taken by Judith Bryant Wittenberg to Temple Drake in *Sanctuary*. Temple, according to Wittenberg, is like Freud's Dora, in that she is devalued and objectified by patriarchy. Unlike Temple, however, Rosa, as I hope to show, writes madness upon us as readers—even as it is being written upon her.

2. From its etymological origin in the Greek word for uterus, *hysteria* has been associated with female deviance. See Juliet Mitchell's discussion of hysteria, femininity, and feminism in *Women: The Longest Revolution* (115–20). Furthermore, as both Mitchell and Charles Bernheimer point out, psychoanalysis itself came into being on the basis of Freud's clinical experience with hysterical patients, almost all of them women. See Bernheimer's brief history of hysteria, especially his analysis of Freud's complex responses to his hysterical patients (Bernheimer, "Introduction: Part One," in Bernheimer and Kahane, *In Dora's Case*, 1–18). In a larger context, Mitchell suggests that psychoanalysis started from an understand-

ing of hysteria, in the sense that it "led Freud to what is universal in psychic construction and it led him there in a particular way—by route of a prolonged and central preoccupation with the difference between the sexes" (*Women* 300–301).

3. As Gerald Langford shows, Faulkner revised the 1865 scene four times to intensify its impact. Moreover, the interconnection of Rosa and Clytie is obvious from a textual history of *Absalom*. In her introduction to *William Faulkner's "Absalom, Absalom!" A Critical Casebook*, Elisabeth Muhlenfeld shows how the character of Raby Sutpen, the vocal woman slave in *Absalom*'s precursor story, "Evangeline," was a combination of Rosa and Clytie, whom Faulkner split into two characters. Clytie and her silence in the novel therefore, Muhlenfeld arguably states, "carry the symbolic weight of all the tragic ramifications of slavery far better than the more voluble Raby. And Rosa . . . could carry much of the narrative burden which had been Raby's" (xxiv).

4. In *Black and White Women of the Old South*, I discussed how this encounter dramatizes biracial female experience under white southern patriarchy. My project here, however, is to reread this incident as an important generator of Rosa's hysterical narrative and as a "mad," hence uninterpretable, space of interactions around race and gender.

5. Gail Mortimer argues that, in Faulkner's narratives, women are constructed as representing a lack of control and a projection of male fear, as "distorted or mythicized beings, the projection of a masculine consciousness at its most vulnerable" (*Faulkner's Rhetoric of Loss* 122). My argument is that their loss generates narrative desire, hence the play of Faulkner's text, hence our pleasure. In a provocative chapter entitled "Significant Absences," Mortimer points to the phenomenon in Faulkner's works of absence encased in shape, citing both Rosa's "small body" and Ellen's "substanceless shell" (87). I differentiate my remarks from Mortimer's in that I am showing how male subjects create "woman" as absence—how they, like Sutpen, see "woman" for what her space represents. What I find most intriguing, though, is how Faulkner enables women to speak out of these tight (non)places and how their desire to do so manifests itself as textual production.

6. Sally Page, for example, believes that young Rosa "falls in love with love" and eventually transfers her desire for "normal fulfillment of herself in love and marriage" from Bon to Sutpen. Her remaining years, Page finds, "are spent in hopeless virginity and furious hatred" (105–7).

7. For an alternative view of Sutpen's identity and motives, see " 'Strange Gods' in Jefferson, Mississippi," in which Richard Poirier finds that the multiple perspectives for *Absalom, Absalom!* suggest that "the act of placing Sutpen in the understandable context of human society and history is a continually necessary act, a never-ending responsibility and an act of humanistic faith" (21).

8. This approach to Rosa Coldfield and her story has proven an irresistible enterprise for some Faulkner critics of decades past. In 1967 Thomas Lorch's "Thomas Sutpen and the Female Principle" argued that in *Absalom, Absalom!* and elsewhere, Faulkner "recognizes female nature as necessary and good, because it provides the living material for the male to shape and elevate" (42). Such views bring serious inquiry about female subjectivity in Faulkner's fiction to a screeching halt.

9. Although it is beyond the purview of this essay to discuss film criticism in any detail, the gendered construction of the gaze is an important element in feminist film theory which informs my thinking. See Teresa de Lauretis, *Alice Doesn't*, and Tania Modleski's "Rape versus Mans/laughter: Hitchcock's *Blackmail* and Feminist Interpretation." In the essay "Desire and Despair: Temple Drake's Self-Victimization," Robert R. Moore seems unaware that looking may be gendered. He says, "We find ourselves on a roller coaster ride of ambivalence as we respond to Temple. If she demands our sympathy and protective impulses, she is also fair game for our sexual fantasies" (114). He argues that Faulkner creates us as an audience of readers who, through our voyeurism, participate in Temple's rape, in "the defilement" of "the self" (the female self, one assumes) (116). This perhaps exaggerated example of the male gaze at work in criticism leads one to ponder, as Modleski does, the problematics of being cast as woman into a critical demeanor constructed by male sexuality.

10. This is Jardine's term in describing configurations of the feminine within Western philosophy and critical theory (*Gynesis* 25).

11. I am reading this passage much more literally than Irwin, who argues that it is evidence of a cycle of revenge among father, son, and father-substitute (122).

12. Unlike, Irwin, who associates castration with repression (88–89), I am more inclined to mediate between Juliet Mitchell's figuring of castration as the splitting of subjectivity and Jane Gallop's redefinition of castration as a theoretical position which frees itself by playing within the uncontrollable spaces between language and subjectivity.

13. Although I think that J. Gary Williams is correct in saying that

Quentin is profoundly influenced by Rosa, I disagree that his "seeing" her at the end of the book is an act of creating her as "a living person" (346).

Works Cited

Baldwin, James. "Everybody's Protest Novel." *Partisan Review* 16 (June 1949): 578–85.

Bernheimer, Charles, and Claire Kahane, eds. *In Dora's Case: Freud-Hysteria-Feminism.* New York: Columbia University Press, 1985.

Brylowski, Walter. "Faulkner's 'Mythology.' " In *William Faulkner's "Absalom, Absalom!" A Critical Casebook,* edited by Elisabeth Muhlenfeld, 109–34. New York: Garland, 1984.

Cixous, Hélène. "Castration or Decapitation?" *Signs* 7 (1981): 41–55.

————. "Sorties: Out and Out: Attacks/Ways Out/Forays." In Hélène Cixous and Catherine Clément, *The Newly Born Woman,* translated by Betsy Wing, 61–132. Minneapolis: University of Minnesota Press, 1986.

Clément, Catherine. "Sorceress and Hysteric." In Hélène Cixous and Catherine Clément, *The Newly Born Woman,* translated by Betsy Wing, 3–39. Minneapolis: University of Minnesota Press, 1986.

Davis, Thadious. *Faulkner's "Negro": Art and the Southern Context.* Baton Rouge: Louisiana State University Press, 1983.

Derrida, Jacques. *Spurs/Eperons.* Chicago, Ill.: University of Chicago Press, 1978.

Diaz-Diocaretz, Myriam. "Faulkner's Hen House: Woman as Bounded Text." In *Faulkner and Women,* edited by Doreen Fowler and Ann J. Abadie, 235–69. Jackson: University Press of Mississippi, 1986.

Faulkner, William. *Absalom, Absalom! The Corrected Text.* New York: Random House, 1986.

Felman, Shoshana. *Writing and Madness,* translated by Martha Noel Evans and Shoshana Felman. Ithaca, N.Y.: Cornell University Press, 1985.

Freud, Sigmund. "Fragment of an Analysis of a Case of Hysteria." In *Standard Edition of the Complete Psychological Works,* edited by James Strachey, 7:7–122. London: Hogarth, 1964.

Gallop, Jane. *Feminism and Psychoanalysis: The Daughter's Seduction.* Ithaca, N.Y.: Cornell University Press, 1982.

Gwin, Minrose C. *Black and White Women of the Old South: The Peculiar Sisterhood in American Literature.* Knoxville: University of Tennessee Press, 1985.

Irwin, John T. *Doubling and Incest/Repetition and Revenge: A Speculative Reading of Faulkner*. Baltimore, Md.: Johns Hopkins University Press, 1975.

Jacobus, Mary. *Reading Woman: Essays in Feminist Criticism*. New York: Columbia University Press, 1986.

Jardine, Alice. *Gynesis: Configurations of Woman and Modernity*. Ithaca, N.Y.: Cornell University Press, 1985.

Jenkins, Lee. *Faulkner and Black-White Relations: A Psychoanalytic Approach*. New York: Columbia University Press, 1981.

Johnson, Barbara. *The Critical Difference: Essays in the Contemporary Rhetoric of Reading*. Baltimore, Md.: Johns Hopkins University Press, 1980.

Lacan, Jacques. *Feminine Sexuality: Jacques Lacan and the École Freudienne*, edited by Juliet Mitchell and Jacqueline Rose, translated by Jacqueline Rose. London: Macmillan, 1982.

Langford, Gerald. *Faulkner's Revision of Absalom, Absalom!* Austin: University of Texas Press, 1971.

Lauretis, Teresa de. *Alice Doesn't: Feminism, Semiotics, Cinema*. Bloomington: Indiana University Press, 1984.

Lorch, Thomas. "Thomas Sutpen and the Female Principle." *Mississippi Quarterly* 20 (Winter 1967): 38–42.

Lyotard, Jean Francois. *The Postmodern Condition: A Report on Knowledge*, translated by Geoff Bennington and Brian Massumi. Minneapolis: University of Minnesota Press, 1984.

Matthews, John T. *The Play of Faulkner's Language*. Ithaca, N.Y.: Cornell University Press, 1982.

Mitchell, Juliet. *Women: The Longest Revolution*. New York: Pantheon, 1966.

Modleski, Tania. "Rape versus Mans/laughter: Hitchcock's *Blackmail* and Feminist Interpretation." *PMLA* 102 (May 1987): 304–15.

Moore, Robert. "Desire and Despair: Temple Drake's Self-Victimization." In *Faulkner and Women*, edited by Doreen Fowler and Ann J. Abadie, 112–27. Jackson: University Press of Mississippi, 1986.

Mortimer, Gail. *Faulkner's Rhetoric of Loss*. Austin: University of Texas Press, 1983.

———. "The Smooth, Suave Shape of Desire: Paradox in Faulknerian Imagery of Women." *Women's Studies* 13 (1986): 149–61.

Muhlenfeld, Elisabeth, ed. *William Faulkner's "Absalom, Absalom!" A Critical Casebook*. New York: Garland, 1984.

Page, Sally. *Faulkner's Women: Characterization and Meaning*. Deland, Fla.: Everett/Edward, 1971.

Poirier, Richard. " 'Strange Gods' in Jefferson, Mississippi: Analysis of *Absalom, Absalom!*" In *William Faulkner's "Absalom, Absalom!" A Critical*

Casebook, edited by Elisabeth Muhlenfeld, 1–22. New York: Garland, 1984.

Weinstein, Philip M. "Meditations on the Other: Faulkner's Rendering of Women." In *Faulkner and Women*, edited by Doreen Fowler and Ann J. Abadie, 81–99. Jackson: University Press of Mississippi, 1986.

Williams, J. Gary. "Quentin Finally Sees Miss Rosa." *Criticism* 21 (1979): 331–46.

Wittenberg, Judith Bryant. "A Feminist *Sanctuary* for Temple Drake?" Paper presented at Modern Language Association Conference, New York, Dec. 1985.

Sutpen's Design

DIRK KUYK, JR.

◆　◆　◆

Y OU SEE, I HAD A DESIGN in my mind." In William
Faulkner's *Absalom, Absalom!* that line occurs more than two-
thirds of the way through the book.[1] Readers, eager or driven to
press on, do not pause to think about it, but the line repays
contemplation. By *design*, Thomas Sutpen certainly means a plan
that he had conceived and had sought to carry out. Design might
mean still more. Because Sutpen was seeking retaliation, *design*
might imply a plan of attack: Sutpen might have formed a design
upon someone or something. Whatever *design* means to Sutpen—
and I think that his meaning is far from fully understood—his
tone, as he speaks the line, expresses neither repentance nor bra-
vado. Sutpen calls the design his own not as an admission or a
claim but as a plain statement of fact. The coldness of his tone
and his lack of shame and remorse have led many readers to
condemn him. They may read *design* ironically, as if Sutpen is
unknowingly condemning himself for a brutal, selfish scheme.
Although *Absalom, Absalom!* is more than the story of Thomas
Sutpen, readers strive to understand his acts and his aims because

they lie in the book's core. We will soon get back to his design; before we do, we need to look into some other implications of the sentence "You see, I had a design in my mind."

Sutpen's verb may be significant. Why does he use the past tense: "had"? Does he mean that he had his design but has given it up or that he still has it? The design was "in my mind"—does that mean that he had never gotten it embodied in the world? Does it mean that he had never even tried to express it until he sat down in General Compson's office and began his account? His opening words, "You see," fix his own roles and General Compson's. Sutpen is the teller; General Compson, the listener; but Sutpen is also the actor in the narrative. Unable to interpret his own story, he is turning to General Compson to interpret it for him. "You see" may not be simply a statement; it is almost a command.

Indeed, many have sought to obey him—have tried to "see." Rosa was the first. General Compson struggled to do so and passed the challenge on to Mr. Compson, who passed it to Quentin, who shared it with Shreve. In 1957 and 1958, while writer-in-residence at the University of Virginia, Faulkner himself grappled with Sutpen's design not as the book's author but as one of its readers. Although he seldom seems to have reread his books, he found *Absalom, Absalom!* so demanding that he resorted to rereading it. Before then his comments had denigrated Sutpen, oversimplified Sutpen's design, and so misrepresented the book, but after rereading it, Faulkner said that the narrators had presented only partial truths. As Faulkner the reader then saw Sutpen, "the old man was himself a little too big for people no greater in stature than Quentin and Miss Rosa and Mr. Compson to see all at once. It would have taken perhaps a wiser or more tolerant or more sensitive or more thoughtful person to see him as he was."[2] Faulkner's words contain a warning that too few have heeded. Critics who have written on *Absalom, Absalom!* believe that Sutpen is quite transparent. They see him as petty and egocentric rather than as "too big," and they seldom seem to have felt that understanding him and his design calls for any special wisdom, tolerance, sensitivity, or thoughtfulness. But once we have grasped exactly what Sutpen's design was, we will see in it less self-serving ambition and more of an aspiration that might actually deserve the word *heroic*.

We will also find that Sutpen's design does not stand in isolation in *Absalom, Absalom!* Other characters have their designs, not only plans that they seek to carry out but also schemes that they have formed to the detriment of others. We will try to understand their aims and motives and to comprehend how their designs mesh or fail to mesh with Sutpen's and with one another's. We will try to see whether their designs came to exist in the world or existed only in the characters' minds. And we will find many characters shifting among the roles of actor, teller, and listening interpreter in a chain that stops only with the reader as the last interpreter and with Faulkner—or, more precisely, *Absalom, Absalom!* itself—crying out, "You see."

"You see, I had a design in my mind," Thomas Sutpen said. How he came to form his design is clear. As a boy Sutpen had moved with his family from the Appalachian backwoods and had settled in a cabin on a plantation in Tidewater Virginia. When he was twelve or thirteen, his father sent him to the plantation house with a message for the owner. Sutpen knocked at the front door. The black butler, obviously carrying out his master's notions of propriety, told the boy "never to come to that front door again but to go around to the back." Sutpen, brought up under the egalitarian code of the mountains, was stunned. He went into the woods to a cave "where he could be quiet and think" (290). He knew "he would have to do something about it in order to live with himself for the rest of his life and he could not decide what it was because of that innocence which he had just discovered he had" (292).

Sutpen never considers vengeance against the black butler because Sutpen knows him to be merely the owner's instrument. Sutpen rejects the notion of killing the owner because "that wouldn't do no good" (293). Soon the boy decides that vengeance against the owner is pointless: "There aint any good or harm either in the living world that I can do to him" (297). Sutpen, with "that innocence instructing him" (297), suddenly finds his design taking shape in his mind:

> "If you were fixing to combat them that had the fine rifles, the first thing you would do would be to get yourself the nearest thing to a fine rifle you could borrow or steal or make, wouldn't it?" and he said Yes. "But this aint a question of rifles. So to combat them you have got to have what they have that made them do what he did. You got to have land and niggers and a fine house to combat them with. You see?" and he said Yes again. He left that night. (297)

> I had a design. To accomplish it I should require money, a house, a plantation, slaves, a family—incidentally of course, a wife. I set out to acquire these. (329)

But by the time those words occur, many other designs have impressed themselves on the minds of readers. That overlay of other designs has, I believe, kept readers from seeing precisely the design that Sutpen had in mind. Eventually I will devote much attention to those other designs, trying to determine how they affect the ways readers have understood the book. Now, however, I will keep focusing on Sutpen's design. What do readers think Sutpen aimed to do? Let us see what critics have said. (The narrator in *Tom Jones* explicates the word *critic* by saying, "By this Word here . . . we mean every Reader in the World."[3] So do I. Therefore, the readers who publish their views will stand in here for all those who do not.)

Readers are essentially unanimous about the nature of his design. Elizabeth M. Kerr speaks for many of them when she says that Sutpen's "grand design" was "to establish an estate and a dynasty . . . on the Tidewater pattern of inheritance through the eldest legitimate son." Cleanth Brooks also finds Sutpen trying to "establish a dynasty." Being sent to the back door made Sutpen change the saying "if you can't beat them, you'd best join them" by adding "you can beat them only by joining them"; and so

Sutpen "dedicated his life to becoming the Tidewater planter." David Paul Ragan says that Sutpen wanted to become, "like Pettibone, a participant in the power structure."[4]

Some critics stress still more that the design has its source in society because society admires those who build dynasties. Ilse Dusoir Lind says that Sutpen chose the "path of social conformity." Donald M. Kartiganer agrees: Sutpen's path leads him to "self-imprisonment in a prevailing social system. . . . His quest is not to create a design, but to accomplish an already existing one, a pattern he can neither understand nor modify to suit himself." Olga W. Vickery writes that "the germ of Sutpen's design is simply his determination to create . . . that pattern which he sees, rightly or wrongly, in Southern society and to conduct his life strictly in terms of its ethical code."[5]

Other critics emphasize the psychic rewards Sutpen will achieve by building his dynasty. David Minter contends that Sutpen aims to "match or even surpass" the plantation owner's "power and grandeur" because Sutpen "wants to avoid the failure that marks his family, particularly his father." Minter says that what Sutpen does, "he does in part for himself, so that he can live with himself for the rest of his life; in part for his forbears . . . ; and in part for the boy he was, or more precisely, for the 'boysymbol' that the boy he was has become."[6] John T. Irwin says:

> Sutpen seeks revenge within the rules of patriarchal power for the affront that he suffered; he does not try to show the injustice of the system, but rather to show that he is as good as any man in the system. If the planter is powerful because he is rich, then Sutpen will have his revenge by becoming richer and more powerful than the planter. And he will pass that wealth and power on to his son, doing for his son what his own father could not do for him.[7]

This critical unanimity is odd in the light of what Sutpen actually accomplished. Having formed his design, he moved with remarkable speed to carry it out. Knowing that "to accomplish my design I should need first of all and above all things money

in considerable quantities and in the quite immediate future"
(303–4), Sutpen went to the West Indies where, he had heard,
"poor men . . . became rich" (302). There he worked as overseer
on a plantation, put down a slave rebellion, and at the age of
twenty married the master's daughter. When he married, he was
"still a virgin. . . . that too was a part of the design which I had
in my mind" (310). He grew wealthy and had a son. At this point
he seems to have acquired absolutely everything called for in his
design, as readers have usually understood it. He ought, then, to
have rested easy.

Sutpen, however, repudiated his wife and child because "I
found that she was not and could never be, through no fault of
her own, adjunctive or incremental to the design which I had in
mind, so I provided for her and put her aside" (300). Although a
reader might join Estella Schoenberg in conjuring up notions that
might account for Sutpen's putting his wife aside—for example,
she might have been illegitimately pregnant, insane, illiterate,
oversexed, or prone to fits[8]—almost all readers think, as I do,
that he had discovered that his wife was partly black. (Eventually
I will try to show why that fact or belief or even rumor would
have impeded the design. But one seeming explanation might as
well be dismissed now. Miscegenation itself would not defeat what
readers generally take to be Sutpen's design. Racial mixing would
not bar him or his wife from high status in the West Indies, and
Sutpen himself did not object to it: Clytie seems to have been
his daughter.) If he were aiming merely at establishing a dynasty
and then "lying in his hammock in the shade, with his shoes off,
receiving drinks brought to him by a servant,"[9] he seems not to
have noticed that he has completed his design. Nor does the
critics' view of his design seem to account for his decision to
remain a virgin until his marriage. Abstinence is neither adjunctive nor incremental to creating a dynasty.

Sutpen's next steps might stir still more doubts about what his
design was. Having come so close to its completion, he abandoned
almost all that he had gained. He left his wife the plantation and
all that went with it except twenty slaves and a sum of money,
made his way to Jefferson, and began once again his effort to

carry out his design. He bought one hundred square miles of virgin bottomland from the Chickasaws. With his slaves and a seemingly kidnapped and certainly imprisoned architect, he built a mansion. By some scheme in which Mr. Coldfield, a respectable merchant and Methodist steward, participated but was ashamed to profit from, Sutpen furnished his mansion with "chandeliers and mahogany and rugs" (50). He married Coldfield's daughter, Ellen, and they had two children, Henry and Judith. Again he has laid the foundation for a dynasty and ought to be ready to recline in his hammock. His design, as the critics have described it, seems for the second time to be complete.

Henry, the scion of the dynasty-to-be, came home for Christmas with a college friend, Charles Bon, from New Orleans. Henry idolized the older, more sophisticated Bon, but what attracted Bon to Henry? Sutpen himself seems to have wondered, and when the boys' friendship lasted through the spring, Sutpen undertook to investigate Bon's background. Mr. Compson's account emphasizes how uncharacteristically Sutpen was behaving:

Sutpen, the man whom, after seeing once and before any engagement existed anywhere save in his wife's mind, he saw as a potential threat to the (now and at last) triumphant coronation of his old hardships and ambition, of which threat he was apparently sure enough to warrant a six hundred mile journey to prove it—this in a man who might have challenged and shot someone whom he disliked or feared but who would not have made even a ten mile journey to investigate him. (125)

Henry brought Bon home in June while Sutpen was away. With encouragement from Henry and from Mrs. Sutpen, Bon and Judith began a courtship. Sutpen, in the meantime, had discovered in New Orleans something about Bon. Expecting that Bon would know that he had been found out, Sutpen may have hoped that Bon would retreat. During the fall, however, the courtship continued, and Sutpen held his hand, again uncharacteristically for "this man of whom it was said that he not only went out to meet his troubles, he sometimes went out and manufactured them" (130). On Christmas Eve, Sutpen acted: he forbade the marriage. When Henry objected, Sutpen justified his decision by revealing something he had discovered in New Orleans. Henry, taking Bon's side, gave his father the lie, and the two young men left Sutpen's Hundred.

Sutpen's stand against the marriage is puzzling. What had he found in New Orleans? How had he justified his stand to Henry? Was the justification that Sutpen had offered his true reason for forbidding the marriage? And, most puzzling of all, why would Sutpen risk his design by estranging Henry in order to stave off the marriage?

A few readers dismiss efforts to answer such questions. Kartiganer, for example, writes that Sutpen withholds his consent "for some unknown reason."[10] Schoenberg goes further. She says that "the many critical attempts to establish the facts and the sequence of Sutpen chronology devolve from, and their errors are partially explainable by, the mistaken premises, first, that *Absalom, Absalom!* is primarily Sutpen's story and second, that the events of the Sutpen story are supposed to have happened. Even in terms of the text, not to say the author's intent, most of them either did not happen or cannot be proved to have happened." For her, Sutpen's story is "*im*material—literally," and so no one need bother trying to figure it out. Yet she undermines her own stand by arguing that Quentin carries the book's action by his "gathering of information, assimilating it, telling it, developing part of it . . . into an elaborate fictional narrative, and bringing his . . . personal involvement in the tale" to a high pitch.[11] Quentin, however, is not unique in carrying out those acts. They describe pretty well what is done by Rosa, Mr. Compson, General Compson, and Shreve; by Faulkner as author; and by the book's readers themselves. Almost all critics have therefore tried to work out Sutpen's motives for barring the marriage. To do so turns out to be more difficult, I believe, than critics have suspected.

Let us take the first question first: What had Sutpen discovered in New Orleans? Mr. Compson told Quentin that Sutpen had found Bon's octoroon mistress and their son there (128). Perhaps Sutpen had even discovered that she and Bon had married in a

non-Christian ceremony. Mr. Compson's view seems correct so
far as it goes; but as he himself feels, it does not go far enough:

> Granted that . . . the existence of the eighth part negro mistress
> and the sixteenth part negro son, granted even the morganatic
> ceremony—a situation which was as much a part of a wealthy
> young New Orleansian's social and fashionable equipment as
> his dancing slippers—was reason enough, which is drawing
> honor a little fine even for the shadowy paragons which are
> our ancestors born in the South and come to man- and wom-
> anhood about eighteen sixty or sixty one. It's just incredible.
> It just does not explain. (123–24)

Mr. Compson's inability to work out a credible explanation frus-
trates him. Like Kartiganer and Schoenberg, Mr. Compson says
that Sutpen, Bon, Judith, and Henry "dont explain and we are
not supposed to know" (124). Unlike those critics, though, he
does not give up. He imagines the four people as chemicals
brought together by a formula incorrectly written or in an ex-
periment improperly performed: "You bring them together in the
proportions called for, but nothing happens; you re-read, tedious
and intent, poring, making sure that you have forgotten nothing,
made no miscalculation; you bring them together again and again
nothing happens" (124–25). With those remarks Mr. Compson
prefaces his account of what Sutpen discovered and why that
discovery led him to bar the marriage. That account has failed
to satisfy readers as it failed to satisfy Mr. Compson himself. Sutpen, we think, must have found more than that.

But the reader must turn many pages before the narrative
offers another explanation. It takes an unexpected form: it comes
from Shreve, the narrator who stands furthest from the Sutpens.
When Henry brought Bon home, Shreve says, Sutpen "looked up
and saw the face he believed he had paid off and discharged
twenty-eight years ago" (331). Quentin agrees and adds a good
many comments that Mr. Compson had made about Sutpen and
Bon as father and son. All of that surprises Shreve, who challenges Quentin: "Your father. . . . He seems to have got an awful

lot of delayed information awful quick, after having waited forty-five years. If he knew all this, what was his reason for telling you that the trouble between Henry and Bon was the octoroon woman?" Quentin replies, "He didn't know it then," and when Shreve asks, "Then who did tell him?" Quentin answers simply, "I did" (332). We have here the answer to our first question: Sutpen had discovered in New Orleans that Bon was his son.

Sutpen surely did not tell Henry all about that during their Christmas Eve confrontation, however. Instead, what Mr. Compson surmised rings true: Sutpen told Henry that Bon had a mistress (possibly a wife) and a child in New Orleans. Mr. Compson's account of Henry's trip with Bon to see the octoroon in New Orleans also fits in with her visit to Sutpen's Hundred and with Clytie's and Judith's ability to find and to help Bon's son, Charles Etienne. Furthermore, when Mr. Compson was sitting on the porch telling Quentin about Sutpen, Mr. Compson had not yet learned who Bon's father was. Mr. Compson's ignorance is itself a faint indication that both Sutpen and Bon had kept Bon's parentage secret. Thus, the answer to our second question: Sutpen justified his decision to Henry by telling him about Bon's mistress (or wife) and child. Two questions remain: Did Sutpen tell Henry the true reasons for forbidding the marriage, and why would Sutpen risk his dynasty to stave off the marriage? To the first of these questions my short answer is no, Sutpen had reasons he was keeping in reserve. Exploring what they were and why he was holding them back will make the second question puzzling and will bring to light more problems with the notion that Sutpen aimed merely at establishing a dynasty.

Let us return to the question of Bon's parentage. Almost all readers believe, as I do too, that Bon is Sutpen's son, although, again, Schoenberg disagrees. The narrative, she says, contradicts the supposition that Bon is Sutpen's son. She rests her argument on two grounds. Bon's gravestone, which Judith ordered, shows Bon to have been born in New Orleans in December 1831. Schoenberg believes that if he were really Sutpen's son, the gravestone would give his birthplace as some island in the West Indies. Is that information wrong then, she asks, because of misinformation or because of subterfuge, Judith's or someone else's? Whatever the case, Schoenberg objects to the narrative's failing to state a motive or to explain how the inscription on the gravestone came to be wrong. While I cannot conceive of Judith sinking to subterfuge, the other possibilities are entirely plausible. And a motive is easy to imagine. Even though Bon was keeping quiet about his origins, he would have to have given himself some background. Bon, then, would be the source of this information. He may have believed it himself; he may not have. No matter which, I see no contradictions there. Schoenberg also asserts that "nowhere in the multiple telling of Sutpen's story by those who could know is there evidence that even Sutpen thought Bon his son."[12] I hope to offer such evidence with Sutpen himself as the witness, but I must still develop the case before bringing Sutpen to the stand.

Although readers do join in taking Bon as Sutpen's son, they quickly separate on exactly why that fact makes Sutpen forbid the marriage. Hyatt Waggoner merely says that Sutpen "could calculate no advantage to be gained by recognizing Bon as his son, and [Sutpen] was not one to be moved by the incalculable."[13] Most critics, though, expend more effort than that in working out the calculations that Sutpen was making. Quentin and Shreve explore the possibility that Sutpen prevents the marriage to prevent incest. But like Quentin and Shreve, most readers find that explanation insufficient. No one regards Sutpen as so appalled at the prospect of incest that he would feel he must stop the marriage at any cost. Indeed, the critics seldom discuss incest as an impediment to Sutpen's plans. I agree: he is pursuing his design so bullheadedly that a little incest would not give him pause.

By far the majority of readers conclude that Sutpen bars the marriage because Bon's mother had "a tinge of Negro blood" and Bon is therefore partly black. Lind says, "The slight fraction of Negro blood, whose denial was Sutpen's crime, is sole cause. Now at last we know what turned father against son." Vickery finds that "Sutpen must choose between his adherence to the concept of pure blood and his own and his son's humanity." The reason for his having to make that choice might seem self-evident: as

Gerald Langford says, "Bon's Negro blood was clearly a threat to the establishment of a dynasty in the antebellum South."[14]

Langford would be indubitably right if Sutpen had meant to found a dynasty on Bon. Since southern culture took "partly black" as "entirely black," no white dynasty could rest on Bon. But Henry, not Bon, was Sutpen's foundation stone. Therefore, Bon's existence would not inherently imperil Sutpen's design if it were simply to found a dynasty. Brooks explains why:

> In view of what is usually written about *Absalom, Absalom!*, the basic security of Sutpen's position needs to be stressed. Suppose that it had become known, either through Sutpen's action or Bon's, that Bon was his son; what, in view of the laws and customs of the time, could Bon have done? He might have created a certain amount of talk. . . . But with [Sutpen's] hundred square miles of plantation and his respectable marriage to Ellen Coldfield, Sutpen could probably have outfaced any charge of bigamy, and by letting the community know that Bon was part-Negro, could have disposed of any notion that Henry was not his legitimate heir.[15]

One could probably make that argument still more strongly. If Sutpen's first wife was partly black, then in Mississippi at the time the marriage would have been illegal. Sutpen could not have made it valid even if he had wished to. Nor could he have in any way legitimized Bon as the child of such a marriage.

Does Langford perhaps mean that Bon's marriage to Judith would threaten the Sutpen dynasty? If people knew either that Bon was partly black or that Bon was Sutpen's son, then, of course, the miscegenation or the incest would make the marriage both illegal and taboo. But who would discover and reveal either of those bits of information? Bon had grown up as not only a white but an upper-class, wealthy white in the sophisticated city of New Orleans; he was studying law at the university (which, one hardly needs to say, admitted no blacks); and no one appears to have doubted his mother's race or his father's name. And, indeed, one might wonder whether a dynasty in a patriarchal society would fall because of a daughter's and sister's scandalous behavior, no matter how great the scandal. In sum, I believe, Brooks's judgment stands: Charles Bon's racial heritage does not threaten the security of Sutpen's dynasty.

Irwin offers an intricate psychological explanation for Sutpen rejecting Bon:

> In the ideal situation, the revenge is inflicted on the same person who originally delivered the affront . . . ; in the other situation, the revenge is inflicted on a substitute. This second situation sheds light on Sutpen's attempt to master the traumatic affront that he suffered as a boy from the man who became his surrogate father, to master it by repeating that affront in reverse, inflicting it on his own son Charles Bon.[16]

Irwin's explanation would make the rejection of Bon the fulfillment of Sutpen's design, the achievement of his revenge by delivering the affront to the surrogate. But Irwin's explanation leaves too much unexplained. Sutpen learned in the spring that Bon was his son. Why, then, would Sutpen, who kept driving single-mindedly toward his goal, wait until the following Christmas to get his revenge? Why not complete his design instantly? And once he had rejected Bon, why did he not get at least a moment's satisfaction from attaining his vengeance and completing his design? Sutpen's own words, passed from General Compson through Mr. Compson to Quentin, undermine Irwin's explanation. Sutpen said that if he were forced to play his "last trump card"—that is, to take the action that definitively rejected Bon— "I destroy my design with my own hand" (341–42). Sutpen's words virtually contradict the idea that rejecting Bon gains Sutpen the revenge that fulfills his design.

Occasionally a critic finds in primogeniture rather than race the reason that Bon poses a problem for Sutpen. For example, Kerr says, "Sutpen himself chose to adopt the laws of primogeniture and refused to recognize Charles Bon, his legitimate elder son and rightful heir by those laws."[17] Of course, as we have already seen, if people regarded Bon as black, then those laws would preclude Bon as either a legitimate son or a rightful heir. But what happens if people take Bon as white? John T. Matthews answers that question by saying that Bon imperils "Sutpen's insemination of a legitimate line. . . . Sutpen cannot acknowledge Charles Bon without accepting a world in which origin and priority have lost their privilege, in which rival sons claim the same father, differing signs the same signified. Sutpen refuses one son and remains loyal to the false authority of dynastic speech."[18] Yet if Sutpen seeks merely to found a dynasty, then his plight is not so grave as that. Fraternal rivalries are just the kinds of conflicts that "dynastic speech" came into being to resolve. Dynastic speech always stands ready to decide questions of origin and priority. It would have to name the rightful heir, but whether it chose Henry or Bon, Sutpen would still have a foundation for his dynasty.

We have reached a crux. Although we know that Sutpen forbade the marriage, we have eliminated all of the widely held reasons for his doing so. He does not seem to have acted to prevent incest. Miscegnation neither offended him nor threatened a dynasty founded on Henry; and primogeniture would have allowed him to found his dynasty on whichever son was his "rightful" heir. Why, then, did he forbid the marriage? What in the world was Sutpen trying to do?

Now it is time to call Sutpen himself to the witness stand so that we can hear him explain his design. His testimony—or, more accurately, my account of his testimony—must pass this test of credibility: it must answer all of the questions, large and small, that the standard interpretations do not answer:

—In Haiti why did Sutpen give up just as he had succeeded or had nearly succeeded in completing his design?

—Why did Sutpen regard his virginity as important to his design?

—Why did Sutpen forbid the marriage?

—Henry killed Bon after the end of the Civil War. In the previous year, however, we heard Sutpen saying that he would have to choose between two courses that would lead to "the same result." We understand, I believe, his first course. If he plays his "last trump card" by telling Henry about Bon, then he expects Henry and Bon to fight. If Henry dies, the Sutpen dynasty will have lost its foundation. If Bon dies, Henry will vanish, as he does, in despair because he will have slain his friend and half brother. All that, Sutpen foresees. But what are we to make of his second course? To take it, he would "do nothing, let matters take the course which I know they will take and see my design complete itself quite normally and naturally and successfully to the public eye, yet to my own in such fashion as to be a mockery and a betrayal of that little boy who approached that door fifty years ago" (342). In this course Bon and Judith would marry; and Henry, kept ignorant that Bon was his half brother, would accept—even welcome— the marriage. The dynasty would go forward. The public eye would regard the design as successful; so would the standard critical interpretations. Why, then, would Sutpen regard this course as a "mockery and a betrayal"? If he were seeking only a dynasty, why would he not then have his design complete and unchallenged?

Scattered throughout *Absalom, Absalom!* Sutpen's remarks reveal much about his design. They call for a close reading that can begin with the rifle analogy that his "innocence" uses to instruct him as his design is coming into being. His innocence teaches him that someone who means to "combat" men with fine rifles would try to get himself "the nearest thing to a fine rifle" he could (297). Since Sutpen means to make his dynasty his weapon, he must have a "fine" dynasty—that is, a dynasty as nearly perfect as possible. The standards of perfection are, of course, not Sutpen's alone; they are the standards of his society. Without wealth a family cannot deserve the name *dynasty*; therefore, Sutpen would, as he says, "require money, a house, a plantation, slaves." A dynasty must extend beyond a single generation: Sutpen would thus "require . . . a family." Since in the society the children must be legitimate, Sutpen would "require . . . incidentally of course, a wife" (329). His family must include a son under patriarchal primogeniture.

Meeting those requirements would not suffice to make a dynasty fine. In Sutpen's place and time those requirements are merely the dynasty's defining traits. A fine dynasty, like a fine rifle, must surpass an ordinary one. Again, the standards are the society's. If society sees blacks as inferior to whites, then a fine dynasty cannot be black. If society regards part-black as entirely black, then neither husband nor wife can be partly black. If society regards, say, an olive skin or even a rumor of blackness as suspicious, then a fine dynasty cannot rest on such suspect foundations. And if female and male virginity are seen as extraordinarily admirable, then the man who founds the finest dynasty will be a virgin. Sutpen is trying to create "the nearest thing" (297) he can to a fine dynasty.

Yet the rifle analogy is not grounded in mere possession. One does not combat men with rifles simply by having similar rifles nor even by having better rifles. No, to use a rifle to combat riflemen, one fires the rifle at them. Sutpen's design, then, must go beyond just having the rifle, beyond just having what the plantation owner had, even beyond having more than he had. If Sutpen aims to have a dynasty, he must also aim to "fire" it at someone.

Who—or what—would he take as his target? Not the black butler or the plantation owner who turned him away. Virtually from the start Sutpen was aiming elsewhere. Again, his analogy itself clarifies his intention. He would have wanted a fine rifle to combat "them that had the fine rifles"; he must have wanted a fine dynasty to combat those who had fine dynasties. The analogy may help us take the next step, too. In fighting those with fine rifles, a man who has gotten a fine rifle would fire it. But how might one use a dynasty against those who have dynasties? How does one fire a dynasty at a dynastic society?

We are now reaching what I take to have been Sutpen's design. He meant, I believe, not merely to acquire a dynasty but to acquire it so that he could turn it against dynastic society itself.

And he meant to do that in an ironic, perhaps even a doubly ironic, way. Quentin repeats for Shreve and for us what Sutpen told General Compson about the design. Because the two boys are, by this time in the book, probing the relationship between Henry and Bon, not inquiring into Sutpen's design, neither Quentin nor Shreve comments on or even seems to notice the meaning of Sutpen's remarks. And few readers seem to have given the passage the attention it deserves. Here is the passage in full with some comments along the way.

> The design.—Getting richer and richer. It must have looked fine and clear ahead for him now: house finished, and even bigger and whiter than the one he had gone to the door of that day and the nigger came in his monkey clothes and told him to go to the back, and he with his own brand of niggers even, which the man who lay in the hammock with his shoes off didn't have, to cull one from and train him to go to the door when his turn came for a little boy without any shoes on and with his pap's cutdown pants for clothes to come and knock on it.

Sutpen is establishing his dynasty in preparation for the moment when "his turn" will come for a little boy to knock on his door. When the boy knocks, the butler will go to the door to do whatever Sutpen has trained him to do. Sutpen may seem to be preparing to reenact his own rejection by inflicting it on a boy who symbolizes the young Sutpen. Quentin, however, tells a different story:

> Only Father said that that wasn't it now, that when he came to Grandfather's office that day after the thirty years, and not trying to excuse now anymore than he had tried in the bottom that night when they ran the architect, but just to explain now, trying hard to explain now because now he was old and knew it, knew it was being old that he had to talk against: time shortening ahead of him that could and would do things to his chances and possibilities even if he had no more doubt

of his bones and flesh than he did of his will and courage, telling Grandfather that the boy-symbol at the door wasn't it because the boy-symbol was just the figment of the amazed and desperate child.

In the last couple of clauses Sutpen is describing himself as "the amazed and desperate child" crouching deep in thought in his cave in the woods. There he had imagined the "boy-symbol" or "figment" representing himself at the door. He must have also imagined himself as a man opening the door or having his butler open it on his behalf. But that figment, that vision, stemmed only from the boy's amazement, desperation, and youth. The boy symbol "wasn't it." The boy symbol at the door was not the design. Instead, Sutpen said

> that now he would take that boy in where he would never again need to stand on the outside of a white door and knock at it: and not at all for mere shelter but so that that boy, that whatever nameless stranger, could shut that door himself forever behind him on all that he had ever known, and look ahead along the still undivulged light rays in which his descendants who might not even ever hear his (the boy's) name, waited to be born without even having to know that they had once been riven forever free from brutehood just as his own (Sutpen's) children were. (325–26)

That is Sutpen's design. He required "money, a house, a plantation, slaves, a family—incidentally of course, a wife" (329)—not for themselves, not because they would enable him to lie in a hammock with his shoes off, not for the social status they would provide, but so as to be ready for the knock on his door. And when the boy, "that whatever nameless stranger," knocked, Sutpen meant to "take that boy in." Sutpen planned to give him more than "mere shelter"; Sutpen meant to take him into his own family. The boy could then "shut that door himself forever behind him" on his past and look into the future toward his descendants—and not just toward a share in the riches of a Sutpen dynasty. In describing the aim of his design, Sutpen looks beyond wealth and power and status and sees lines of children, the boy and his descendants, "riven forever free from brutehood just as his own (Sutpen's) children were."

The rifle analogy, not yet stretched quite to its breaking point, may serve us one last time. To return the fire of those with fine rifles, one shoots back. The similar rifle fires in the opposite direction. The plantation owner had the little boy turned away; Sutpen will open the door and welcome the "nameless stranger" into his family. The dynastic society's bullet had struck the boy Sutpen with such tremendous force that Sutpen the man has never recovered. As he draws a bead on dynastic society, Sutpen aims to fire back the highest velocity bullet he can. He wants his return shot to strike with maximum impact.

Yet since he knows that the society wears armor to protect itself, he must design a bullet that will pierce that armor. If he lacks money, a house, a plantation, and slaves when he opens the door, his bullet would be a dud. To invite the boy in to have a share of little or nothing would seem meaningless to dynastic society. Sutpen's act would not bear on it at all. If he is wealthy but lacks a family, dynastic society would explain his act away by saying something like "You can't take it with you. No wonder he took in that ragamuffin. He needed somebody to take care of him in his old age, and he can keep him there by promising to remember him in his will." If Sutpen's wife is partly black, society would, as we have seen, judge their union to be illegal and taboo. To open the door to a white boy and invite him into such a household would, in the eyes of society, be to besmirch the status of even a nameless stranger. If Sutpen's wife is even rumored to be black, society would use the rumor to protect itself against the significance of Sutpen's act. If he has a family but no son, dynastic society would still shield itself with "When he dies, his name will vanish. He had to take that boy in. Sutpen needed an heir." In sum, then, Sutpen must have everything that dynastic society admires so that, when he opens the door and takes the boy in, society will be unable to snatch up any fact or rumor and take shelter behind it. The bullet he has designed will then strike home.

Sutpen's design would free the boy and his descendants forever from the backwoods brutehood in which Sutpen grew up and from which he raised himself. Yet in shaping that design, Sutpen remains faithful to his innocent boyhood belief in what we might call an egalitarian noblesse oblige. In Tidewater Virginia, he had learned that

> there was a difference between white men and white men not to be measured by lifting anvils or gouging eyes or how much whiskey you could drink then get up and walk out of the room. That is, he had begun to discern that without being aware of it yet. He still thought that that was just a matter of where you were spawned and how; lucky or not lucky; and that the lucky ones would be even slower and lother than the unlucky to take any advantage of it or credit for it, feel that it gave them anything more than the luck; that they would feel if anything more tender toward the unlucky than the unlucky would ever need to feel toward them. (282)

From the start, then, Sutpen meant his design to teach society the lesson that those lucky enough to have risen above brutehood should at least care about the feelings of the unlucky. Through his design Sutpen would not just preach this lesson but teach it by his own example. He would reach down and lift up one of the unlucky, a little boy, a nameless stranger knocking at his door. He may have imagined that the people lucky enough to have power would witness him opening the door, feel shame at their own hardheartedness, and change their ways. (But if his design had succeeded, those people would not, I suspect, have understood it any better than, say, most readers have. Sutpen's trouble was, indeed, innocence.)

For Sutpen as a boy even to conceive of such a design required a powerful act of imagination. His conception did not spring from the traditional source of such ideas: from the Christian maxim "love thy neighbor as thyself" exemplified in such stories as that of the Good Samaritan. Sutpen's upbringing seems to have been without religion. Nor did the conception simply grow out of Appalachian egalitarianism. While the mountain people he came from would never have sent a caller around to the back door and might have been "tender toward the unlucky" (282), taking a nameless stranger into the family surely would have lain beyond their ken. The design, of course, reaches even further than that. Sutpen intends to free the stranger's descendants from brutehood forever and, by doing so, to strike at the heart of the patriarchical structure on which not only the southern plantation but also Western culture itself had been based. That is the conception, the design, that sprang full-grown from the boy's mind.

If conceiving the design is a triumph of the imagination, Sutpen's single-minded effort to carry it out is an impressive act of determination. Rosa, the Compsons, Shreve, and the people of Yoknapatawpha look on not only in puzzlement but in awe. And so, I think, should we as we watch a man bound by time and caught in the flux of events dare to imagine this design and then dare to try to consummate it.

In another sense, too, the design is an anomaly. Faulkner was writing the book in the 1930s, in the midst of the Great Depression. Plenty of nameless strangers were knocking at front doors. Many were sent around to the back. Householders might offer a meal in exchange for a chore or give the stranger a handout, but few considered taking the stranger in and freeing him and his descendants from brutehood forever. (The social legislation of the New Deal, however, might be said to spring from a conception a little like Sutpen's.)

Readers who accept this view of Sutpen's design will find their experience of reading *Absalom, Absalom!* considerably altered. They will, rightly, continue to object to him using other people as objects to put in place, ready for the knock at the door. Yet although his means of completing his design remain ruthless and wrong, his end is now seen not as selfish aggrandizement but as an attack on the immorality of dynastic society. *Absalom, Absalom!* may, then, call upon us to answer the question that Mr. Compson, speaking of Judith, asks Quentin: "Have you noticed how so often when we try to reconstruct the causes which lead up to the actions of men and women, how with a sort of astonishment we find ourselves now and then reduced to the belief, the only possible belief, that they stemmed from some of the old virtues? the thief who steals not for greed but for love, the murderer who kills not out of lust but pity?" (150).

As we will see in more detail later, this view of Sutpen's design authenticates some of the narrators' observations that otherwise seem inappropriate. Rosa, for example, senses that Sutpen stands larger than life even though she comprehends nothing of his design except that she believes, according to the third-person narrator, that it was to be an "assault upon . . . respectability" (42); and Mr. Compson conceives of Sutpen as a figure of irony and tragedy. We may share Mr. Compson's feelings as we read Quentin's account of the moment in which Sutpen heard the knock, opened the door, and

Henry said, "Father, this is Charles" and he . . . saw the face and knew that there are situations where coincidence is no more than the little child that rushes out onto a football field to take part in the game and the players run over and around the unscathed head and go on and shock together and in the fury of the struggle for the facts called gain or loss nobody even remembers the child nor saw who came and snatched it back from dissolution;—that he stood there at his own door, just as he had imagined, planned, designed, and sure enough and after fifty years the forlorn nameless and homeless lost child came to knock at it and no monkey-dressed nigger anywhere under the sun to come to the door and order the child away; and Father said that even then, even though he knew that Bon and Judith had never laid eyes on one another, he must have felt and heard the design—house, position, posterity and all—come down like it had been built out of smoke, making no sound, creating no rush of displaced air and not even leaving any debris. (333)

This account contains two kinds of irony. What its narrators, Quentin and Mr. Compson, are saying has dramatic irony: Although neither of them has perceived the essence of Sutpen's design, their analysis of his feelings is true, but true in a way beyond their comprehension. They imagine that Sutpen foresees only the fall of his dynasty, but as he himself says to General Compson, he has also foreseen another possibility—an ironic success. For the "coincidence" that brings Bon to the door is itself ironic: Sutpen cannot open the door to him as a nameless stranger because Bon is his son.

Sutpen recognizes his own plight. Seeing himself caught in that ironic dilemma, he goes to General Compson to review his actions and to discuss the dilemma. Sutpen begins by framing the questions he wants to answer: "You see, I had a design in my mind. Whether it was a good or a bad design is beside the point; the question is, Where did I make the mistake in it, what did I do or misdo in it, whom or what injure by it to the extent which this would indicate" (329). Next, he sketches the way his dilemma arose out of his marriage in Haiti:

I had a design. To accomplish it I should require money, a house, a plantation, slaves, a family—incidentally of course, a wife. I set out to acquire these, asking no favor of any man. I even risked my life at one time, as I told you, though as I also told you I did not undertake this risk purely and simply to gain a wife, though it did have that result. But that is beside the point also: suffice that I had the wife, accepted her in good faith, with no reservations about myself, and I expected as much from them. . . . I accepted them at their own valuation while insisting on my own part upon explaining fully about myself and my progenitors: yet they deliberately withheld from me the one fact which I have reason to know they were aware would have caused me to decline the entire matter, otherwise they would not have withheld it from me—a fact which I did not learn until after my son was born. (329)

Sutpen's words here allow readers to begin inferring his reason for setting his first wife aside. The Haitian family had "deliberately withheld" a fact that, if revealed, would have made him refuse the marriage. Sutpen's context—"I [explained] fully about myself and my progenitors; yet they . . ."—implies that his wife and her parents had deliberately withheld a fact about her progenitors. The fact is, furthermore, one that revealed itself when the baby was born and, as Sutpen will soon add, precluded the woman and the child from having a part in his design. The likeliest inference is that Sutpen saw the baby, grew suspicious, questioned his wife or her parents, and learned that she was partly black. (Incidentally, although a few readers have thought that Sutpen might have set aside his wife because her baby was not his, Sutpen's phrasing here contradicts that. He says, unequivocally, "my son.")

Although the marriage had cost him "wasted years," he had sought an annulment that would be more than just, and his wife had agreed to it:

> I made no attempt to keep not only that which I might consider myself to have earned at the risk of my life but which had been given to me by signed testimonials, but on the contrary I declined and resigned all right and claim to this in order that I might repair whatever injustice I might be considered to have done by so providing for the two persons whom I might be considered to have deprived of anything I might later possess: and this was agreed to, mind; agreed to between the two parties. (330)

We have already heard Sutpen call his Haitian wife's baby "my son." Now Sutpen thinks himself ready to look ahead across the "more than thirty years" between that time and the moment when Bon stood at the door. Later Sutpen will say that the dilemma he faced with Bon at the door devolved out of his situation in Haiti (342). Sutpen's own words provide each of those bits of evidence, and all of those bits, linked together, support most readers' belief that Sutpen knows Bon to be his son.

But before Sutpen can move to his present dilemma, he feels obliged to recapitulate his previous difficulty. (At the ellipsis below, Quentin breaks off quoting Sutpen. The ellipsis represents a ten-page digression in Quentin's narrative but no gap, I believe, in Sutpen's.)

> And yet, and after more than thirty years, more than thirty years after my conscience had finally assured me that if I had done an injustice, I had done what I could to rectify it— . . . I was faced with condoning a fact which had been foisted upon me without my knowledge during the process of building toward my design, which meant the absolute and irrevocable negation of the design; or in holding to my original plan for the design in pursuit of which I had incurred this negation. I chose, and I made to the fullest what atonement lay in my power for whatever injury I might have done in choosing, paying even more for the privilege of choosing as I chose than I might have been expected to, or even (by law) required. (330, 341)

For himself—and for General Compson—Sutpen is obviously re-confirming that he has treated his first wife at least justly. On discovering the hidden fact, he had faced a painful choice. He sets out the options he had. (A flaw in parallel structure clouds his meaning. Faulkner probably intended to contrast *condoning* with *holding*, but the word *in* before *holding* throws the two gerunds out of balance.) The first of Sutpen's options was to stay with his wife and their new son on the Haitian plantation. To have taken that option would have "meant the absolute and irrevocable negation" of his design. If his design were merely to create a dynasty, his statement would make no sense, but, as we have seen, his statement is consistent with a design that leads up to opening the door and taking in the nameless stranger. So he takes his second option—"holding to my original design"—and sets his wife aside.

His recapitulation complete, Sutpen is ready to pick up the line of thought that he began with: "And yet, and after more than thirty years." Here are the words with which he describes his dilemma at finding Charles Bon at his door: "Yet I am now faced with a second necessity to choose, the curious factor of which is not, as you pointed out and as first appeared to me, that the necessity for a new choice should have arisen, but that either choice which I might make, either course which I might choose, leads to the same result" (341). We might take the word *faced* literally. In Haiti, Sutpen must have realized he had to make his first choice when he looked at the baby's face. Now, looking at that face again, he sees that he must choose again. But this time he knows that either choice he makes will prevent him from completing his design. Nevertheless, he does have a choice: he can choose either of two ways to fail. His first alternative is "Either I destroy my design with my own hand, which will happen if I am forced to play my last trump card" (341–42). This is the choice he eventually makes. He plays his last trump when he tells Henry enough to drive him to kill Bon, go into hiding, and remove himself as the foundation of the dynasty. Actually, Sutpen slightly overstates the case here. Although he appears to foresee what Henry will do, Sutpen does not realize that he himself will make two more attempts—with Rosa and Milly—to father a son and thus once again stand ready to complete his design by opening the door to the stranger. Reestablishing his design does remain possible; all he needs is another son qualified to be his heir. Still, Sutpen is essentially right, for despite his tenacity he will never again stand ready to answer the nameless stranger's knock.

If Sutpen were seeking no more than a dynasty, then the first alternative would plainly be fatal to his design. His second alternative, however, would appear to complete it, as he himself says. He might either play his last trump card "or do nothing, let matters take the course which I know they will take and see my design complete itself quite normally and naturally and successfully to the public eye" (342). That is, he will have the public effect he is seeking if he allows Bon and Judith to marry and takes Bon fully into his family. Again, I think, he overstates. If he were, say, to make Bon co-heir with Henry, the public eye might widen a bit with surprise. Sutpen would be displaying uncommon generosity for a father-in-law—and less than common sense in a society in which primogeniture preserves large holdings from fragmentation. But merely to surprise people would hardly satisfy Sutpen; he is more likely to be aiming a blow at the public eye. But even if his second alternative were to have the public effect his design seeks, Sutpen would nevertheless reject it. He would know its effect to be a fraud. His design would complete itself to the public eye and "yet to my own in such fashion as to be a mockery and a betrayal of that little boy who approached that door fifty years ago and was turned away, for whose vindication the whole plan was conceived and carried forward to the moment of this choice, this second choice devolving out of that first one" (342). Critics who believe that Sutpen seeks only a dynasty have scanted this part of Sutpen's explanation, which makes their view untenable. Judith and Bon's marriage would have been unlikely to disturb the dynasty in any way and surely not in a way that would mock and betray the little boy. But if the design calls for getting everything ready to open the door to the nameless stranger, Sutpen cannot open it to Bon. Bon is disqualified for a half dozen reasons, but for Sutpen, I think, the first five do not count. First, Bon is not nameless (although he does not bear his father's name). Second, since he is Henry's friend and college classmate, he is not a stranger. Next, at thirty years of age, he is no little boy. Nor is he impoverished as Sutpen had been when he knocked at the plantation house door. (In fact, Bon seems roughly as well-to-do as Sutpen himself.) Fifth, since Bon is or might be partly black, Sutpen could not legally take him openly into the family. (He might be included covertly as Clytie and Charles Etienne were, but that kind of inclusion would not suffice in fulfilling the design.) Those five disqualifications, strong as they may be, would not deter Sutpen, I believe, but the sixth does. Sutpen cannot open the door and take Bon in because Bon is his son. The father has an obligation to his son—an obligation, by the way, that Sutpen believes he has already kept. Sutpen's design calls for him accepting someone to whom he has no societal obligations whatever. Therefore, to open the door and take his own son into the family would indeed be "a mockery and a betrayal" to Sutpen's eye, no matter how the public eye viewed it. Sutpen therefore rejects his second alternative and begins telling Henry more and more until Henry kills Bon.

Notes

1. Subsequent quotations from *Absalom, Absalom!* are cited parenthetically in the text. Quotations follow the 1986 edition, *Absalom, Absalom! The Corrected Text* (New York: Random House, 1986).

2. Frederick L. Gwynn and Joseph L. Blotner, eds., *Faulkner in the University* (New York: Vintage, 1959), 274.

3. Henry Fielding, *Tom Jones* (1749; reprint, New York: Norton, 1973), 302.

4. Elizabeth M. Kerr, *William Faulkner's Gothic Domain* (Port Washington, N.Y.: Kennikat, 1979), 38; Cleanth Brooks, *William Faulkner: Toward Yoknapatawpha and Beyond* (New Haven, Conn.: Yale University Press, 1978), 293; David Paul Ragan, *William Faulkner's "Absalom, Absalom!" A Critical Study* (Ann Arbor, Mich.: UMI Research Press, 1987), 112.

5. Ilse Dusoir Lind, "The Design and Meaning of *Absalom, Absalom!*" in *William Faulkner: Three Decades of Criticism*, ed. Frederick J. Hoffmann and Olga W. Vickery (New York: Harcourt Brace Jovanovich, 1963), 298; Donald M. Kartiganer, *The Fragile Thread: The Meaning of Form in Faulkner's Novels* (Amherst: University of Massachusetts Press, 1979), 88; Olga W. Vickery, *The Novels of William Faulkner: A Critical Interpretation* (Baton Rouge: Louisiana State University Press, 1959), 94.

6. David L. Minter, *William Faulkner: His Life and Work* (Baltimore, Md.: Johns Hopkins University Press, 1980), 154.

7. John T. Irwin, *Doubling and Incest/Repetition and Revenge: A Speculative Reading of Faulkner* (Baltimore, Md.: Johns Hopkins University Press, 1975), 98.

8. Estella Schoenberg, *Old Tales and Talking: Quentin Compson in William Faulkner's "Absalom, Absalom!" and Related Works* (Jackson: University Press of Mississippi, 1977), 81–82.

9. Brooks, *William Faulkner*, 293.

10. Kartiganer, *Fragile Thread*, 93.

11. Schoenberg, *Old Tales and Talking*, 75, 135, 134.

12. Ibid., 80–81.

13. Hyatt Waggoner, *William Faulkner: From Jefferson to the World* (Lexington: University of Kentucky Press, 1959), 166.

14. John Lewis Longley, *The Tragic Mask: A Study of Faulkner's Heroes* (Chapel Hill: University of North Carolina Press, 1963), 118; Lind, "Design and Meaning," 288; Vickery, *Novels*, 96; Gerald Langford, *Faulkner's Revision of "Absalom, Absalom!"* (Austin: University of Texas Press, 1971), 9.

15. Brooks, *William Faulkner*, 298.

16. Irwin, *Doubling and Incest*, 116–17.

17. Kerr, *William Faulkner's Gothic Domain*, 39.

18. John T. Matthews, *The Play of Faulkner's Language* (Ithaca, N.Y.: Cornell University Press, 1982), 157.

"The Direction of the Howling"

Nationalism and the Color Line in Absalom, Absalom!

BARBARA LADD

◆　◆　◆

ALTHOUGH STORIES OF THE SLAVEHOLDER'S mixed-race children were immensely popular prior to the Civil War, most were written, as one might expect, by northern writers intent on, or at least not opposed to, stirring public sentiment against slavery. The white southern writer tended to avoid the subject. After the Civil War, however, mixed-blood characters began to appear with some frequency in the work of white southern writers like George Washington Cable, Joel Chandler Harris, Grace King, Kate Chopin, Mark Twain, and, later, William Faulkner. The issue of passing was of particular interest to many of these writers; they often depicted characters traditionally classified as "quadroons" or "octoroons," not solely to indicate that these characters had more white ancestry than black, but also to suggest their origins in the colonialist slave cultures of the Deep South and the Caribbean where they were associated with a distinct caste of free persons of mixed blood relatively unknown in the slaveholding areas of the Upper South—creoles of color. Consistent with this cultural legacy, in many of these Deep South texts the octoroon is initially attributed not with an African origin, but with a European, that is, a French or Spanish, one; the figure seldom carries any telltale sign of African ancestry. It is well into *The Grandissimes,* for instance, before the young German-American Joseph Frowenfeld learns that his dark and elegant landlord Honoré Grandissime is anyone other than a white creole. Nor, to take another example, is Armand's ancestry known until the very end of Chopin's "Désirée's Baby." In Alice Morris Buckner's *Towards the Gulf,* we are never sure if the innocent young wife carries the "fatal drop" or not. And William Faulkner's Charles Bon is taken for a white creole for a long time before he is "reconstructed." This "mistake" in identifying the octoroon as a French or Spanish creole is strategic and points to questions and anxieties that the white southerner had about his or her own future in a nationalistic and increasingly imperialistic United States.

The most salient feature of the octoroons as they are constructed in these texts is their capacity to delineate the political and cultural repressions and displacements, the submerged or forgotten history that underlies the dream of U.S. national unity. In so many of these texts, the personal history of the octoroon—his origin in a slave culture, alienation from the father, even the memory of a dead, sometimes anonymous, or monstrously rendered mother—is a psychologized recapitulation of the nationalist narrative; the octoroon's tragic fate, typically death or exile to Europe, is the destiny that always attends the past in any dream of U.S. redemptive nationalism. In most of these texts the figure is inscribed with the threatening characteristics of the displaced colonialist culture—she is almost always "aristocratic," a true product of a European-style and colonial class system, often superfluous both economically and politically, completely unsuited to the economic and political life of the American republic. The presence of the octoroon, as a sign of transgression of American racial as well as cultural ideology, is associated with the southern white protagonist's review, critique, and confirmation of his or her own political and cultural entitlements. In the octoroon, the white author creates alternative political and cultural selves, selves that for one reason or another have to be rejected, scapegoated, or otherwise silenced, but versions, nevertheless, of the postbellum white southerner in terms of the political and cultural history of the Deep South.[1] One of the most profound achievements of *Absalom, Absalom!* is its power of commentary on this (and at times its own) use of the creole of color. In *The Grandissimes,* for example, lying beneath the scapegoating of unacceptable legacies in the exile of the quadroon woman and the suicide of the octoroon man, one discerns a faint suggestion that the white heroes might someday once again have to face their own troublesome history of slavery. It is a suggestion that becomes reality in *Absalom, Absalom!* where the economy of American national innocence is itself thematized and the economy of the text is one of historical reclamation. That Charles Bon should, in following his American father (and Martinican grandfather) into the frontier wilderness of Mississippi, be transformed from "Charles Good, Charles Husband-Soon-to-be" into decadent white creole, into brother, into "the nigger that's going to sleep with your sister," and that he should then eventuate in the figure of Jim Bond, the "one nigger Sutpen left," whose howling in that wilderness has no direction, cannot be traced toward New Orleans, toward the West Indies, nor finally eastward toward Europe—a howling traceable nowhere, in fact, except inward—is the final reclamation of a damning history by Quentin Compson, as he himself lies displaced and shivering in a "cold known land."[2]

The reasons for the assignment of a French or Spanish origin to the octoroon stem directly from the history of colonization and miscegenation in the Deep South (especially Louisiana, which is this figure's site of origin in so many of these works) and particularly from the very different methods of classifying the offspring of Anglo- or Euro-African liaisons there. Prior to the Louisiana Purchase in 1803, racial classification in the creole Deep South was much more complex than in the Anglo upper South, where the status of a mixed-blood child followed that of the mother from the very beginning of the eighteenth century. Consequently, in the upper South, the figure of the mixed-blood person was classed officially and metaphorically as part of the race that was defined as "slave," a legal/political nonentity. In the Deep South, however, traditions were different. Until the Louisiana Purchase, racial classifications were based, in some ways, upon the status of the father. Children of white fathers were more easily manumitted in the Deep South, and fathers acknowledged those children more frequently than in the upper South. Children could inherit from the white father's estate more easily. Furthermore, legalized marriages between white men and black women were possible, if rare. Throughout the West Indies (including New Orleans), these children of European colonists and African women constituted a separate caste and were recognized, by law as well as by sentiment, as bearing some legitimacy as carriers of European "blood" or "culture." They could, and often did, fight against slaves during insurrections. Many identified, strongly, with the European homeland, sometimes being sent to France to be educated and, in many cases, emigrating to France where they bore even less of the stigma of African descent, it having been decreed at one point that any slave or former slave who once set foot in the French homeland would be forever free.[3] The consequence is that the mixed-blood person possessed some power of economic and political agency in these cultures and often exercised a considerable economic and political role with respect to the colony's relationship to the homeland.

The cession of colonialist Louisiana to the nationalistic United States in 1803 overturned this system of race and caste in the Louisiana Territory. The biggest difference between France and the United States with respect to racial policies derived from the fact that the French government, like many colonialist governments, found it useful to pursue a policy of assimilation between its own agents on distant frontiers and other populations. This practice had produced an intermediate black creole caste which provided the home government (as well as white creoles, or white persons born in the colonies) with assistance in the acculturation of alienated populations—that is, slaves and natives—in the colony, but because of the distance between the homeland and the colony (and for other reasons) did not threaten the "integrity"—status quo—of the colonialist government. Yet the United

States was not acquiring a new colony. The nationalistic United States was acquiring the Louisiana Territory to be a part of its expanding nation; the racist ideology of American nationalism (like many other nationalisms) had never been particularly hospitable to amalgamation. What happened was the attempted replacement of an assimilationist colonial policy with respect to racial relationships by a segregationist and nationalist policy which demanded that one prove one's status as white in order to be assimilated to any degree whatsoever into the redemptive New World nation.[4]

Initially, creoles of color seem to have had some hopes that the new American government in Louisiana would augment their status, but the segregationist ideology of the United States not only prevented any such thing from happening, but tended to eradicate the distinctions of caste already in existence. Creoles of color were in a difficult situation. They negotiated with Governor William C. C. Claiborne and his successors for a number of years in an effort to preserve some of their traditional rights of caste, but the segregationist United States had no place for them except as "free blacks" or (to use the legal term) "free men/women of color"—a class of persons the United States was already, in the 1820s, beginning to persecute in various ways. Many creoles of color emigrated to France during this period.

Whereas white racial purity had been an important commodity prior to the cession, afterward it became absolutely essential to upper-class creoles intent on maintaining their status. Creoles had to insist on it if they could do so—and they would do so, vehemently. "Creolism," or the worship of the supposedly "pure" European inheritance of the creole elite, originated in the West Indies in the revolutionary years of the late eighteenth century when blacks and mulattoes rebelled against slavery and French rule. Ironically, it seems to have functioned as a means of legitimation. Because Europeans as well as Americans had doubts about the capacities of mixed races for self-government, the reputation of a creole as "white" thus carried with it an important kind of cultural validation. But creolism increased in Louisiana during the years following the cession. Members of the creole elite began to insist that the word itself, where capitalized, always referred to the white descendant of a French or Spanish colonist, with the emphasis on "white." In actuality, "creole" (capitalized or not) had long been used in both North and South America in several different ways to classify various groups of people (as well as to classify plants, architecture, language, art, religion, political authority, and just about everything else) with respect to their place in relation to New World colonies and Old World powers. In France's Caribbean holdings (which included Louisiana and much of the Deep South) during the seventeenth and eighteenth centuries, the word was used irrespective of race to designate someone (or something) born in the colonies rather than in the French or Spanish homeland.[5] And it makes sense, of course, that in an outlying colony, where the government of the homeland finds it useful to pursue a policy of assimilation, the possession of wealth by members of the intermediate racial caste would in some instances work to break down taboos regarding intermarriage between whites and certain members of that caste. Under the new American government, however, assumptions about race, culture, and politics were vastly different.

Despite the insistence of some creoles upon white racial purity (and despite the fact that many were "white" even by U.S. standards), the association of "creole" with suggestions of colonialist race mixing persisted in the American context. As late as 1854, some American politicians in Louisiana attempted to ensure their victory by charging that their creole opponents possessed African ancestry, a charge that was by that time a de facto basis for political disfranchisement. Alexander Dimitry, one of the oldest and most "elite" of New Orleans creoles, found his own son-in-law, George Pandely, removed from office because of a supposed trace of African inheritance.[6] But the association of creoles with the slave population was not always so exclusively focused on biological "traces and taints." More often it seems to have derived from the tendency of Anglo Americans (many of whom were already uncomfortable with the presence of slavery in the United States) to associate creoles—regardless of whether they believed those creoles to be biologically "tainted" or not—with the colonialist site of slavery, miscegenation, and political and cultural degeneration. As Europeans, as Roman Catholics, and even as victims of slave insurrections, seizures of property, and torture, creoles were carriers of "traces and taints" that Americans feared as challenges to their own redemptive mission in the New World. At one point, during Thomas Jefferson's reelection campaign in 1800, U.S. congressman Robert Goodloe Harper wrote home to South Carolina that the antislavery French were about to launch an invasion of the southern states from bases in St. Domingo—an indication that the creole threat was not solely based on the specter of black revolution.[7] For a time, Americans, terrified of the effects on their own slaves of contact with refugees from the black and mulatto revolutions of the West Indies, prohibited immigration into ports at Charleston and New Orleans. It was not only black creoles who were feared, but white ones as well; the latter carried servants with them but even if servants were prohibited from entering the ports, these white refugees would talk of what they themselves had experienced. It was sometimes the fear of the effects of rumor, of talk, that made Americans distrust even white creoles. They too carried "news" that might threaten the supposed peace of the U.S. slave states. John Rutledge in 1787 reported to the Fifth Congress on the insurrectionary activities of West Indian slaves, concluding in righteous American fashion—"sufficient for the day is the evil thereof"—and advising that southern states "shut their door against any thing which had a tendency to produce the like confusion in this country."[8]

There is no doubt something biblical about Rutledge's style, but there is something equally biblical about the general American fear of rumor, of news from either "senile" Europe or "savage" Haiti. That is because there was something biblical about the way the New World nation envisioned itself as redemptive, as innocent, as untouched (or "unconfused") by history. The ethos of national innocence made it perfectly logical to link white creoles and black as constituting an intricately interconnected challenge to the mission of the United States. In 1804, while debating the kind of government most appropriate to the newly acquired Louisiana Territory, disagreement hinged on the effect of granting

a republican form of government to subjects of European mon-
archy. If they were not ripe for liberty, the consequences for the
United States could be dire. An exchange between Benjamin
Huger, a U.S. representative from South Carolina, and John Jackson, from Virginia, demonstrates very clearly exactly what those
consequences were imagined to be. Huger, arguing that creoles
were unfit to rule themselves, asserted that they "ought to be
looked upon as a certain portion of people among us [slaves] and
treated as such." Jackson objected to the analogy, but took the
opportunity to issue a plea for freedom. "I believe," he said, "that
man is the same, whether born in the United States or on the
banks of the Ganges, under an African sun or on the banks of
the Mississippi, and that a love of liberty is implanted in his nature."⁹ This is no doubt an instance of one of the early skirmishes
in the American debate over southern slavery, but it is more
relevant to this argument that black slaves would be implicated
in that debate as rhetorical surrogates in what was supposed to
be a discussion of the fitness of white creoles for republican self-
rule.

Black surrogacy makes sense, of course; it was supposed at this
time that the white creole created the man of mixed blood, educated him, gave him rights withheld from men of African descent, and in that way paved the way toward the terrifying revolutions that eventually replaced white with supposedly
degenerate mulatto governments in Haiti. (Similar suppositions
would be made with respect to the relationship between the white
American slaveholder and the slave during the mid- and late
nineteenth century in the United States.) Under the circumstances, it is no wonder that white Americans like Huger feared
Europe's presence in the New World—Europe was seen as the
source of those mulatto governments since it was presumably
French revolutionary idealism and the political pressure of France
and Great Britain to abolish slavery in the Caribbean colonies that
had led to those governments. Both France and Great Britain
even went so far as to recognize the mulatto government of Haiti,
the second independent republic in the New World (the first being
the United States itself). For slaveholders and speculators, for

whom manifest destiny, the Monroe Doctrine, and the "benevolent institution" of slavery were concepts essential to the understanding of America's messianic mission, such recognition may have been only one more example of Old World complicity with African insurrectionists in a threat against the political and economic integrity of the United States. It is within this context of anxiety that we should perhaps understand the speed with which the coming of Claiborne and the U.S. government into the Louisiana Territory resulted in a redefinition of the mixed-blood person as part of the "black," hence "slave," population. In other words, this redefinition of the creole of color was an attempt to supplant a long tradition of assimilationism which enabled those descendants of white fathers to "aspire" to (but probably never to attain) something resembling the status of the European colonist.

This particular historical and discursive context exerted a real fascination for postbellum southern writers. In it they found the same issues that would reappear in the discourse surrounding the reconstruction of the South in their own eras—race and nationalism, assimilation and segregation, black surrogacy or the moral "contamination" of the slaveholder by the slave, as well as the cultural effects of racial hybridization or amalgamation versus what might be termed racial purity, homogeneity, or (even more insidiously) "integrity." In Cable's postbellum generation and perhaps largely through Cable's work and influence there developed a tendency to represent the defeated South as "creole," to attempt to read the reconstruction of the postbellum white southerner in terms of the nationalization of white creoles during the cession years. On their surfaces, texts like *The Grandissimes* or the stories of *Old Creole Days* are optimistic reconciliation tales where white creoles become Americans or are displaced by those who do. But the complexity of the historical discourse about "creoles"—"real" or metaphoric creoles, political or literary discourse—in the American context, the very indeterminacy of the word "creole" itself especially where its racial referents were concerned, permits what Foucault might term the excavation of a counternarrative, a narrative that ran submerged in the story Cable may have wanted to tell of our nation's progress toward redemptive unity, toward a kind of political millennium wherein history would be transcended. It is a counternarrative of division and recalcitrance and defeat by history. Faulkner's *Absalom, Absalom!* will pursue this counternarrative with as much diligence as Cable's texts pursue the reconciliationist dream of reunification and transcendence of tragic history.

As I have already suggested, the term "creole" has operated as a kind of traveling (and changeable) stage upon which the drama of race and nationalism in the Deep South is enacted. When Cable appropriated the term in the 1870s in order to define the South's own complex relationship to colonialism, to slavery, and to U.S. ahistorical nationalism, he seems to have been unprepared for the outrage his characters would elicit from the elite creoles of New Orleans who were concerned not only about what they perceived as caricatures of themselves but by Cable's suggestions of race mixing among the creole elite, a suggestion it had long been essential to deny. Hence Cable's scrupulous acknowledgment in *The Creoles of Louisiana* that Creoles (capitalized) define themselves as the *white* descendants of European colonists. But the mere necessity for such insistence belies its problems, as Cable concedes when he writes that "there seems to be no more serviceable definition of the Creoles of Louisiana than . . . that they are the French-speaking, native portion of the ruling class." He is even more direct about this in an entry written for the ninth edition of the *Encyclopedia Brittanica*, where he says that the "better class" of creole in New Orleans appears to be white although "the name they [Louisiana creoles] have borrowed . . . [from the West Indies] does not necessarily imply, any more than it excludes, a departure from a pure double line of Latin descent."[10]

The newly intensified debate in the 1880s and afterward over the definition of "creole" reminds us that once again, in the post–Civil War era, the question of who might be or might become an American had resurfaced, and the implicit racism of the U.S. national mission made it once again necessary that the color line be reaffirmed. The speed with which Claiborne and the U.S. government divested creoles of color of their hopes for citizenship after the Louisiana Purchase (which took a couple of decades) is outdone by the speed with which the United States divested freedmen of their hopes after the Civil War. It took less than one decade to decide that the freedman would not become an active participant in national life except through the mediation of former white masters. The cultural debate about the capacities of the former slaveholder continued, however, in much the same fashion as the debate over the capacities of the white creole during the years following the cession. The questions were the same: the impact of slavery on the moral fiber of the former slaveholder, the slaveholder's fitness for self-government, and the impact of the former slaveholder's assimilation upon the body politic. An editorialist for the *New York Tribune* summed up a too-familiar argument: "Wherever slavery existed, there the moral sense was so blunted and benumbed . . . that the white population as a whole is to this day incapable of that sense of honor which prevails elsewhere."[11]

Despite the persistence of some suspicion that the former slaveholder was, like the creole who so often represented him in the discourse, tragically compromised—morally if not genetically— by his intimacy with the savage and the senile, the rhetoric of southern redemption was largely inspiriting. In an 1882 address to the graduating class at the University of Mississippi, Cable called for southerners to transcend the past, to put history behind them. In this talk, he objected to the phrase "New South," suggesting that we aim for the "No South": "Does the word sound like annihilation? It is the farthest from it. It is enlargement. It is growth. It is a higher life."[12] Yet neither the reality of political and economic life in the South nor the literature of the period bears out the promise of Cable's optimistic rhetoric. The white southerner's return to the reunified nation during the significantly named Redemption Era that followed Reconstruction was less a transcendence of southern history in a redemptive national body than a return to the white southerner of the rights to reconstitute, or attempt to reconstitute, a racial order which imitated, in some respects, that of antebellum years. And, predictably enough, it was less a redemption from than a renewal of certain racist assumptions about the proper relationship between black and white in the United States. It also revealed the continuing assumption that it was the white southerner's particular history and nature that would fit him to deal with the dangerous African American. There is in this assumption something of the idea that Emerson had attributed to the abolitionist: that "the negro [and] the negro-holder are really of one party."[13]

It might have been expected that the fundamental racism of the American culture would result in a "redemption" that amounted to the return of the African American to a semislave status and the return of the white South to a marginal status with respect to a national mission imagined in terms of its capacity to transcend history. Certainly the politics of the Redemption Era returned the southern white man to power in the South but also led to the South's increasing political, economic, and cultural isolation and to a growing—because related—southern hysteria about the dangers of "amalgamation." This hysteria seems to have developed from the white southerner's awareness, at least on some level, that the color line was little more than a reflection of the political, cultural, and economic alienation of selected populations, that he himself was, in some respects, alienated by that very color line from the U.S. national mission, and that to be alienated in the United States was, whatever the color of your skin, to be "black."

Lest this sound a bit extreme, we might recall that it is the putative "blackness" of the mysterious stranger who appears "white" that preoccupied the white southern writer, as it preoccupied the U.S. court system during these years.[14] This preoccupation was based on the belief that political and economic equality for the freedman would inevitably lead to "social equality," to the "contamination" of white bodies with black blood, to the "degeneration" of white civilization in the South. These terrors themselves reflected doubts—on the part of the white southerner as well as the rest of the nation—about the white southerner's capacity to accomplish the transcendence of history that was required before he could be effectively redeemed. They also reiterated the issues of assimilation versus segregation that had preoccupied the nation during the original cession of the Louisiana Territory to the United States and echoed against a new reality, the reality of imperialism, which ironically placed the white American abroad in the same position in which the white southerner had been placed on the domestic front.

This complex history of cultural displacement is of particular relevance to *Absalom, Absalom!* where the creole becomes the means through which post–Civil War white southerners dramatize their own recalcitrance. In a sense, *Absalom, Absalom!* will eventually appropriate the figure of the creole of color as he is constructed by earlier white writers like Cable, but Faulkner's text also transfigures the construction in ways that result in a stronger, more deliberate, and less qualified critique of the ahistorical nationalism that would seek to deny or transcend U.S. complicity with Europe and with Africa in the development of a New World nation. In *Absalom, Absalom!* unlike so much of the earlier literature, there is not even the illusion of a happy ending—no marriage, no dynasty, no legitimate offspring.

In this work, the hubris of an American innocent, Thomas Sutpen, creates a retributive agent in the figure of Charles Bon, a mystery whom we never see, who never speaks except through the mouths of those who tell his story, who has no identity independent of their projections.[15] The fact remains, however, that the significance of Charles Bon—like that of the dark Honoré in *The Grandissimes*—evolves from the relationship between the history of the Deep South with respect to U.S. nationalistic expansion in the early nineteenth century and the political, rhetorical situation of the white southerner in the years after the Civil War. It is also important to note that the construction and reconstruction of Charles Bon recapitulates the construction and reconstruction of the creole Deep South as site of the struggle between an ahistorical ideology of American transcendence of history and American history itself. In other words, the issue of race mixing and the effort to keep the mixed blood out of the white family (or nation) in *Absalom, Absalom!* is a return, through the medium of psychological family drama, to the issue of assimilation versus segregation of the creole as it was defined and discussed in the political discourse of American nationalism between 1803 and the beginning of the Civil War.

Charles Bon, that "durn French feller" (133), appears suddenly in the middle of frontier Mississippi. He comes—at least initially we are told he comes—from New Orleans, the site of the colonialist culture represented by so many of the octoroons in U.S. literature. And like so many of them he possesses a fatal (and fatalistic) creole sophistication and later, much later, for some speakers (and only for some speakers), the "taint" of African ancestry—a detail that is considered fact by most Faulkner scholars and probably comes as close to fact as any other detail concerning Bon, which is to say not very close at all. The real fact, of course, is that the conversation that supposedly reveals Bon as black is not included in the text, which leaves open the possibility that Quentin might have misconstrued, or invented, such a conversation for his own purposes. The reason for the murder of Charles Bon by Henry Sutpen in 1865 becomes one of the novel's central mysteries—as central as the mystery of Thomas Sutpen's character to which that murder is intricately tied—and the need to create a satisfactory explanation for that murder becomes an obsession for each speaker.

We, as readers, do not know exactly why Henry Sutpen killed Charles Bon. All we can be sure of is that, for all of the speakers except Miss Rosa, Henry was driven by some necessity for preserving his family's (and the nation's) purity. In fact, what we are more than likely meant to know is that the story of the murder constructed by each speaker is remarkably representative of that speaker's sense of his own defeat within a specific historical context. In other words, whether the "purity" that Henry is seen as protecting is constructed in terms that are nationalistic, familial, or racial depends upon who the speaker is, or rather *when* he is. Repeatedly, Faulkner warns us that the story is "invented" (335) by the tellers of the tale, and "true enough" to boot, but that the telling of the story is a matter of "hearing and sifting and discarding the false and conserving what seemed true, or fit the preconceived" (316). Under the circumstances Faulkner's decision to embed the truth in the drama of performance, to bind infor-

mation so tightly to interpretation, leads the reader to ask not
only who or what Charles Bon was—whether he was black or
white, possible son or would-be husband—but to ask who and
what the speakers are with respect to the Charles Bon they construct. And it is clear that who and what they are has everything
to do with history as it happened in the Deep South in the years
between the cession of the Louisiana Territory and the early twentieth century. It is the relationship of two postwar generations—
represented by Jason Compson and his son Quentin, respectively—to that history (which in this text takes the form of the
"preconceived") that makes the tale. The final irony is that whatever the rationale, the murder itself did happen and, instead of
releasing the Sutpens and those whom they represent from the
tragedies of their own history, served to accelerate their decline
into that history. In this sense, *Absalom, Absalom!* is as much a novel
about the return of a tragic history to the American South—in
the guises first of white creole decadence, then of blackness, and
in the form of retributive justice—as *The Grandissimes* and other,
earlier octoroon stories are stories of the attempted (and often
failed) expulsion of history in the exile of the man of mixed blood
and extranational loyalties.

There is little doubt that Faulkner wrote *Absalom, Absalom!* out
of a deep familiarity with the political and cultural situation in
both New Orleans and Haiti, especially as it was perceived by and
important to nineteenth- and early twentieth-century southerners such as the ones upon whom Jason and Quentin Compson
were modeled. Faulkner's familiarity with this context should not
be surprising, given his Deep South origins; the arrival of his own
most famous ancestor, William Clark Falkner, in the southwest-
ern frontier during the first half of the nineteenth century when
Mississippi was still very much frontier and creole New Orleans
was a newly acquired southern terminus (hardly sixty miles
south); and his own time in the French Quarter of New Orleans
and in France in the mid-1920s.

Thomas Sutpen lives in French Haiti from the early 1820s to
1833. He serves for a time as overseer on a sugar plantation owned
by a French planter; he "subdues" an uprising of Haitian slaves

who threaten the planter with their voodoo in what is probably one of the many skirmishes that made up the long and bloody Haitian revolution of the late eighteenth and nineteenth centuries; he marries Eulalia, the planter's daughter by a Spanish creole; his son, Charles Bon, is born in 1829; and Sutpen makes the "discovery" that causes him to repudiate Eulalia in 1831, two years before he arrives in Yoknapatawpha County and not long before his spurned wife arrives, with their son, in New Orleans—still a logical destination for a West Indian creole at this time.

That a man like the young Sutpen, obsessed with his redemptive design, should end up in the West Indies is probable. Despite the U.S. refusal to recognize the mulatto government of Jean Paul Boyer, Haiti, of all the West Indian islands, was of great economic importance to the United States. The Caribbean was the logical theater for dreams of American expansion in the pre–Civil War era (as it would be once again in Quentin Compson's era) since the desire for expansion had certainly not been exhausted by the acquisition of the Louisiana Territory. What did happen between that time and the years preceding the Civil War was the development of a more articulate ideology of expansion in which the idea of the design as redemptive was more pronounced and more intricately entangled with the ideology of race and slavery. Throughout the pre–Civil War era, dreams of worldly wealth for white Americans and dreams of a millennial civilization, or terrestrial paradise, where even the enslavement of the darker races could be seen as a step toward lifting them out of such darkness and into the light of God's righteous millennium, were united in that rhetoric. By extension, it was of great importance to preserve the American nation from contamination by decadent Europe and its leveling influence, already visible in the formation of Haiti as the first mulatto government in the New World. The question—of course, the same question that Americans put to themselves in their debate over national assimilation of white creoles—was whether such preservation was possible. It was a question that would be readily appropriated by the postbellum white American as a way to explain the South's defeat as somehow preordained. Just as importantly it was a question that would be readily appropriated by William Faulkner as the key to the construction and reconstruction of Charles Bon and the means through which Faulkner might explore the implications of his own generation's imperialist designs.

In the light of Faulkner's critique of millennialist ideology, it is certainly of some ironic import that the architect for Sutpen's mansion should be a colonialist Frenchman from Martinique, because in so many ways the slave culture that the Anglo planter in the Deep South inherited (if not the slave culture he envisioned) was established upon a West Indian, predominantly French and Spanish, foundation. During the time that Sutpen's mansion is going up, the architect, "in his formal coat and his Paris hat and his expression of grim and embittered amazement lurked about the environs of the scene with his air something between a casual and bitterly disinterested spectator and a condemned and conscientious ghostamazement . . . not at the others and what they were doing so much as at himself, at the inexplicable and incredible fact of his own presence" (38). Later, Charles Bon will share not only a French cultural identification but also the Frenchman's spectral relationship to the American slaveholder:

> From the moment when he [Bon] realized that Sutpen was going to prevent the marriage if he could, he (Bon) seems to have withdrawn into a mere spectator, passive, a little sardonic, and completely enigmatic. He seems to hover, shadowy, almost substanceless, a little behind and above all the other straightforward and logical, even though (to him) incomprehensible, ultimatums and affirmations and defiances and challenges and repudiations, with an air of sardonic and indolent detachment like that of a youthful Roman consul making the Grand Tour of his day among the barbarian hordes which his grandfather conquered. (93)

Bon, like the French architect (who may be, at least rhetorically and symbolically, the "grandfather" referred to), is a ghostly spectator who seems condemned to haunt the site of a former life.

Despite the intricate historical relationships among New World slave cultures, the expansion of the United States during the early nineteenth century placed the colonialist cultures of Europe in just this position with respect to the developing nation in the New World, a nation that defined itself as the working out in a New World wilderness of a providential design impossible in the corrupt atmosphere of Europe. That this French architect should so clearly prefigure Charles Bon suggests that Faulkner was well aware of the inevitable persistence of the displaced in any design which sought to transcend a historical relationship among various cultures and peoples.

It is the persistence of history in the New World—in the discourse of New World speakers—and its capacity to undermine official American innocence that seems most to interest Faulkner. His rich historicism is strikingly apparent in his handling of the voices that construct and reconstruct the story of Charles Bon, constructing and reconstructing themselves in the process. According to Rosa Coldfield, who came of age in the antebellum South—and for whom the Civil War is a consequence rather than a cause—Bon's murder is inexplicable except as the inevitable consequence of Sutpen's, the American innocent's, own demonic nature (15). For Rosa, Bon is "Charles Good, Charles Husband-Soon-To-Be," an unseen prince who is nothing less than a miracle, a civilized man on the Mississippi frontier. Thus for Rosa, the marriage between Judith and Bon is "forbidden without rhyme or reason or shadow of excuse" (18). But according to those speakers who came of age after the Civil War, including Jason Compson and his son Quentin, the murder is made necessary by Bon's nature, not by Sutpen's—at least that is the kind of motivating cause these speakers pursue with greatest energy. Not surprisingly, these are the speakers for whom the Civil War has become a kind of originary moment wherein the Sutpens, like their textual descendants the Compsons, find their motive and rationale.

Jason and Quentin Compson are nevertheless quite different as speakers, and their stories of Bon—of the South's (and of America's) repressed history—diverge, especially insofar as race figures into the stories, chiefly because for Faulkner they represent two distinct generations whose understanding of the United States and of their own relationship to the United States and to the history of slavery and race in the Deep South is very different. Although both imagine Bon as a creole possessed of the expected creole decadence and capable of corrupting the innocence of Sutpens, it is only in Quentin's narrative that Bon is constructed as black. For Jason—whose understanding of Bon and of the South's defeat seems to have developed free of the impact of U.S. imperialism and radical racist ideas of race and culture (which became popular only in the late 1880s, long after Jason would have first heard of Bon and begun to formulate his own understanding)— Bon is simply "the curious one" in this American frontier, "apparently complete, without background or past or childhood," a man who invades an "isolated puritan country household" and seduces both brother and sister in a way more inevitable than deliberate (93). For Jason, preoccupied with the scene of a colonizing and corrupting European empire and its impact on the American Deep South, the white creole Bon is representative of a retributive power perceived as culminating in his inheritance of the French architect's ability to "curb the dream of grim and castlelike magnificence" (38) toward which Sutpen aims. The difference between Jason and his antebellum forebears, of course, is that the postbellum Jason Compson identifies *himself* more closely with the white creole Bon than with the Sutpens. Charles Bon is, in Donald Kartiganer's words, Jason Compson "writ large," a man "equipped with a cynicism that rivals Mr. Compson's own," and, fundamentally, a man who shares with Jason Compson the kind of cultural superfluity that results from having inherited, like the French aristocrats in Faulkner's early manuscript "Elmer," "an old and splendid thing worn out with time."[16] It is difficult to resist Kartiganer's reading, for the South's defeat in the Civil War has left Jason in the very position he constructs for Bon, as "complete [yet] without background . . . a mere spectator" (93). Jason's heroic ancestors are separated from him not only by time or death but by a kind of political legitimacy to which he, like the white creole, can no longer aspire; unlike him, they are "not dwarfed and involved but distinct, uncomplex who had the gift of loving once or dying once instead of being diffused and scattered creatures drawn blindly limb from limb from a grab bag and assembled, author and victim too of a thousand homicides and a thousand copulations and divorcements" (89). In this passage Jason reveals his own sense of confused and violent origins as well as the alienation of the southerners whom he represents from the ordering power of a nationalistic discourse, an alienation traceable to 1865 and, in this text, to the murder of Bon.

When Jason attempts to explain that murder, he resorts predictably to the terms of his own compelling narrative of the encounter of the nationalistic American and the colonizing European. Henry Sutpen, the "legitimate" ("puritan") son of Thomas Sutpen, might have found that Bon had to be killed for the fatal French assimilationism which allowed him to maintain, in a semblance of legitimacy, an octoroon woman and their son (100)—a story which recapitulates the response of the segregationist United States to the existence of the intermediate caste of creoles of color in the Caribbean and reflects, in terms of domestic/sexual history, American distrust of the French as authors of the black revolutions in the Caribbean. In murdering Bon, then, Henry (according to the logic of Jason Compson's version of events) may have been attempting to preserve Thomas Sutpen's vision of order and hierarchy from the example of Europe. That Bon maintained a black family and perhaps even carried their pictures with him must have seemed to Henry a violation of the very terms upon which civilization must be established. One must note, however, that for Jason the threat (and the seductive promise) of "racemixing" is situated in the female octoroon, whom he imagines as a creature utterly powerless to challenge or threaten the white estate except as a tool of the colonist. The relish with which Jason describes her home in New Orleans, closed and hidden, its crumbling walls and old doorkeeper like a figure from a French woodcut, confines her threat within the displaced colonialist culture—far removed by the ideologies of race, gender, and nation from any possibility of a serious claim to the white estate, except through the agency of the European colonist (112–13).

It is, however, Quentin's appropriation and deployment of this horror of confused and violent origins in his reconstruction of Charles Bon himself as a "white nigger" that is of greater significance. It is, after all, Quentin Compson as "commonwealth" (12), as heir of southern history, its final dying original, who completes—and is himself completed by—the story begun by Rosa Coldfield and continued by Jason. It should not be surprising that a white southerner of Quentin's generation, caught between a history that associates him with Africa and with Europe and a political rhetoric that would assimilate him to a nationalistic, increasingly imperialistic, and racist ideal, would dramatize his situation with respect to the very best representative of that situation, the creole man of mixed blood.

Central to Quentin's reconstruction of Bon are the preoccupations of his own turn-of-the-century South with questions of white racial purity and the American mission. In his revision, black Haiti replaces white creole New Orleans as the locus for Bon, who eventually becomes a representative of that troubled "mulatto nation"—as well as a harbinger of America's own assimilation to a like future through the inevitable "amalgamation" that racists of Quentin's generation felt would result from any recognition of blacks as equal citizens of the United States. The extent and the nature of this cultural hysteria are most visible in the work of radical racists like Thomas Dixon, Jr., and Robert Lee Durham. There is little question that in the work of these writers the octoroon has been characterized very differently than by Cable and other Deep South writers of his generation. In these explicitly racist fictions, the octoroon figure is marked by an inclination to sexual excess and violence associated with images of "African" savagery, his or her white skin nothing more than a mask to hide the destructive fires associated with the heavily sexualized "dark continent," a place that ostensibly exists prior to history and political order and the site of a radical chaos which is presented as a danger to the American redemptive mission. Of

course Quentin's narrative eventually does work its way around
to this sexualized vision of an African Bon, but the development
of this Bon as part of a longer historical process of "inventing"
Bon serves as a means of textual containment and commentary
on that vision. As a matter of fact, it is really not very far, in
terms of metaphorical development, from Jason's creation of Bon
(and by extension of *himself*) as cynical or fatalistic European
charged with the seduction of the South through the unveiling
of the white Negro—the beautiful octoroon woman or "apotheosis of chattelry" (112)—to Quentin's creation of Bon (and by
extension of *himself*) as the white negro, a man who has inherited
both the violence and the illegitimacy, and whose blood demands
vengeance. Both Jason's and Quentin's accounts are dramatiza-
tions of the white southerner's sense of his own construction by
postbellum history. By extension one might also note that Bon's
capacity to contain all of history in this new role of "nigger"
(corrupt European and dispossessed elder brother as well as "nigger")—as if the "white nigger" is indeed the "supreme apotheosis"
not only of chattelry but of all of history—offers us some sense
of the extremity of Quentin's position as both American and as
southern heir to a past he cannot transcend.

Equally important to the reconstruction of Bon is the context
of U.S. imperialism. What Theodore Roosevelt called the New
Nationalism may have been the logical outcome of the reunion
of North and South after Reconstruction, but by the end of the
century, nationalism had become imperialism—at the very least,
what Benedict Anderson calls "official nationalism" had become
useful rhetorically for the agenda of empire. At the turn of the
century the imperialistic designs of the United States tapped
the same racist ambitions and anxieties in white Americans that
the expansionist designs of slaveholders had tapped a half century
before.[17] The concurrent rise of U.S. imperialism abroad and radical racism inside the United States, the latter holding that
blacks—freed from the civilizing influences of slavery—were ret-
rogressing into savagery and would eventually die out in the
competition with whites, was no coincidence. One might, in fact,
read the hysteria of radical racism as an appropriation, on the

domestic front, of the imperialistic agenda of redemption, the burnings and dismemberments of black bodies a dramatization on the physical body of the effects of colonization on the black cultural bodies of Cuba, Puerto Rico, and the Philippines, acquired by the United States in the Spanish-American War. The U.S. agenda was quite clear. Albert Beveridge may have said it best:

> God has not been preparing the English-speaking and Teutonic peoples for a thousand years for nothing but vain and idle self-contemplation and self-admiration. No. He made us master organizers of the world to establish system where chaos reigned. He has given us the spirit of progress to overwhelm the forces of reaction throughout the earth. He has made us adept in government that we may administer government among savage and senile peoples. Were it not for such a force as this the world would relapse into barbarism and night. And of all our race He has marked the American people as His chosen nation to finally lead in the redemption of the world.[18]

Beveridge made this speech to the U.S. Senate at the turn of the century, marshaling in only a few lines the kind of rhetoric that William Faulkner would conjure in his development of Quentin as both victim and agent of such imperialist ideology.

Quentin's narrative begins in the winter following his discovery of Henry Sutpen in the old mansion. What this means is that it begins after he has supposedly learned that Bon was black. Nevertheless, Quentin does not reveal this putative solution to the text's various mysteries until very late in the story, allowing the detail of miscegenation to seem to be arrived at by a process of deduction from the premise of Bon's origins in a colonialist slave culture—a process that recapitulates the psychopolitical drama of the white southerner in the novel, whose own origins in a colonialist slave culture eventually lead to his defeat and alienation. At first, we know only that Charles Bon is a mysterious French creole, but as Quentin's story unfolds, Bon is transformed from colonialist creole into Thomas Sutpen's elder son into "the nigger that's going to sleep with your sister" (358). In other words,

Quentin's narrative transforms Charles Bon from a man who had, at a prior stage of history (Jason Compson's), some—albeit negligible—claim upon the white estate (a claim to assimilation) into someone who cannot possibly, according to the conventional logic of American radical racism, sustain any such claims.

It is here that the extent of Quentin Compson's own alienation from the ordering power of the nationalist discourse becomes most evident. Quentin's Charles Bon—Quentin Compson "writ large"—wants the father's recognition more than he wants his father's daughter. Bon's lawyer (never mentioned in Jason's story and certainly more believable as a product of the imaginations of two turn-of-the-century college students than as a realistic representation of antebellum legal counsel) is more intent on pressing the claims of the (at this point) white and creole Bon on the American father's estate than in pressing his suit of love. In fact, the *"daughter? daughter? daughter?"* (309) is hardly more than a means for acquiring some portion of entitlement to that estate. Bon's ultimatum, implicit but nevertheless clear enough, requires either recognition by the American father and all it entails or incestuous marriage to the daughter. It is also implicit, but clear enough, that the ultimatum is designed to lead to the father's recognition of Bon and not to Bon's marriage to Judith. What it does lead to, as Quentin imagines it, is Thomas Sutpen's revelation to Henry that Bon is not white, a revelation that changes everything. Bon's claims to the white estate are rendered absolutely monstrous, and Bon is transformed from alienated son into "the nigger that's going to sleep with your sister," an agent for the destruction of the white estate.

It is here that the post-1890 context out of which Quentin constructs his story becomes most evident. The phrase that Bon uses during his final confrontation with Henry—"the nigger that's going to sleep with your sister"—would not likely have been used in the South of 1865, when Charles Bon is supposed by Quentin Compson to have uttered it, although it had become a racist rallying cry by the turn of the century when Quentin Compson constructs this imaginary scene. (It is indeed fascinating that Quentin attributes that line to Charles Bon himself, as if giving the character an opportunity to comment, somewhat prematurely, upon his own development as a construct.) In Quentin's South, a South growing more and more isolated from the rest of the country, the terms "black" and "brother" became just reconcilable enough in the rhetoric of radical racism which claimed that the black man wanted nothing so much as the white woman, just possible enough to function as the white southerner's ultimate nightmare of alienation. As African, as "black beast," as "the nigger that's going to sleep with your sister," and yet as brother nonetheless, Charles Bon represents all that the post-1890 white southerner most feared: the gradual usurpation of political, familial, and economic purity—legitimacy, recognition by the national body or by the father—by a mulatto brother or brother-in-law, a usurpation almost always associated with the degeneration of a proud civilization into a "mongrel" future.

What this substitution of "nigger" for "brother" suggests is the existence in Quentin's narrative of a perceived necessity, played out in a rhetorical maneuver, of denying the Fifteenth Amendment, of denying, in effect, that one can be *both* black and brother. In 1913, Senator James K. Vardaman spoke directly to this point: "I unhesitatingly assert that political equality for the colored race leads to social equality. Social equality leads to race amalgamation, and race amalgamation leads to deterioration and disintegration."[19] What Vardaman and those for whom he spoke reveal in such statements is the fear of the degeneration of their own lines, political as well as familial. Under the circumstances, it is relatively easy to see that what the white racist is attempting to protect by refusing to acknowledge a black man as brother or "social equal"—the purity of the family line as a kind of metaphor for citizenship and rights to govern—is in *Absalom, Absalom!* exactly what such a policy does not protect, precisely because of the possibility that an unrecognized (and unrecognizable) black son might, through passing unknown into the white family, violate laws against miscegenation as well as incest. Ironically, Thomas Sutpen's refusal to acknowledge his mulatto son, to give him the father's name which would "place" him with respect to his lineage (a placing that had been possible in the Caribbean cultures that preceded the coming of Americans like Sutpen into the Deep South), is exactly what precipitates the dual threats of incest and miscegenation.

If we recall, for a moment, Quentin's often-discussed obsession with his sister Caddy—the incestuous desires that lead him in *The Sound and the* Fury to transform his own virginity into the sign of incest consummated and reified—the nexus of issues of racial (familial) purity and national legitimacy in the novel becomes clearer as the site of the white southerner's own struggle for cultural redemption, for an escape from history into the millennial New World nation of the United States. Bon is Quentin himself writ large in the language of his own defeat as a construct who almost, but not quite, gets away with the incest Quentin imagines that he has committed, longs to have committed, and fears desperately that he has committed—an incest that, as John Irwin has suggested, operates as a metaphor for origination and authority in Quentin Compson but also carries with it the threat, as well as the promise, of death.[20]

"Amalgamation is incest," wrote one Mississippian as early as 1854: "Impurity of race is against the law of nature. Mulattoes are monsters. The law of nature is the law of God. The same law which forbids consanguinous amalgamation forbids ethnical amalgamation. Both are incestuous."[21] It is a powerful equation when read in terms of Quentin's narrative of race and sex, where the monster who must be destroyed, the figure who "owns the terror," is both black and brother—despite the rhetoric that would deny that relationship—in other words a dramatization of the white racist's most nightmarish vision of his own future under the new dispensation. If the supreme apotheosis of slavery is the octoroon woman, the supreme apotheosis of emancipation, in the mind of a radical racist, may be the "white nigger." It is particularly important in this reading of Quentin Compson's paradoxical desire for and rejection of the "black" brother that this is a phrase used at this time not only to refer to the octoroon but also to describe certain kinds of traitorous whites who exhibited what was perceived as "morally black" behavior—incest, for example.[22] Quentin's incestuous desires are thus not only configured as the logical outcome of his own loss of cultural legitimacy which could effectively "name" and thereby "place" him (in a parallel of the black creole's loss of such legitimacy during the cession years), but they do indeed redefine him as a "white nigger," as "morally black"; they make him, in a sense, "the nigger that's going to sleep with your sister." As a matter of fact, Shreve McCannon, Quentin's audience and cocreator for the story, suggests this very thing. "You've got . . . one nigger Sutpen left," he tells Quentin at the end of *Absalom, Absalom!*

> I think that in time the Jim Bonds are going to conquer the western hemisphere. Of course it won't quite be in our time and of course as they spread toward the poles they will bleach out again like the rabbits and the birds do, so they won't show up so sharp against the snow. But it will still be Jim Bond; and so in a few thousand years, I who regard you will also have sprung from the loins of African kings. (378)

The subtext, of course, is that Quentin himself has already, in some sense, "sprung from the loins of African kings." Shreve's prophecy makes it apparent that, already, through a process of constructing the story in terms of the most deadly fear, assimilation/amalgamation, it is the white southerner himself who finally and ironically "owns the terror" (369–70) because he has been transformed (or has transformed himself), through the rhetoric of defeat as it is used in a racist and nationalistic culture, into the victim, into the European and African ghosts whom the United States, obsessed with its own ahistorical uniqueness, fears so intensely. In other words, when a nation envisions itself in ahistorical and millennialist terms, as new and as redemptive, it denies its relationships to the past, even to the history of its making. The consequence for a white southerner who had been prior to his defeat by the United States at the very center of a southern nationalism that envisioned itself in terms remarkably similar to those of the United States (as redemptive) is that—by the logic of his own rhetoric—he has become through his defeat the inheritor of history as well as the bearer of prior displacements in his own.

In the climactic scene between Henry Sutpen and Charles Bon at the gate to Sutpen's mansion, the segregationist ideal is enforced. No marriage takes place between Charles Bon and Judith Sutpen. By all the lights of radical racist ideology, this is preservation, the laying of foundations for a sunny future. But in Faulkner's text, the segregationist dream is subverted into its own nightmare. Instead of progress, redemption from the sins of the fathers, and transcendence of history, we are left with degeneration, damnation, and submergence into history. The fact is that Quentin fails. It is not so much that he fails to penetrate the mysteries of the past—that failure is inevitable. The more significant failure is that he reconstructs Charles Bon in the same terms, according to the same economy of exclusion that his fathers had used in their construction of America on the preposterous ideal of transcendence of history. Like his fathers, Quentin is incapable of reading his own kinship with those populations alienated by New World ideology as anything other than a sign of his own degeneracy. Quentin's is a failure of imagination, an inability to rewrite the old stories. Quentin solves no mystery of Charles Bon; he solves no murder. Bon remains invisible; the murder remains unexplained; and Quentin remains as much a victim of the past as his many fathers.

But if Quentin's status as a victim of history makes him a compelling representation of the southerner of Faulkner's generation, it also makes him equally compelling as a representation of Faulkner's future American. Certainly Shreve's metaphor of migration suggests that the implications of amalgamation are not exclusively for that region of the United States known as the "South," although one has to acknowledge that the alienated status of the American South at this period is essential to the story. The reality of implication suggests, instead, that in *Absalom, Absalom!* the South is not only a discrete region within the geographical borders of the United States, but a phase within the narrative of nationalism, a tropic site wherein that narrative originates and from which it flees. The power of *Absalom, Absalom!* is to be found in its capacity to subvert, on southern terrain, those rhetorical strategies the United States has used to constitute itself as a coherent and culminating entity, distinct from its colonialist past and slavery. Carolyn Porter observes of *Absalom, Absalom!* that "by the time we find out what is going on, we are already implicated in it."[23] For all of its engagement with the alienating discourses of racial, national, and regional divisions, *Absalom, Absalom!* is a study in implication.

Notes

1. I am focusing on the construction of this figure in the work of white writers. African-American writers have used the figure of the creole of color often, and in ways very different from those devised by whites. Certainly, in African-American literature as in Anglo-American literature, the octoroon is an alienated figure; however, in much African-American literature, she is also an index of racial progress, and the drama often moves the character from an alienated condition to an identification with and commitment to the African-American community. For a good discussion of the use of the mixed-blood figure in African-American literature, see J. Dickson Bruce's *Black American Writing from the Nadir: The Evolution of a Literary Tradition, 1877–1915* (Baton Rouge: Louisiana State University Press, 1989), 11–55.

Furthermore, it is important to acknowledge that in Anglo-American literature the submergence (not to be mistaken for the complete eradication) of Africa as site of the octoroon's origins may be evidence of an anxiety around the issues of race that is deeper than any political anxieties associated with the Old World. Be that as it may, neither Cable's Honoré Grandissime, free man of color, nor William Faulkner's Charles Bon possesses any of the expected tags of African ancestry—strange shiverings around slaveyards, uncanny resemblances to black characters, and so on. It is the meaning of the characteristics the figure does possess that is of primary interest in this study.

2. William Faulkner, *Absalom, Absalom!* (New York: Random House, 1936), 148, 358, 378, 250. All further quotations from *Absalom, Absalom!* are from this edition and cited in parentheses in the text.

3. Gwendolyn Midlo Hall's recent *Africans in Colonial Louisiana: The De-*

velopment of Afro-Creole Culture in the Eighteenth Century* (Baton Rouge: Louisiana State University Press, 1992), especially her chapter "The Pointe Coupée Post: Race Mixture and Freedom at a Frontier Settlement," is invaluable for an understanding of race mixing and passing on the French colonialist frontier.

For discussions of the traditions of classifying children of black-white liaisons in the Deep South and the West Indies and the political and economic consequences of the cession of the Louisiana Territory to the United States, see also Ira Berlin, *Slaves without Masters: The Free Negro in the Antebellum South* (New York: Random House, 1974), 97–98; Carl Degler, *Neither Black nor White: Slavery and Race Relations in Brazil and the United States* (New York: Macmillan, 1971), 226–45; Laura Foner, "The Free People of Color in Louisiana and St. Domingue," *Journal of Social History* 3 (Summer 1970): 406–30; Winthrop Jordan, *White over Black: American Attitudes toward the Negro, 1550–1812* (New York: Norton, 1977), 167; James Kinney, *Amalgamation! Race, Sex, and Rhetoric in the Nineteenth-Century American Novel* (Westport, Conn.: Greenwood, 1985); John G. Mencke, *Mulattoes and Race Mixture: American Attitudes and Images, 1865–1918* (Ann Arbor, Mich.: UMI Research Press, 1979), 1–36; and H. E. Sterkx, *The Free Negro in Antebellum Louisiana* (Rutherford, N.J.: Fairleigh Dickinson University Press, 1972).

The following discussions focus specifically upon the coming of the United States into the Louisiana Territory: Alice Dunbar Nelson, "People of Color in Louisiana," *Journal of Negro History* 1 (1916): 361–76, and 2 (1917): 51–78; Donald E. Everett, "Émigrés and Militiamen: Free Persons of Color in New Orleans, 1803–1815," *Journal of Negro History* 38 (1953): 377–402; Thomas Marc Fiehrer, "The African Presence in Colonial Louisiana," in *Louisiana's Black Heritage,* ed. Robert R. MacDonald, John R. Kemp, and Edward F. Haas (New Orleans: Louisiana State Museum, 1977); and Charles Barthelemy Rousseve, *The Negro in Louisiana* (New Orleans, La.: Xavier University Press, 1937), 47–48; the speech by Robespierre included in the appendix, "Speech on the Condition of the Free Men of Color in the French Colonies," 173–74; and a series of documents under the heading "Legislation Restricting Free People of Color," 175–78.

4. For a discussion of the different policies of nationalist and colonialist expansion, especially as worked out in the Deep South context, see Arnold R. Hirsch and Joseph Logsdon, eds., *Creole New Orleans: Race and Americanization* (Baton Rouge: Louisiana State University Press, 1992), especially the essays by Joseph G. Tregle, Jr., "Creoles and Americans," and Gwendolyn Midlo Hall, "The Formation of Afro-Creole Culture." The introduction to part 2, "The American Challenge," is also useful.

For a discussion of nationalism and its connections to ideas of "race" as well as for a good discussion of race in the creole New World, see Benedict Anderson's *Imagined Communities: Reflections on the Origin and Spread of Nationalism,* rev. ed. (New York: Verso, 1991).

5. Hirsch and Logsdon, *Creole New Orleans,* 60, 98, 132ff.

6. Ibid., 98.

7. Jordan, *White over Black,* 388.

8. Ibid.

9. Ibid., 389–90.

10. George Washington Cable, *The Creoles of Louisiana* (New York: Scribner's, 1885), 41, 42; *Encyclopedia Brittanica,* 9th ed. (1984), s.v. "New Orleans."

11. *New York Tribune,* 30 August 1879.

12. George Washington Cable, "Literature in the Southern States," in *The Negro Question: A Selection of Writings on Civil Rights in the South,* ed. Arlin Turner (New York: Doubleday, 1958), 44.

13. *The Journals and Miscellaneous Notebooks of Ralph Waldo Emerson,* vol. 13, *1852–1855,* ed. Ralph H. Orth and Alfred R. Ferguson (Cambridge, Mass.: Harvard University Press, 1977), 198.

14. See Eric Sundquist's discussion of the *Plessy v. Ferguson* case and its impact on American literature of the era in "Mark Twain and Homer Plessy" in his *To Wake the Nations: Race in the Making of American Literature* (Cambridge, Mass.: Harvard University Press, 1993).

15. In calling Sutpen an "American innocent," I follow critics like Cleanth Brooks and Carolyn Porter for whom Sutpen is, in Porter's words, "no less American for being Southern, and no less Southern for being American" (*Seeing and Being: The Plight of the Participant Observer in Emerson, James, Adams, and Faulkner* [Middletown, Conn.: Wesleyan University Press, 1981], 209). See also Cleanth Brooks's important discussion of the character of Thomas Sutpen in *William Faulkner: The Yoknapatawpha Country* (New Haven, Conn.: Yale University Press, 1963), 11ff., 296.

16. Donald Kartiganer, *The Fragile Thread: The Meaning of Form in Faulkner's Novels* (Amherst: University of Massachusetts Press, 1979), 81–82; William Faulkner, "Elmer," *Mississippi Quarterly* 36 (Summer 1983): 410.

17. Anderson, *Imagined Communities,* 83–111.

18. Quoted in Ernest Lee Tuveson, *Redeemer Nation: The Idea of America's Millennial Role* (Chicago, Ill.: University of Chicago Press, 1968), vii.

19. Quoted in Joel Williamson, *The Crucible of Race: Black-White Relations in the American South since Emancipation* (New York: Oxford University Press, 1984), 379.

20. John Irwin, *Doubling and Incest/Repetition and Revenge: A Speculative Read-*

ing of Faulkner (Baltimore, Md.: Johns Hopkins University Press, 1975), 64, 82–94.

21. Henry Hughes, *A Treatise on Sociology: Theoretical and Practical* (Philadelphia: Lippincott, Grambo, 1854), 31.

22. Williamson, *Crucible of Race,* 466.

23. Porter, *Seeing and Being,* 49.

Absalom, Absalom! Haiti, and Labor History

Reading Unreadable Revolutions

RICHARD GODDEN

◆ ◆ ◆

IN 1791 SLAVES REVOLTED on San Domingo. "The world's richest colony" was overrun in a black revolution whose forces "defeated the Spanish; inflicted a defeat of unprecedented proportions on the British, and then made their country the graveyard of Napoleon's magnificent army."[1] By 1804 the Americas had their first black national state, the independent republic of Haiti. In 1823 Thomas Sutpen leaves Virginia for the West Indies where, in 1827, he puts down an uprising among slaves on a French sugar plantation on Haiti. As due recompense, he marries the owner's daughter and achieves a son (1829). The dates are important since they indicate that Faulkner has the hero of *Absalom, Absalom!* earn the properties upon which he will eventually base his plantation "design" improperly. There were neither slaves nor French plantations on Haiti in 1827. Faulkner's chronology creates an anachronism that rewrites one of the key facts of nineteenth-century black American history, in what looks suspiciously like an act of literary counterrevolution.

Those Faulkner scholars who notice the anachronism urge error; I am unconvinced.[2] The Haitian revolution had lasting consequences for the slaveholding states of the South where, during the 1790s, white panics about slave revolts were endemic. Indeed, "Saint Domingo [became] the symbol for black liberation struggles throughout the hemisphere and touched off a series of new insurrectionary attempts." Gabriel Prosser in 1800, Denmark Vessey in 1822, Nat Turner in 1831—to turn to the major North American black rebellions is to discover allusions to Haiti.[3] Nor does the Haitian example fade with the onset of the Civil War; in 1864, in Natchez, ex-slave Mississippi soldiers in the Union Army reacted violently when the city's military commander tried to force freedmen to work abandoned plantations; a northern missionary, S. G. Wright, "trembled," fearing "blood equalling the day of vengeance in the island of Hayti."[4] Mary Chesnut's diary entry for 14 July 1865 notes that "on our place our people were all at home—quiet, orderly, respectful and at their usual work. In point of fact things looked unchanged. There was nothing to show that any one of them had ever seen a Yankee or knew that there was one in existence." However, she follows her reassuring observations with a piece of unattributed gossip: "We are in for a new St. Domingo all the same. The Yankees have raised the devil, and now they cannot guide him."[5]

In the South, Haiti is synonymous with revolution, and whether that be positively or negatively viewed it is not something about which southern authors with an interest in antebellum history lightly make mistakes. Moreover, the evidence of *Absalom, Absalom!* suggests that Faulkner knew more than enough about San Domingo to put its revolution in the right century. He knew that Haitian soil is a cemetery on the grandest scale. Accounts of the colony's eighteenth-century slave population vary, but historians agree that death rates were extremely high; Rod Prince reckons the total number of slaves imported between 1681 and 1791 at 864,000, and adds that "some estimates have suggested that the equivalent of the entire number of slaves was replaced every twenty years."[6] Faulkner notes that the earth, "manured with black blood from two hundred years of oppression and exploitation . . . cried out for vengeance."[7] He knew that

French planters were leading purchasers in the eighteenth-century slave trade. C. L. R. James puts the figure for slave imports around 1789 at 40,000 per year, a figure that translates into Faulkner's sense of an island poised between Africa, ravaged by slavers, and America, seat of rational slave production: "A little island . . . which was the halfway point between what we call the jungle and what we call civilization, halfway between the dark inscrutable continent from which the black blood . . . was ravished by violence, and the cold known land to which it was doomed" (202).[8] It is likely that he knew that Vodun (voodoo) was the initial language of revolt on San Domingo (during the days prior to the insurrection, Sutpen finds signs made from pigs' bones, feathers, and rags, signs which he does not recognize as such [207]), and that the French territory was adjacent to a Spanish colony (Sutpen's mother-in-law "had been a Spaniard" [203]). Knowing even part of this, he surely knew "1791."

Why then pretend otherwise, when to do so implies that Toussant L'Ouverture's revolution did not happen? The answer may, finally, prove anything but counterrevolutionary. Consider the manner in which Sutpen suppresses the anomalous uprising; on the eighth night of seige

> he just put the musket down and had someone unbar the door and then bar it behind him, and walked out into the darkness and subdued them, maybe by yelling louder, maybe by standing, bearing more than they believed any bones and flesh could or should. . . . maybe at last they themselves turning in horror and fleeing from the white arms and legs shaped like theirs and from which blood could be made to spurt and flow as it could from theirs and containing an indomitable spirit which should have come from the same primary fire which theirs came from but which could not have, could not possibly have. (204–5)

Leaving aside the maybes for a moment, it seems that Sutpen triumphs by demonstrating white supremacy: what he suffers establishes an absolute separation between white and black insofar as their points of origin or "primary fires" differ. White proves stronger than black and causes black to vanish. However, allowing that Sutpen said only that he "subdued them," the maybes indicate that the fuller account derives from the story's line of transmission. The line is clear: Sutpen told General Compson (1835), who told it to his son, who told Quentin, who tells Shreve (1910). The options for anecdotal elaboration are several, but since it is the general to whom we owe the detail of Haiti's bloody horticulture and the general to whom Sutpen shows his scars (205), it is probably the general who gives us the "spurt and flow" scenario. In which case, two planters of similar social origin talking in 1835, four years after the Turner uprising, combine to construct a story that affirms their interest in clear-cut racial mastery, albeit an authority tempered in rebellious fires. Given white "primary fire," insurrections will fail and revolutions fade. The supposition is General Compson's, and the recognition that slavery is an undeclared state of war, in which black revolution is a permanent risk, is Sutpen's. His behavior as a slaveholder in Mississippi is eccentric but plain: on a regular and ritualized basis he organizes and participates in single combat with his slaves. While clearly slave codes were designed to police the peculiar institution on the understanding that black conspiracy was a fact of planter life, and while it is certain that compulsory pass systems, complex patterns of surveillance, and "the obligatory involvement of all white members of the community in the implementation of the laws" indicate what one historian calls "a strung-out society" (strung out because the blacks were "in the South in such numbers and in such manner as they were"), that behavior "was recurrently rebellious."[9] It is also undeniable that few southern planters, other than at times of disturbance, systematically viewed their slaves as black Jacobins. To do so would have been to credit them with a will quite beyond the capacity of chattel or a "Sambo." The peculiar institution peculiarly demanded that its managers view their slaves as a threat but also, and simultaneously, as children of limited will, as Sambos to be loved through subordination.

There is little of kindness in Sutpen, who has no time for

Sambo. He fights African Americans out of Haiti who are physically his equal. As Haitians they embody that which the plantocracy most fears and must deny—the spirit of revolution. In the aftermath of 1791, North Carolina passed a law prohibiting the entry of all West Indian slaves over the age of fifteen, for fear that they might incite a general slave rebellion; three years later (1798) Governor Samuel Ashe, "seeking to suppress the ideology of the Haitian Revolution," issued a proclamation urging that the landing of all Negroes from the islands be stopped.[10] To suspend the importation of bodies is not to block news of their acts; as late as 1840, slaves in South Carolina were interpreting information from Haiti as a projection of their own freedom.[11]

Sutpen imports his Haitian archaisms in 1832. In 1833 he appears in Yoknapatawpha County, "takes up land, builds his house" (305), and fights his slaves. The house is complete by 1835: the fighting continues, as far as I can tell, until about 1850. Sutpen's persistent and systematized combat is without historical precedent, as is Faulkner's dating of the San Domingo uprising. However, read together, these anomalies make absolute historical sense. Given that Faulkner wishes to foreground the continuous potential for revolution within the institution of slavery, he needs Haiti, the only successful black revolution. Given that he wishes to characterize the plantocracy as a class that suppresses revolution, he requires that his ur-planter suppress the Haitian revolution and go on doing so. Had Sutpen's design needed only "money in considerable quantities" (196), as Sutpen claims, Mississippi, as a rapidly evolving frontier society, would have provided him with ample and historically accurate opportunities. Witness the career of Sutpen's contemporary General Compson, who in 1811 entered Yoknapatawpha in possession of "a pair of fine pistols, one meagre saddle bag. . . . [and] a stronghocked mare"; it is doubtful whether Sutpen's maritime wages amount to as much by the time he lands in San Domingo (approximately 1820), but neither arriviste arrives with more than a little, and both found dynasties.[12] Furthermore, had Faulkner merely wished to add the capacity to quell slave insurrection to the list of "design" "ingredients" (211), he could, with veracity, have located his hero's first

forays, during the 1830s, almost anywhere in the lower South—
though South Carolina or Mississippi would have been ideal, since
with populations divided almost equally between black and white,
opportunities for "impudence and insubordination" were many
and always liable to induce violent reaction.[13]

My point is finally a simple one: in Sutpen's slaves Faulkner
creates an anomalous archaism; they are historically free and yet
doubly constrained, by a fiction (*Absalom, Absalom!*) and by a counterrevolutionary violence (Sutpen's) that is necessary to the work-
ings of the plantation system. Sutpen's fights give true title to
each measure of labor control in the antebellum South. Southerners might recognize that when Sutpen "enter[s] the ring" with
one of his slaves, he does so with "deadly forethought," not
merely to retain "supremacy [and] domination" (21), but to enact
the preemptive counterrevolution, crucial to the authority of his
class. Furthermore, the fights are staged as social education. At-
tended by white and black (who form "a hollow square . . . white
faces on three sides . . . black ones on the fourth" [20]), the scenes
in barn and stable are part of a class apprenticeship; Sutpen's son
is required to attend at least once, and his daughters (white and
black) watch illicitly. The origin of Sutpen's beaten slave allows
Faulkner to posit the slave as black Jacobin (hence Haiti) prior to
having the planter put him down. Of course, this cannot be
openly acknowledged in any study of the imagination of masters,
around 1830–1850 (hence the suppression of 1791).

Sutpen's belief in the abrasive primacy of his "primary fire"
(205) cannot entirely disguise the suspicion that, in getting into
the ring in the first place, he has compromised his own "domination," that is to say, his own whiteness. James Snead notes how
often in *Absalom, Absalom!* "white" becomes "black," or in his terms,
how frequently "Sutpen and blacks are twinned," this being con-
spiciously true of Sutpen and his "wild Negroes" (27). We are
assured that they "belonged to him body and soul," yet despite
being extensions of his will, they impose their bodily form on
him, so that when they fight, "they should not only have been
the same color, but should have been covered with fur too" (20);
when they work, only beard and eyes distinguish the master, "the

bearded white man," from the "twenty black ones"; all stand "stark naked beneath the croaching and pervading mud" (28). Snead pursues the evidence of crossing in terms of miscegenation: "These mergings would be less noteworthy if they did not originate in Sutpen's merging with the one black whom he most wants to distance, his son Charles Bon."[14]

I, however, wish to pause in order to consider merger implications at the level of labor—after all, Sutpen works in the mud with his slaves (28) and harnesses himself to the capstan of a brick kiln with his slaves (27), in order to produce a property that is exclusively his own. His mastery (white), embodied in Sutpen's Hundred ("Be Light" [4]), derives from the labor of the slaves, and is experienced by a master who almost made himself black to get his plantation built. To turn from what Sutpen does in constructing a plantation to what he thinks he does (that is, to chapter seven) is to find evidence suggesting that his violent enactment of white supremacy explicitly contradicts his own fuller sense of master-slave relations. From what he tells General Compson, it is clear that he suppresses Haiti—to which one might add that he also suppresses Hegel. I say this because "Lordship and Bondage," chapter four of Hegel's *Phenomenology of the Mind*, stands as a useful gloss on Sutpen's account of his childhood experience, particularly that of being turned from a planter's door by a black butler.

Here is Hegel, considerably reduced. The lord seeks absolute, because independent, authority. At the moment of his supremacy he is troubled because he recognizes, in objects through which he represents that supremacy (to himself), labor that is not his own. He knows that his lordship depends upon the labor of the bound man: "Just when the master had effectively achieved lordship, he really finds that something has come about quite different from an independent consciousness. It is not an independent consciousness, but rather a dependent consciousness that he has achieved."[15] The trauma of recognition involves him in an unpassable contradiction; the lord must extract from his lordship the very materials that define it ("in order to become certain of [himself] . . . as a true being").[16] Meanwhile, the bound man exists in an equally problematic relation to objects of labor; having experienced himself as a negation, or as nothing other than an extension of his lord's will (one "whose essence of life is for another"), he too is troubled because he recognizes, in the independent existence of those things made by his hand, the negation of his own prior negation by the lord: "Shaping and forming the object has . . . the positive significance that the bondsman becomes thereby the author of himself as factually and objectively self-existent."[17] Such a moment is uncomfortable in that it requires that the bound man experience both the death of his dependent self and the emergence of an independent self: "Precisely in labour, where there seems to be some outsider's mind and ideas involved, the bondsman becomes aware, through his rediscovery of himself by himself, of having and being a 'mind of his own.' "[18] Where the master risks his masterful self in the appreciation that the objects of his desire are the products of the slave's hand, the slave risks his abject self in the consciousness that his labor not only postpones the master's satisfaction but also produces an object "that is permanent" and remains "after the master's desire is gratified."[19]

Central to Hegel's understanding of "the forms of servitude" are two notions: first, that of "recognition," which occurs when a "distinct" self, whether bound or binding, comes to a "completer realization of self in another self"—a process which involves loss "of its own [or initial] self, since it finds itself as an other being."[20] The "other" is, for the master, the slave and his works; for the slave, the "other" is simply his work. Hegel describes the moment of "recognition" as "death," since each self "risks its own life" as it engages in "a life and death struggle"[21] to "come outside itself" into another. Politically speaking, masters must deny "recognition" if they wish to retain their goods and satisfactions. Slaves have several options along a more or less revolutionary spectrum: they can play dead, that is, they can pretend to be the chattels that they know themselves not to be; alternatively, they may pilfer, feign illness, and slow the pace of work; or they can conspire and revolt. Whatever their decision, the bound have before their eyes artifacts that prove their independence. For, Hegel, the slave's "recognition" derives directly from his works.

TO RETURN TO SUTPEN'S METHODS of labor control, I have argued that his fights with Haitian slaves embody his recognition that slavery rests on a continuous repression of revolution. Yet in chapter seven, far from tracing the inception of his plantation design (212) to a nascent sense of white supremacy, he roots that design in the interdependency of slave and master: the key image is a black butler's "balloon face" (189). In 1835, as they pause from hunting the absconded French architect, whose recapture is essential to the completion of the dynastic house, Sutpen describes to Grandfather Compson the house upon which his house is founded. What Sutpen tells the general is his own genesis (c. 1820), central to which is a black face, inside a white door, sending a poor white child around to the back:

> *But I can shoot him.* (Not the monkey nigger. It was not the nigger any more than it had been the nigger that his father had helped to whip that night. The nigger was just another balloon face slick and distended with that mellow loud and terrible laughing so that he did not dare to burst it, looking down at him from within the half-closed door during that instant in which, before he knew it, something in him had escaped and— he unable to close the eyes of it—was looking out from within the balloon face just as the man who did not even have to wear the shoes he owned, whom the laughter which the balloon held barricaded and protected from such as he, looked out from whatever invisible place he (the man) happened to be at the moment, at the boy outside the barred door in his patched garments and splayed bare feet, looking through and beyond the boy, he himself seeing his own father and sisters and brothers as the owner, the rich man (not the nigger) must have been seeing them all the time—as cattle, creatures heavy and without grace, brutely evacuated into a world without hope or purpose for them, who would in turn spawn with brutish and vicious prolixity, populate, double treble and com-

pound, fill space and earth with a race whose future would be
a succession of cut-down and patched and made-over garments
bought on exorbitant credit because they were white people,
from stores where niggers were given the garments free, with
for sole heritage that expression on a balloon face bursting with
laughter which had looked out at some unremembered and
nameless progenitor who had knocked at a door when he was
a little boy and been told by a nigger to go around the back):
But I can shoot him. (189–90)

As Hegel might have put it, the self "has come outside itself"
with a vengeance.[22]

Grandfather Compson will later call Sutpen's problem "innocence" (178); he is wrong. Sutpen's solution is innocence; his
problem is his disorienting insight into the dependencies of slave
production. What he sees is traumatic because it leaves him no
possibility of an unenslaved life. Stated at its most phenomeno-
logical, which is how Sutpen experiences it, he knows that what
he breathes is the breath of slaves, and that he will breathe it no
matter where he sits in the hierarchy.

His first move is to remove himself. He "crawls" into a hole
in the ground, a "cave" made by a fallen tree where he sits "with
his back against the uptorn roots" (186). His regression is twofold,
from human nature to nature, and from cotton production to
self-sufficiency (that of the hunter; the cave is a "den beside [a]
game trail" [188]). Both removals are illusory. In the cotton South,
the earth itself is a fact of labor, whose meaning is inseparable
from the dominant form of work. Sutpen knows this, at least in
1835, since he prefaces his description of the cave with an earlier
memory. As a boy, he and his sister had refused to give way to
a coach approaching from behind; the black coachman swerved
in time, but only just; and Sutpen found himself "throwing vain
clods of dirt after the dust as it spun on": "[K]nowing, while the
monkey-dressed nigger butler kept the door barred with his body
while he spoke, that it had not been the nigger coachman that
he threw at at all, that it was the actual dust raised by the proud
delicate wheels, and just that vain" (187). Faulkner shares Sutpen's

evaluation: in a letter to Harrison Smith (February 1934) he sum-
marizes *Absalom, Absalom!* as follows: "Roughly, the theme is a man
who outraged the land, and the land then turned and destroyed
the man's family."[23] "Clod," "dust," "land"—inorganic matter becomes an agent (whether as target or destroyer) only because it
is marked by human projects. As Sartre puts it:

> I need only to glance out of the window: I will be able to see
> cars which are men and drivers who are cars . . . and instru-
> ments (pavements, a thoroughfare, a taxi rank, a bus stop. . . .
> proclaiming with their frozen voices how they are to be used).
> . . . These [are] beings—neither thing nor man, but practical
> unities made up of man and inert thing.[24]

To apply this Parisian glance to the cotton lands of the antebellum South is to see "clod" and "dust" as "beings" insofar as they
are "worked things" that consequently issue imperatives and contain futures. Virginian "dust" early in the nineteenth century is
an ensemble of human practices, chief among them slavery, but
to Sutpen on a dirt road, standing in it, the dust is that which
will make him its thing, least among its many things (lumpen
labor). Of course, it can do this only because, as the container of
persistent practices, it contains a sentence that some men have
passed on other men.[25] Under other systems, dust issues alternative instructions, hence Sutpen's boyhood regression to memories of self-sufficiency. In the mountains of western Virginia (c.
1807–1820), land was what you hunted over—it "belonged to
anybody and everybody" (179)—a property in common from
which men took only what they needed and could hold onto.
Sutpen's concern with the "mountain man" who "happened to
own a fine rifle" (185, 192) obeys the imperative of those lands at
this time.

But Sutpen, with his back to an uprooted tree in 1820, recalls
mountains to which his "woodman's instinct" can no longer return him (183); furthermore, he recollects his prior self as he
hunts his plantation architect in 1835. The mountains of 1807
look irrelevant from the cotton lands nearly thirty years later,

and their values are anachronistic: small wonder that Sutpen tells General Compson that "his own rifle analogy" could not help with the black butler (192).

Very little can. Sutpen is forced to fall back on labor—almost all that he has experienced—to take the "measure" of what he has seen (188). He catalogs the forms of work that he knows. Hunting (irrelevant). His father's Tidewater tasks, unspecified beyond tenancy (irrelevant, since the butler does not bother to inquire after the message that Sutpen carries from his father to the planter). His sister's brutal domestic work at the washtub (irrelevant, since she is little more than things in process, "a shapeless . . . calico dress," an "old man's shoes," "pumping" (190). The work of the master (inessential because slight, consisting of little more than the receipt of drinks while in a "barrel stave hammock" [184]). Indeed, so minimal is the master's labor that Sutpen speculates whether he who has a servant to put the glass in his hand and to pull the boot from his foot also has others to chew, swallow, and breathe for him (180). If so, the master does not live. He is dead and his servants do his living for him. The labor of the slave (essential, since the slave's services to the lord's body give that body its substance, "protect" that body [190], and provide it with the vantage point from which it may dismiss, as irrelevant, the labor of surrounding bodies).

The implications of Sutpen's labor list would appear plain: he who would be master must have "niggers and a fine house" (192), which is why Sutpen goes to the West Indies. However, to be master is also to depend upon the labor that you dismiss, to be all but dead, and to rest enclosed in the head of a slave. Mastery on such terms is difficult. Sutpen becomes a planter in Mississippi (1835) only because what happens in Haiti (1827) allows him to repress what he saw in eastern Virginia (1820). Put tersely, Sutpen can raise his plantation because, having experienced slavery as the suppression of revolution, he can, in his own defense, displace his knowledge that the master's mastery depends upon the body and the consciousness of the bound man. Again, Haiti is the key, but repression is not easy. The fights with the Haitian slaves (1835–1850), read within this sequence, mark the return and control of repressed materials: only by "gouging" at the revolutionary eyes (20) on the "balloon face" can Sutpen preserve the separateness of his "primary fire" (205). Of course, in demonstrating that his whiteness does not depend upon blackness he contradicts himself, since to those who watch in the barn, his whiteness turns black: "and Ellen [saw] not the two black beasts she had expected to see but instead a white one and a black one, both naked to the waist and gouging at one another's eyes as if they should . . . have been the same color" (20).

Sutpen constructs his integrity as master through a combination of violence and innocence. The latter term, appealed to by most who tell the story, derives from General Compson and the conversation of 1835, during which the general offers a detailed account of its origin, rooting "innocence" in labor experience. Having returned from plantation threshold to tenant cabin, the boy rethinks the house servant's refusal to consider his father's message:

And then he [Sutpen] said that all of a sudden it was not thinking, it was something shouting it almost loud enough for his sisters on the other pallet and his father in the bed with the two youngest and filling the room with alcohol snoring, to hear too: *He never even give me a chance to say it*: it too fast, too mixed up to be thinking, it all kind of shouting at him at once, boiling out and over him like the nigger laughing: *He never give me a chance to say it and Pap never asked me if I told him or not and so he cant even know that Pap sent him any message and so whether he got it or not cant even matter, not even to Pap; I went up to that door for that nigger to tell me never to come to that front door again and I not only wasn't doing any good to him by telling it or any harm to him by not telling it, there aint any good or harm either in the living world that I can do to him.* It was like that, he said, like an explosion—a bright glare that vanished and left nothing, no ashes nor refuse; just a limitless flat plain with the severe shape of his intact innocence rising from it like a monument; that innocence instructing him as calm as the others had ever spoken, using his own rifle analogy to do it with, and when it said *them* in place of *he* or *him*, it meant more than all the human puny mortals under the sun that might lie in hammocks all afternoon with their shoes off. (192)

I quote at length in order to emphasize the labor-based nature of the trauma, and to explore the manner of the cover-up. As so often on this day, agency is composite ("mixed up"). Sutpen receives warning of his irrelevance—because of the irrelevance of his words—from a voice whose status is unclear. The "something" that shouts is not a "thought" and, given its apparent availability to others in the room, would appear to derive from outside of the boy's consciousness. Whatever shouts at him (his voice, an interior voice, the voice of another or others) resembles "nigger laughing" and so in this context may well owe its origin to the problematic "balloon face." As some "thing" carried on the master/black's breath, addressing an issue of labor and identified most consistently by the impersonal pronoun "it," it becomes a vocalization of the very "things" that work produces. Since masters, according to the boy, do not work, and since the voice declares that the labor of poor whites has no substance, the thing that speaks is the work of the slave's hand. Other pronouns prove polyvalent: witness the "he" who "never give [the boy] a chance to say." Sutpen has earlier identified an italicized "he" as "(not the nigger now either)" (191). However, his parentheses occur prior to the problems of "it," and consequently the pronoun ("he") retains its tendency to shift between planter and house servant; in which case, the "he" whom Sutpen acknowledges as beyond harm is master and slave in the fullness of their interdependency.

Sutpen recognizes that he and his class cannot affect the master class; his recognition, involving a simultaneous acknowledgment that the substantiality of the master is inextricable from the works of the slave, is explosive. But Sutpen's term, "explosion," is modified in the telling. The labor materials so central to the boy's trauma are suppressed. The speaking "things" are silenced, and in their place "innocence" instructs. The awkward "it" is simplified so that "when it said *them* in place of *he* or *him*," "it," innocently renamed, refers to the planter as a class type whose unenigmatic properties are to be countered by possession of equally unenigmatic properties ("land and niggers and a fine house"). The modification is achieved in two swift steps. Step one: "explosion" is replaced by a synonym, "bright glare," whose emphasis falls less on damage than on illumination; brightness so obscures the work of dark hands that neither ashes (dark marks) or refuse (refusal) remain. I am reminded of Quentin's equally hygienic *"Be Light"* (4), where biblical reference and architectural expectation as to plantations and whitewash ally to obscure twenty Haitians and one master, united in labor and mud. Step two: in the space made by erasure, a "monument" of overtly sexual design is raised, its shape both phallic and "intact." Gone is Sutpen's debilitating vision of slave production as the free passage of black bodies into white through labor. Instead, "innocence" grants male authority by expelling the black body from the white, which, cleansed of traumatic stain, may claim integrity. Sex displaces labor to cast integrity as virginity, deriving not from Sutpen but from Rosa Coldfield; "intact" complements Sutpen's claim to have been a virgin on his wedding night (200), but its shape is hymeneal and echoes Mr. Compson's vision of Rosa's hymen-rampant:

> Perhaps she even saw herself as an instrument of retribution: if not in herself an active instrument strong enough to cope with him, at least as a kind of passive symbol of inescapable reminding to rise bloodless and without dimension from the sacrificial stone of the marriage-bed.[26]

Asked (in 1862) by Ellen (her sister) to save Judith (her niece), Rosa (according to Mr. Compson) installs herself in Sutpen's Hundred to await Sutpen's return from the Civil War (1865). More particularly she installs herself in the bed chamber, where her spectral slightness serves, in a metaphorical reworking, to heal her sister's hymen; the repair protects Judith by gathering her back (unborn) into the generic integrity of Coldfield womankind. This fantasy belongs to Mr. Compson (by way of Quentin), but takes its preoccupations from the cult of southern womanhood, which raised the standard of the unbreachable hymen in order to counter fears over miscegenation.[27] My point here, however, is merely to note just how far the antecedents of a single word—"intact"—have carried us from an "explosion" as it is used in 1820. Sutpen's experience is all too easily lost under the interpretive parentheses of his narrators. Mr. Compson and Quentin combine to translate labor fears into sexual fears, thereby producing a more local and manageable problem. Sutpen's sexuality will eventually bring his house down; it does not and cannot bring down the plantation as a system of production.

OF COURSE, TO BLAME NARRATORS is to simplify Sutpen, who in 1861 can no longer afford to see what he saw in 1820. After Haiti, and with Sutpen's Hundred built, he has to control his memory. However, his transition to full planter status remains awkward: for three years, between 1835 and 1838, with house built and cotton in the ground, he refuses to emerge through marriage into dynasty (29), and instead uses his property against the grain of its imperatives. He retains himself in archaic form as "a fine rifle" (185), employing his house as a hunting lodge; implicitly, he is loath to commit himself to full slave production and to its peculiar form of mastery. In 1864, after twenty-three growing seasons, Sutpen may be said successfully to have pursued the public logic of his wealth; as a result, on entering General Compson's legal office to renew their conversation, he can deny his earlier insight, describing "the boy-symbol" as "just the figment of the amazed and desperate child" (210).

To gloss, the practice of slaveholding has allowed him to repress his knowledge of the interdependence of slave and master. Further, three years into the Civil War, he is prepared to compound repressions by declaring a complete absence of class antagonism between slaveholding and nonslaveholding whites. Tenant and planter, upcountry yeoman and black belt lord elide as he tells his class ally how, if a "nameless" boy came to his "white door" now, "he would take that boy in" (210). As one elected Confederate officer to another, with the war going badly and desertion particularly high among yeomen from the hill counties, Sutpen needs a vision of southern unity. He, and every other planter, on "look[ing] ahead along the still undivulged light rays," hopes to see a Confederate future, with white "doors," "bigger" and "whiter" than their Virginian prototypes still intact, and at each of them, if necessary, a poor white child welcomed into an independent slaveholding republic. Without such images, planter hegemony, strained to a breaking point by 1864, could not hope to counter yeomen claims that this was "a rich man's war and a poor boy's fight."[28] Sutpen's reworking of the boy at the door is a piece of Confederate utopianism that still has resonance in 1910 for at least one grandchild of the plantocracy. Shreve interrupts Quentin's retelling to observe, "Dont say it's just me that sounds like your old man" (210). Quentin extends the echo: "*Maybe we are both Father. . . . Yes, we are both Father. Or maybe Father and I are both Shreve, maybe it took Father and me both to make Shreve or Shreve and me both to make Father or maybe Thomas Sutpen to make all of us*" (210). Given that his Harvard fees derive from the sale of some of his grandfather's landed property, Quentin is, in a very real sense, Sutpen-made, a product of planter efforts to ensure their class's continuity.

Failure to hear Sutpen's insistence that the boy at the door would be admitted "now," in 1864, deprives the image of historical and political specificity. Dirk Kuyk rewrites 1864 as 1933 when, "in the midst of the Depression . . . plenty of nameless strangers were knocking at front doors," so Sutpen becomes a New Dealer, seeking "to teach society the lesson that those lucky enough to have risen above brutehood should at least care about the feelings of the unlucky."[29] Further to the right stands Carolyn Porter's Sutpen, whose career, "conducted in the name of equality," is dedicated to "vindicating the American dream itself."[30] Both descend from Sutpen out of Cleanth Brooks, whose antecedents are Henry James's *The American* and F. Scott Fitzgerald's *The Great Gatsby*, literary representations of a generically "American neurosis."[31] Sutpen, like Newman and Gatsby, is a self-made pursuer of an "abstract idea" which, since its form is "money" and its practice "the Protestant work ethic," may be said to be "a characteristically American aberration."[32] These Sutpens show scant concern for a dependent labor system: indeed, each celebrates "the idea that the cash nexus offer[s] a permissible basis for human relations"— anathema to the antebellum planter.[33] They are "capitalist entre- preneurs," whose intense and various espousals of "human per- fectibility" (Brooks), "the principle of social equality" (Porter), and radical egalitarianism (Kuyk) must presumably be premised upon a thoroughly bourgeois faith in the individual as free, equal, and autonomous.[34]

Such Sutpens bear no traceable relation to the boy of 1820, or indeed to the man revising that boy in 1864. However, Brooks would seem to have a point when he reminds us that Sutpen believes that his first wife will not object to being put aside, be- cause Sutpen "was willing to make a just and even generous property settlement for her benefit."[35] Brooks cites the cash nexus, and certainly there is much talk of "valuation," "schedules," "compensatory amounts of time," and two-party agreements (212). But this is not simply the language of bourgeois contracts. Sutpen breaks his marriage when he learns that Eulalia is black; as a free black woman in the West Indies she may freely enter contractual agreements, but were she to visit the South she would have to prove her free status and without proof would be des- ignated a slave, sans contractual rights. Her child (as Haitian born) would similarly be free but required to prove it and would therefore stand constrained by popular assumption. His ability to enter into contracts would also be compromised, unless he chose to "pass." Sutpen enters into contracts with persons who, on racial grounds, in the antebellum South, have no contractual rights. Sutpen neglects to tell General Compson why he repu- diates Eulalia, but knowing what Quentin and Shreve suppose about her antecedents, we may read his market lexicon both as inappropriate and as contrived to obscure racial trauma. Brooks misses the historical subtext. Sutpen's discovery that his first fam- ily is "black" marks the return of his childhood recognition that a white skin emerges from a laboring black body; whether that labor produces property as cotton or property as person is less significant than the fact that Eulalia's child is potentially a white dynast in a black skin. So read, "explosion" rather than "abstract" calculation informs the repudiation.

Brooks mistakes Sutpen's motives. Porter makes a stronger case for the structural nature of his design. Her case runs: Sutpen's "dream of parental authority," far from tying him to Genovese's pre-bourgeois planters, typifies the degree to which he and they espouse market liberalism, since paternalism was throughout the first half of the nineteenth century another name for the nastier forms of bourgeois appropriation.[36] Sutpen, a "grandiose" father, "merit[ing] the analogy with King David implied by the novel's title," allows Faulkner to explore the self-contradicting logic of market paternalism, which "logically dictates that fathers exile and repudiate their sons."[37]

But Sutpen is no kind of paternalist: he treats his Haitians as Jacobins not as children. Nor, despite his interpreters, does he regard Bon as a son; in this instance, neither paternity nor miscegenation is *his* problem. Witness how he names his Haitian child; Quentin, citing his father and his father's father, notes: "Father said he probably named him himself. Charles Bon. Charles Good. . . . Grandfather believed, just as he named them all—the Charles Goods and the Clytemnestras" (213–14).[38] Bon: good: goods—the pun is cruelly obvious and is recognized as apt by a tradition whose authority over labor extended to the naming of new slaves, whether new by birth or purchase. Planters were entitled to declare their title or property within a slave by naming that slave as they wished, and in so doing they deadened the slave's right by birth to human connections. Orlando Paterson describes this renaming as "natal death."[39] Sutpen does not deny his son his patronym, since Eulalia does not give birth to a son but to goods, and in naming him as such Sutpen declares Bon dead and himself an owner, not a father. Faulkner's choice of Jim Bond, as the name of Bon's grandson, indicates his concern for the complex latencies of nomination. Quentin encounters the simpleton Jim Bond on his visit to Sutpen's Hundred in 1909: after telling of that visit, he takes to his Harvard bed, "rigid" and silently quoting from "The Raven": "Nevermore of peace. Nevermore of peace. Nevermore Nevermore Nevermore" (298–99).

Poe's black bird is an obscurely wise headache, and in quoting it Quentin may well be attending, through its choric word, "nevermore," to the choric cry of another obscure blackbird. "Jim

Bond," in the context of "The Raven," euphoniously yields "Jim Crow" because the semantics of the pun, "bond," would have it so. "Bond," whether as "shackle" or "binding agreement," contains the idea of constraint. The name was presumably given at Jim's birth (1882), and although the network of Jim Crow laws, disfranchising southern blacks, was not fully in place as a legal system until the 1890s, one of the first instances of such legislation was adopted by the Tennessee legislature in 1881.[40] Jim Bond is birdlike in another sense; he is that which cannot be caught. He can be heard, but Quentin and Shreve agree, "they couldn't catch him" (301, 302); further, Quentin admits on the novel's final page that he "still hear[s] him at night sometimes." Jim Bond may have vanished when Sutpen's Hundred burned in 1910, but his howling persistence in Quentin's head (whether or not annotated as black wisdom liable to split white skull) provides Shreve with the pattern for his final and infamous joke:

> I think that in time the Jim Bonds are going to conquer the western hemisphere. Of course it won't quite be in our time and of course as they spread towards the poles they will bleach out again like the rabbits and the birds do, so they won't show up so sharp against the snow. But it will still be Jim Bond; and so in a few thousand years, I who regard you will also have sprung from the loins of African kings. (302)

Just as Minerva, having been eaten in fetal form, along with her mother, by Jupiter, her father, sprang black and birdlike from the paternal skull, so Jim Bond, constrained to be little more than a loud thing, will prove seminal once it is recognized that his blackness, as that which gave substance to white bodies, also provided them with their true patronym. The joke is metamorphic: Bond's bleached-out bird, under pressure from "snow," transforms into semen, becoming a flutter in the "rabbit" loins of an African king. By means of innuendo and contortion Shreve suggests that his and Quentin's heirs (like Bon's before them) will eventually descend from a great black father. His is a joke against white paternalism, which turns the novel upside down in a manner owing

much to Sutpen's key recognition of 1820. Shreve, like the boy
at the door, though with different emphasis, points out that white
"comes" from black, an insight that allows him to retell the Sutpen story, in its last and most minimal form, as a story of black
paternity.

Quentin, still in bed, still "rigid," but now "panting," is
shocked, not by a reworking of the one about miscegenation (*"I'm
the nigger that's going to sleep with your sister"* [286])—he's already heard
that earlier in the evening—but by his own response to the joke
and to the question that follows it, "Why do you hate the
South?":

> "I dont hate it," Quentin said, quickly, at once, immediately;
> "I dont hate it," he said, *I don't hate it* he thought, panting in
> the cold air, the iron New England dark; *I dont. I dont! I dont hate
> it! I dont hate it!* (303)

His reaction is automatic but not immediately meaningful. That
which he does not apparently hate—"the South"—appears too
generic to signify anything in particular. What significance there
is seems, in the first instance, to reside in euphony. The rhythm
of denial precisely recalls Quentin's earlier use of Poe's negatives:
he offered five "Nevermores." Poe's raven croaked the word seven
times. Quentin gives us seven denials. Moreover Quentin's two
reiterations echo one another in their format, both consisting of
two phrases, one short, one longer, each staccato. I labor their
affinity because rhythm is not customarily considered a key se-
mantic element outside a poem. Yet here, Quentin's denial, recalling his prior use of Poe's denial, also calls into itself an awkward signifying chain running from the raven and the crow,
through Bond and Eulalia to Bon, and so to Sutpen's designation
of his son as goods. If all *that* falls into place as an archaeology
imminent within the repetition, semanticizing its euphony, what
is it that Quentin denies?

The manner of that denial is difficult, given that by saying
"no" so often he seems to contradict himself, affirming his hate.
But either way, affirm or deny, what object does he address? Of

what southern thing or event does he think? My answer is unnervingly specific—"Bon," not as a person (fictional or real) but as an associative path through a collection of words, leading back to Sutpen's act of naming, that is, to the owner's translation of a nominal son into real property (Sutpen believes, quite literally, that he has paid [220] in acres and slaves for Eulalia's labor and "goods"). As I have already argued, Sutpen's choice of the name "Bon" derives from and represses a prior event (being turned away from the planter's door). By calling the slave who comes from his own white body "goods," Sutpen disclaims his earlier vision of the master's white mastery emerging from the body of black labor. "Bon" proves to be less a name than a collection of verbal traces obstructing the trauma to which they refer. This "Bon" is what Quentin sees, and does and does not hate

Since "Bon" comes to mean so much, I had best reprise how so much meaning came upon it. My attempt to explain a single act of naming (Bon) led me to a set of names (Bon, Eulalia, Bond). Attracted by the euphonies, puns, contortions, and distortions released by their conjunction, I find that I have discovered a labyrinth, zigzagging through space and time from Haiti to Harvard, and from 1820 to 1910. My textual stratagems would be entirely pointless and lacking in any functional relation to *Absalom, Absalom!* without the instigatory force of Sutpen's traumatic experience in eastern Virginia. What he saw was in effect slave labor's primal scene, which scarcely happens before it is repressed, and to which no planter or planter's child or grandchild can give credence. He witnessed the simple and debilitating truth of slave production, that the master's body is made by the slave's work: a fact that casts ethnic interdependency as white dependency. It should be stressed that in the antebellum South sexual production literally resembled cotton production, insofar as both yielded a crop that could be taken to market. With the banning of the overseas trade in slaves (1808), miscegenation was always liable to become another way in which slaves made goods for masters. By naming Bon for property, Sutpen suppresses a trauma whose force continues to distort the working of the very word through which he attempted suppression. In pursuing

"Bon" and its network of related names, I have produced an interminable decipherment, which at any and every point risks reencrypting that story's unbearable truth.

That truth would not trouble a capitalist. After my detour through "Bon," I return now to what prompted it, to Carolyn Porter's claim that Sutpen's paternalism makes him a typical liberal capitalist of the first half of the nineteenth century. It is undoubtedly true that the antebellum planter was "deeply embedded in the world market," in that his products tied him to the Western capitalist order.[41] Cotton, sugar, and tobacco are the staples of Europe's midcentury consumer boom. However, it is equally apparent that at the level of production, rather than distribution or consumption, his preferred labor relations are distinct from the labor relations of those with whom he trades. Indeed, the southern planter class stood in increasingly hostile relation to the northern bourgeoisie, eventually choosing "to wage a 'civil war' in order to break free from its political and economic ties within a bourgeois national state."[42] The bone of contention was slavery and the South's determination to defend its distinctive system of labor.

Since Sutpen's design is to become a planter, he is perhaps best understood through his status as a distinctive labor lord. Had he been a northern capitalist he would have paid wages, thereby declaring himself independent of his free employees, since, in the bourgeois marketplace, those who contract together, whether as the purchaser or seller of labor, do so under the assumption that each of them is a free and independent unit. Contract is an institution that both separates and equalizes its signatories, or so the story goes; a contract to exchange wages for labor is at least nominally noncoercive, implying that those who sign do so freely and even equally insofar as both parties are property owners (one of the means of production [plant], the other of the means to labor [body]). "Everyone shall be free, and shall respect the freedom of others. . . . Everyone possesses *his own* body as free tool of his will."[43]

Manifestly, under slavery, the bound laborer is not free, and any suggestion that he might possess rights or will, independent of the will of his lord, strikes at the working of the entire system because it threatens the grounds upon which the owner owns and uses the slave. Bourgeois contract turns on "partial relations," which direct the owner to ignore aspects of a worker's person or circumstance that are unrelated to production.[44] Slave production turns on relations of personal dependency, which are "total," involving the whole lives of masters and the whole lives of slaves.[45] Of course, the whole life of a slave is wholly negated if she is reduced to a chattel; nonetheless, even total subordination (without which basic precept slavery cannot work) commits the owner to the whole life-as-living-death of the owned, in a way that bourgeois paternalism (freed by contract to be as finally irresponsible as it may wish) only pretends to do.

Planters were bound by ties of interdependency to their bound labor. They could and did disguise this fact in all manner of ways, but they could not and did not perceive their activities through the language of bourgeois individualism, since as Fox-Genovese and Genovese put it, "opportunities for individual autonomy" were limited in the antebellum South.[46] Which is another way of saying, contra Brooks and Porter, that Sutpen is no capitalist because he founds his design on relations quite other than those between capitalist and free labor. Sutpen's vision of the consequences of mutual dependence as white dependency lead him away from paternalism as a language through which to address the relations of slavery. Paternalism does not suppress enough for Sutpen because, in its presentation of the master as father to an extended black family, it not only posits black gratitude in return for white responsibility but implies filial rights, thereby contradicting "the principle of submission" lying "at the heart of the master's self-justification."[47] Haiti allows Sutpen to go for total submission, becoming Judge Rifkin sans sensitivity, because having experienced a private revolution in Virginia and having enacted a necessary counterrevolution in Haiti, he can do nothing else— at least if he wishes to keep his property.

The return of Bon to Sutpen is, for Sutpen, the return not of a son but of a slave. Sutpen has no apparent difficulty withholding his paternal acknowledgment because he does not see Bon as

his child but as his goods. Indeed, it is as goods and not as a son
that Bon threatens him. The threat derives not from miscegenation but from labor, since Bon reminds Sutpen of "the actual
condition of things" under slave production—that every master
and every master's son is a black in whiteface. My remark is not
intended rhetorically. Faulkner stresses that Sutpen is "faced"
(219) with a "face" (214). When he sees Bon ride up to Sutpen's
Hundred in 1859, he sees his own features on a male slave:

> "and he saw the face and knew" ... "—saw the face and
> knew." ... and Father said that even then, even though he
> knew that Bon and Judith had never laid eyes on one another,
> he must have felt and heard the design—house, position, pos-
> terity and all—come down like it had been built out of smoke.
> (214–15)

The form of their meeting is resonant of Virginia:

> He stood there at his own door, just as he had imagined,
> planned, designed, and sure enough and after fifty years the
> forlorn nameless and homeless child came to knock at it and
> no monkey-dressed nigger anywhere under the sun to come
> to the door and order the child away. (215)

To decipher, however, on the basis of what Sutpen knows, is
to recover the butler and to see what Sutpen saw in 1820. The
recurrence of slave labor's primal scene revises the status and
position of the subjects involved. The boy who is and plays Sutpen is a slave (black goods); the master who is and plays the
"monkey nigger's" part is, despite his name (Sutpen), black goods.
Faced with this, Sutpen has no option—he must turn the boy
(and the insight) from the door, or lose the door. To extend the
logic of the insight is to appreciate the extent of the "explosion";
should Bon marry Judith, Sutpen's Hundred will not only be a
materialization of black work but its inheritors will lose their
euphemistic patronym (Sutpen), becoming goods (Bon) in name
as well as fact. As a result, the white master's nominal authority,

along with his nominal irony, will vanish "like . . . smoke." As in the 1820s, so in the 1860s, Sutpen responds by using Haiti on Virginia, meeting revolutionary recognition with counterrevolutionary violence. Henry will kill Bon at his father's bidding, but in so doing he will kill that which manufactures mastery. Consequently, Henry vanishes to all intents and purposes as he pulls the trigger. He returns to a diminished plantation "*to die*" (298), a "wasted yellow face" with "wasted hands," who is "already a corpse" in 1909 because, as a planter who killed his own most vital part (labor), he has been a corpse since that act in 1865.

Critics who speculate on what might have happened had Sutpen let matters take their course, allowed Bon to marry Judith, and become (in a region without primogeniture law) co-heir with Henry, miss the point. Sutpen plans to accumulate by means of slave production, and consequently his accumulations are founded on a primary repression of the fact that mastery is made by bound labor. Bon's presence disables that repression, so that Sutpen cannot keep the labor truth down; he therefore knows that, complete or incomplete, his design is vitiated. He tells General Compson, in 1864, that if he does nothing, "let[s] matters take the course which I know they will take and see my design complete itself quite normally and naturally and successfully to the public eye," what results will be "a mockery," "a betrayal of that little boy who approached that door fifty years ago and was turned away, for whose vindication the whole plan was conceived and carried forward to the moment of this choice" (220). To vindicate that boy he had to repress what the boy saw, and to go on doing so for nearly a half century (the years of major slave production in the South). When that is no longer possible, when the unrepressed child (Bon, or white as black goods) finally becomes father to the man (as his posterity), then the man as planter may as well be dead. If Sutpen lets "the design complete itself," care of Bon, he must witness his own dynastic body become what it always was—black property.

Sutpen considers his design "a mockery" (220) because it rests on an "initial mistake" (219) that is the "sole cause" of its failure (218). In this he is right, except that he nominates the wrong mistake, directing the general's attention, at least in 1864, to the Haitian marriage. Although he never quite says as much, Bon becomes Sutpen's way of repressing his own founding narrative. Sutpen's mistake lies here: he uses miscegenation, barely confessed in 1864, to mystify labor fear, more fully confessed in 1835. The earlier story is deeply disruptive of planter properties, and in 1835, less committed to those properties, he almost said as much to the general. However, neither then nor thirty years later can he bear full witness to the boy's insight into the labor facts of the master's matter.

As a labor lord Sutpen cannot let the revolution in his own consciousness be readable to himself or to others. In this, at least, he is successful; his labor trauma passes almost unremarked by interpreters in and outside the novel. While it is fair, therefore, to say that repression delivers the goods both cognitively and politically, it must be added that Faulkner marks Sutpen's chief repressive device (counterrevolution, care of Haiti) as a mistake. Put crudely, repression in Haiti in 1827 is, quite literally, an impossible counterrevolution. Interpreters should not have been misled, yet it remains entirely understandable that they were and are. It will not have escaped attention that *Absalom, Absalom!* is almost unreadable; as a record of an attempt by a planter and his class descendants to tell the story of planter accumulation, it is the product of characters who, in order to live with themselves and their properties, have to make themselves more or less unreadable to themselves and to others. Repression, cognitive and political, is their cast of mind, yielding stories that contort, distort, evade, and displace what they know.

It would be a mistake to read the novel's difficulty as raising primarily epistemological questions. While readers must ask, Who knows what, when, and how? this should not—critics to the contrary—induce a crisis of knowledge culminating in some form of the unanswerable question, How can they (or we) know at all?[48] In *Absalom, Absalom!* a novel designed to explore a repressive class design, difficulty begs the altogether more answerable question, How can those who know so much repress so much of what they know? As with most things in this novel, Sutpen is

there first: apparently motivated by a desire to make himself in-
telligible he holds two conversations, separated by thirty years.
The first, a story about labor experience, is so concealed under
the second, a story about marital innocence, that decipherment
leads to encipherment. Mystification depends upon overlap. Were
the two stories manifestly different, the second would not encrypt
the first. However, because the second half of Sutpen's conversation appears to continue the first, right down to starting at the
point where the first part ceased (the marriage), distortion can
occur under the guise of resolution. So, one "error," the Virginian
decision to become a labor lord when the consequence of such
lordship is perceived as bondage, becomes another, the Haitian
decision to marry a woman whose "Spanish" mother is found to
have been black. Similarly, one child at the door (Sutpen), subjected to labor trauma, becomes another child at the door (Bon),
subjected to another and familial trauma. In each instance, affinity disguises the degree to which Sutpen's narratives are collu-
sively cryptic. For example, while it is true that a master's sexual
use of a female slave results in large part from the more general
condition of slave labor, miscegenation cannot be said to express
the essence of that condition.[49] Yet the interference of Sutpen's
two stories, one with another, promotes a reading of Bon not as
goods but as miscegenation-produced son. Alternatively, while it
is true that the history of the Sutpens is familial, in the South
the family as "household" always extends beyond the family as
Oedipal unit—which is simply to say that Sutpen, the father, is
also a man who does not take sugar in his coffee, who fights
slaves, who allies with merchant capital, and who is elected a
Confederate officer.[50] Yet because the link between Sutpen, parts
1 and 2, appears to be Eulalia as wife and mother, rather than
Eulalia as route to slave properties, Freud and not Hegel has provided the prevalent critical glossary to the novel.

It remains the case that if the labor truth is missed, it is because
Sutpen would have it so. He tells his second story in order to
avoid unbearable truths in his first. Since he renders himself unreadable, it is perhaps understandable that so many have compounded his unreadability. The nature and consequence of their

collusive repression is the substance of yet another essay on *Absalom, Absalom!*

Notes

1. Eugene Genovese, *From Rebellion to Revolution* (Baton Rouge: Louisiana State University Press, 1979), 85.

2. See Dirk Kuyk, Jr., *Sutpen's Design: Interpreting "Absalom, Absalom!"* (Charlottesville: University Press of Virginia, 1990), 85.

3. The quotation is from Sylvia Frey, *Water from the Rock: Black Resistance in a Revolutionary Age* (Princeton, N.J.: Princeton University Press, 1991), 231. On black rebellions, see Genovese, *From Rebellion*, 95; William Freehling, *Prelude to Civil War: The Nullification Controversy in South Carolina, 1816–36* (New York: Harper, 1969), 58–60; and Stephen Oates, *The Fires of Jubilee: Nat Turner's Fierce Rebellion* (New York: Mentor, 1973), 12, 17.

4. Herbert Gutman, *The Black Family in Slavery and Freedom, 1750–1925* (Oxford: Blackwell, 1976), 24.

5. C. Vann Woodward, ed., *Mary Chesnut's Civil War* (New Haven, Conn.: Yale University Press, 1981), 834.

6. Rod Prince, *Haiti: Family Business* (London: Latin American Bureau, 1985), 11.

7. William Faulkner, *Absalom, Absalom!* (1936; reprint, New York: Random House, 1986), 203. Subsequent references to this edition will be included in the text.

8. C. L. R. James, *History of Negro Revolt* (London: Race Today Publications, 1985), 9.

9. Frey, *Water from the Rock*, 235; Joel Williamson, *The Crucible of Race: Black/White Relations in the American South since Emancipation* (New York: Oxford University Press, 1984), 31.

10. Frey, *Water from the Rock*, 232.

11. Alfred Hunt, *Haiti's Influence on Antebellum America: Slumbering Volcano in the Caribbean* (Baton Rouge: Louisiana State University Press, 1988), 145–46.

12. William Faulkner, "Appendix Compson: 1699–1945," in *The Sound and the Fury* (New York: Norton, 1987), 227.

13. See Vernon Lane Wharton, *The Negro in Mississippi: 1865–1890* (New York: Harper and Row, 1965), 11–13, and Freehling, *Prelude to Civil War*, 11, 363–67.

14. James Snead, "The 'Joint' of Racism: Withholding the Black in

Absalom, Absalom!" in *Modern Critical Interpretations: William Faulkner's "Absalom, Absalom!"* ed. Harold Bloom (New York: Chelsea House, 1987), 124.

15. G. W. F. Hegel, *The Phenomenology of the Mind*, vol. 1, trans. J. B. Baillie (New York: Macmillan, 1910), 184.

16. Ibid., 176.

17. Ibid., 182, 186.

18. Ibid., 187.

19. Ibid., 186.

20. Ibid., 173, 175, 176.

21. Ibid., 179, 176.

22. Ibid., 176.

23. Joseph Blotner, ed., *Selected Letters of William Faulkner* (New York: Vintage, 1978), 78–79.

24. Jean-Paul Sartre, *Critique of Dialectical Reason*, vol. 1 (London: Verso, 1982), 323. See also 178–79.

25. Ibid., 328.

26. Given his labor trauma, it is understandable that Sutpen adopts continence as a shield against mingling and copresent bodies.

27. See W. J. Cash, *The Mind of the South* (1941; reprint, London: Thames and Hudson, 1971), 86; Richard Gray, *Writing the South: Ideas of an American Region* (Cambridge: Cambridge University Press, 1989), 189; and Williamson, *Crucible of Race*, 303–8.

28. Quoted in Stephen Hahn, *The Roots of Southern Populism: Yeomen Farmers and the Transformation of the Georgia Upcountry, 1850–1890* (New York: Oxford University Press, 1983), 133.

29. Kuyk, *Sutpen's Design*, 20, 22.

30. Carolyn Porter, *Seeing and Being: The Plight of the Participant Observer in Emerson, James, Adams and Faulkner* (Middletown, Conn.: Wesleyan University Press, 1981), 222.

31. Cleanth Brooks, *William Faulkner: Toward Yoknapatawpha and Beyond* (New Haven, Conn.: Yale University Press, 1979), 299.

32. Ibid., 296, 294, 299.

33. Eugene Genovese notes that the pre-bourgeois spirit of the planters meant that they "could not accept the idea that the cash nexus offered a permissible basis for human relations." Brooks quotes him in *William Faulkner*, 294. I have modified Brooks's use of the Genovese quotation.

34. Porter, *Seeing and Being*, 222; Brooks, *William Faulkner*, 299; Porter, *Seeing and Being*, 236; Kuyk, *Sutpen's Design*, 21.

35. Brooks, *William Faulkner*, 295.

36. Porter, *Seeing and Being*, 234.

37. Ibid.

38. Quentin's observation is strange since, at least nominally, General Compson knows neither that Bon is Sutpen's son nor that he is black. Quentin may be exaggerating his grandfather's point, or he may be hinting at his own suspicion that the general had worked out Sutpen's paternal secrets.

39. Orlando Paterson, *Slavery and Social Death: A Comparative Study* (Cambridge, Mass.: Harvard University Press, 1982), 8.

40. C. Vann Woodward, *The Strange Career of Jim Crow* (New York: Oxford University Press, 1959), xvi.

41. Elizabeth Fox-Genovese and Eugene Genovese, *Fruits of Merchant Capital: Slavery and Bourgeois Capital in the Rise and Expansion of Capitalism* (New York: Oxford University Press, 1983), 5.

42. Mark Tushnet, *The American Law of Slavery: Consideration of Humanity and Interest* (Princeton, N.J.: Princeton University Press, 1981), 232.

43. Johann Fichte, *The Science of Rights* (Philadelphia: Lippincott, 1869), quoted in Evgeny Pashukanis, *Law and Marxism* (London: Ink Links, 1978), 114. My discussion of contract is heavily informed by Pashukanis's chapter on "Commodity and Subject," 109–33.

44. Tushnet, *American Law of Slavery*, 6.

45. Ibid.

46. Fox-Genovese and Genovese, *Fruits of Merchant Capital*, 131.

47. Ibid.

48. Eugene Genovese, *Roll Jordan Roll: The World the Slaves Made* (New York: Random House, 1972), 91.

49. Contemporary observers agree that, after emancipation, miscegenation between white men and black women was much reduced. Freedom blocked white access to the quarters, while segregation functioned to separate black and white lives. See Williamson, *Crucible of Race*, particularly chap. 7.

50. Where the northern "home" narrows socials relations into an essentially private, feminized, and familial space (Oedipal), the southern "household" necessarily links private to public and locates familial relations within production relations (anti-Oedipal). "Within households, personal ties cross class-lines. Slave-holders and slaves participated in a shared imaginative universe that could shimmer with mutual affection or . . . shatter in mutual antagonism." Elizabeth Fox-Genovese, *Within the Plantation Household: Black and White Women in the Old South* (Chapel Hill: University of North Carolina Press, 1988), 27; also see 37–99.

Remarks on *Absalom, Absalom!*

WILLIAM FAULKNER

◆ ◆ ◆

THE FOLLOWING REMARKS BY FAULKNER came in response to questions from students at the University of Virginia in April 1957 and at Washington and Lee University in May 1958. They are included in *Faulkner in the University: Class Conferences at the University of Virginia 1957–1958*, ed. Frederick L. Gwynn and Joseph L. Blotner (Charlottesville: University of Virginia Press, 1959). These remarks constitute the closest thing to an interview Faulkner ever gave concerning *Absalom, Absalom!*

Q. Who is the central character of *Absalom, Absalom!*? It seems so obviously to be Sutpen, yet it's been said that it's also the story of Quentin, and I was wondering just who is the central character?

A. The central character is Sutpen, yes. The story of a man who wanted a son and got too many, got so many that they destroyed him. It's incidentally the story of Quentin Compson's hatred of the bad qualities in the country he loves. But the central character is Sutpen, the story of a man who wanted sons.

Q. Sir, in the same book I was wondering what is supposed to be the reader's attitude toward Mr. Coldfield, the father of Ellen?

A. Well, my attitude is that he was a pretty poor man. I don't know what the reader's attitude might be, but I still felt compassion and pity for him, but he was a poor man in my opinion.

Q. Sir, what sort of a deal was made between Goodhue Coldfield and Sutpen in reference to the bill of lading? They pulled some sort of deal.

A. I don't remember. That book is so long ago to me, but Coldfield was a petty, grasping man and Sutpen was a bold, ruthless man, and Sutpen used Coldfield's pettiness for his, Sutpen's, ends, but I don't remember exactly what it was. . . .

Q. In another class you stated that you seldom have the plot of your novels worked out before you begin to write, but that they simply develop from a character or an incident. I was wondering if you remember what character or what incident caused you to write *Absalom, Absalom!*?

A. Sutpen.

Q. You thought of that character and then—

A. Yes, the idea of a man who wanted sons and got sons who destroyed him. The other characters I had to get out of the attic to tell the story of Sutpen.

Q. I've been looking for Sutpen's—the reason for Sutpen's downfall, Mr. Faulkner, and it seems to me that the Civil War played a part in it. Is that true?

A. Yes.

Q. But that's not the main reason?

A. No, I used the Civil War to—for my own ends there. Sutpen's country was wrecked by the Civil War, but that didn't stop Sutpen, he was still trying to get the son, still trying to establish a dynasty. He was still trying to get even with that man who in his youth had said, Go to the back door.

Q. Mr. Faulkner, what was the particular significance of having Wash Jones, a very humble man, be the instrument through which Sutpen met his death? Does that relate back to the social stratum from which Sutpen himself came and have there a sort of ironic effect? Just what was the idea of that?

A. In a sense. In another sense Wash Jones represented the man who survived the Civil War. The aristocrat in the columned house was ruined, but Wash Jones survived it unchanged. He had been Wash Jones before 1861, and after 1865 he was still Wash Jones and Sutpen finally collided with him. . . .

Q. How much of the story of *Absalom, Absalom!* is reconstructed by Shreve and Quentin? How does the reader know which to accept as objective truth and which to consider just a [reflection] of their personalities?

A. Well, the story was told by Quentin to Shreve. Shreve was the commentator [who] held the thing to something of reality. If Quentin had been let alone to tell it, it would have become completely unreal. It had to have a solvent to keep it real, keep it believable, creditable, otherwise it would have vanished into smoke and fury.

Q. Sir, along that same line, you mentioned at the English Club that you had had to lay aside *Absalom* at one point, to resume it later on. I wonder if it might not have been the point where toward the end of Miss Rosa's section—where you might have felt that she was running away with you, because right after that, Shreve comes in. Is that in your memory at all, sir?

A. I can't say just where it was that I had to put it down, that I decided that I didn't know enough at that time, maybe, or my feeling toward it wasn't passionate enough or pure enough, but I don't remember at what point I put it down. Though when I took it up again I almost rewrote the whole thing. I think that what I put down were inchoate fragments that wouldn't coalesce and then when I took it up again, as I remember, I rewrote it. . . .

Q. Is the title of *Absalom, Absalom!* taken from the passage in the Bible found in Second Samuel?

A. Yes.

Q. Did you write the novel with this episode in your mind or did you first write the novel and then realizing the similarity in the name—?

A. They were simultaneous. As soon as I thought of the idea of the man who wanted sons and the sons destroyed him, then I thought of the title. . . .

Q. Sir, how good a judge of his own work do you think any writer can be?

A. He is—can judge only in whether it's good enough to suit him or not, otherwise, he's probably a rotten judge of it, because he gets involved personally and he refuses to recognize the bad sometimes and he insists that the mediocre is first-rate, because he is involved personally.

Q. And conversely, may fail to appreciate?

A. That's right.

Q. Mr. Faulkner, is there any purpose in the repetition on the same sets of characters throughout your writing?

A. No, only that I have led a—all of my life has been lived in a little Mississippi town, and there's not much variety there. A writer writes from his experience, his background, in the terms of his imagination and his observation. That would be the explanation, I think. . . .

Q. It's been said that you write about the secret of the human heart. Is there one major truth of the human heart?

A. Well, that's a question almost metaphysical. I would say if there is one truth of the human heart, it would be to believe in itself, believe in its capacity to aspire, to be better than it is, might be. That it does exist in all people. . . .

Q. I was wondering whether Charles Bon in *Absalom, Absalom!* ever had suspicions of who his father was.

A. I think he knew. I don't know whether he—his mother probably told him. I think he knew.

Q. Was it a conscious knowledge, would you say, or unconscious knowledge?

A. Probably it was a conscious knowledge in the sense that his mother had told him who his father was. It may be that he didn't believe it, or didn't know or didn't care. I think—I don't believe that he felt any affinity with Sutpen as father and son, but probably his mother had told him and—that she had been deserted and if anything, if he did believe it, he hated Sutpen, of course.

Q. Sir, do you—according to Nathaniel Hawthorne, the greatest sin was the violation of the human heart. Would you say that you think along those lines as far as what the greatest sin could be or the greatest crime or characteristic of sin? Would you agree with that statement?

A. Yes, yes, I agree with that. . . .

Q. Mr. Faulkner, throughout your work there seems to be a theme that there's a curse upon the South. I was wondering if you could explain what this curse is and if there is any chance of the South to escape.

A. The curse is slavery, which is an intolerable condition—no man shall be enslaved—and the South has got to work that curse out and it will, if it's let alone. It can't be compelled to do it. It must do it of its own will and desire, which I believe it will do if it's let alone.

Q. Was the reaction of the people to Sutpen's second marriage—when no one showed up at [the wedding] . . . —was that reaction caused by the people's dislike of his life or his social errors or because of their not being told why—where he got his money?

A. Oh, he had violated the local mores. They feared him and they hated him because of his ruthlessness. He made no pretense to be anything else except what he was, and so he violated the local mores and they ostracized him. Not in revenge at all, but simply because they wanted no part of Sutpen. . . .

Q. Is Sutpen meant to be a completely depraved character, something like Claggart in *Billy Budd* or Iago in *Othello*, or is he meant to be pitied?

A. To me, he is to be pitied. He was not depraved—he was amoral, he was ruthless, completely self-centered. To me, he is to be pitied, as anyone who ignores man is to be pitied, who does not believe that he belongs as a member of a human family, of *the* human family, is to be pitied. Sutpen didn't believe that. He was Sutpen. He was going to take what he wanted because he was big enough and strong enough, and I think that people like that are destroyed sooner or later, because one has got to belong to the human family, and to take a responsible part in the human family. . . .

Q. In *Absalom, Absalom!* which you said you didn't remember very well last time, do you happen to remember when Charles Bon realizes that Sutpen is his father? Is it before or after he leaves New Orleans to go to the university?

A. I should think that his mother dinned that into him as soon as he was big enough to remember, and that he came deliberately to hunt out his father, not for justice for himself, but for revenge for his abandoned mother. He must have known that, that must have been in his—the background of his childhood, that this abandoned woman never let him forget that.

Q. Does the New Orleans lawyer have personal gain in mind in helping Bon and his mother?

A. Possibly, yes. Yes, when he located Sutpen, knew that Sutpen was a wealthy man in his time, yes, he thought there would be gain, but Bon didn't want gain, he wanted revenge, for his mother.

Q. How far do you think the relationship between Charles Bon and Sutpen parallels what you consider the general racial situation in the South?

A. It was a manifestation of a general racial system in the South which was condensed and concentrated as the writer has got to do with any incident or any character he takes, for the reason that he hasn't got sixty years. He has got to do his job in—between the covers of a book, but—that is, epitomize a constant general condition in the South, yes. . . .

Q. Sir, are you conscious of any similarity between Thomas Sutpen and Flem Snopes? They are—I don't suppose there's any comedy in *Absalom* anywhere, and there's a great deal of course in *The Hamlet* and *The Town*, but both of them are—have a grand design and are unscrupulous about getting in—they use people.

A. Well, only Sutpen had a grand design. Snopes's design was pretty base—he just wanted to get rich, he didn't care how. Sutpen wanted to get rich only incidentally. He wanted to take revenge for all the redneck people against the aristocrat who told him to go around to the back door. He wanted to show that he could establish a dynasty too—he could make himself a king and raise a line of princes. . . .

Q. This callous attitude of Sutpen and Flem Snopes, this ability

to use people without realizing they're people, sort of dehuman-
izing them, it seems to gradually get worse as they go from country into towns and cities. Is that a definite, is that a conscious
thing?

A. It didn't get worse because they came into cities. They had
to come into cities to find more people to use. But it got worse
because of the contempt which the ability to use people develops
in anyone. There are very few people that have enough grandeur
of soul to be able to use people and not develop contempt for
[them]. And that—the contempt for people—came not because
they moved to the city but out of success. . . .

Q. Did [Sutpen] acknowledge Clytemnestra as his daughter?

A. No. Well, that would not have mattered because Clytemnestra was a female. The important thing to him was he should
establish a line of dukes, you see. He was going to create a dukedom. He'd have to have a male descendant. He would have to
establish a dukedom which would be his revenge on the white
[*sic*] Virginian who told him to go to the back door. And so he—
to have a Negro, half-Negro, for his son would have wrecked the
whole dream. If he couldn't—if he had thought that it would
ever be exposed that Bon was his son, he may have killed Bon
himself. If it had ever come to that point, he would have destroyed Bon just as he would have destroyed any other individual
who got in his way. . . .

Q. I'd like to go back to Charles Bon. . . . I have the impression
that up until very near the end of the book that he does not
realize he is part Negro. . . . At what point does he find this out
and how does he find it out?

A. I think that Bon knew all the time that his mother was
part Negress, but during Bon's childhood that was not important.
He grew up in the Indies or in New Orleans where that wasn't
too important. His mother was a wealthy woman. She could have
called herself a Creole whether she had Negro blood along with
the French or not. It became important only when Bon realized
that it was important to his father. I think that Bon got into that
business—well, of course, because he formed a friendship with
Henry and felt that Henry, the ignorant country boy, had given

him a sort of worship, an admiration and a worship which he enjoyed. Then—when he saw the sort of stiff-necked man that Henry's father was and knew that that was his father too, he in a way had given his father a chance to say, I will acknowledge you, but if you—I do openly and you stay here, you will wreck what I have devoted my life to, and so take my love and go, I think Bon would have done it. But this old man was afraid to do that. And Bon tempted him to hold him over the coals in— partly in revenge on his treatment of his—Bon's—mother, until Bon got involved too deeply. No, Bon knew that he was a Negro, but until he found it was important to Sutpen, that wasn't important to him. That he was a gentleman, had been well bred, cultured, much better bred and cultured than Henry himself was.

Q. Did Bon love Judith, or . . . ?

A. I think he loved her, I think that he loved her. He knew that if she knew that he was part Negro, with her training and background it would have destroyed her too. . . .

Q. Mr. Faulkner, in *Absalom, Absalom!* does any one of the people who talks about Sutpen have the right view, or is it more or less a case of thirteen ways of looking at a blackbird with none of them right?

A. That's it exactly. I think that no one individual can look at truth. It blinds you. You look at it and you see one phase of it. Someone else looks at it and sees a slightly awry phase of it. But taken all together, the truth is in what they saw though nobody saw the truth intact. So these are true as far as Miss Rosa and as Quentin saw it. Quentin's father saw what he believed was truth, that was all he saw. But the old man was himself a little too big for people no greater in stature than Quentin and Miss Rosa and Mr. Compson to—see all at once. It would have taken perhaps a wiser or more tolerant or more sensitive or more thoughtful person to see him as he was. It was, as you say, thirteen ways of looking at a blackbird. But the truth, I would like to think, comes out, that when the reader has read all these thirteen different ways of looking at the blackbird, the reader has his own four- teenth image of that blackbird, which I would like to think is the truth.

Q. Mr. Faulkner, Mr. Coldfield in *Absalom, Absalom!* retreats into the attic when the war between the states starts. Now, why did he do that? Was it because he was a sort of conscientious objector, or was he all or part coward?

A. No, he was probably by religious scruples a conscientious objector. Also, he was very likely a Unionist. That he hated that threat to the dissolution of the Union. That he hadn't enough courage to do anything about it except to hide his head in the sand. But I think that he was probably a Unionist. He probably came from eastern Tennessee, where the people were Unionists at that time. His background was a tradition of fidelity to the United States as it was. He had no agrarian tradition behind him in which slavery was an important part of it. . . .

Q. Sir, speaking of those two books, as you read *Absalom, Absalom!* how much can a reader feel that this is the Quentin, the same Quentin, who appeared in *The Sound and the Fury*—that is, a man thinking about his own Compson family, his own sister?

A. To me, he's consistent. That he approached the Sutpen family with the same ophthalmia that he approached his own troubles, that he probably never saw anything very clearly, that his was just one of the thirteen ways to look at Sutpen, and his may have been the—one of the most erroneous. Probably his friend McCannon had a much truer picture of Sutpen from what Quentin told him than Quentin himself did.

Q. But it's still Sutpen's story. It's not Quentin's story.

A. No, it's Sutpen's story. But then, every time any character gets into a book, no matter how minor, he's actually telling his biography—that's all anyone ever does, he tells his own biography, talking about himself, in a thousand different terms, but himself. Quentin was still trying to get God to tell him why, in *Absalom, Absalom!* as he was in *The Sound and the Fury*. . . .

Q. May I ask what you think of James Joyce?

A. James Joyce was one of the great men of my time. He was electrocuted by the divine fire. He, Thomas Mann, were the great writers of my time. He was probably—might have been the greatest, but he was electrocuted. He had more talent than he could control. . . .

Q. Pertinent to that, I'd like to ask why is it that Mississippi seems very active in a literary way and yet we don't find the same phenomenon in New Jersey.

A. Well, that's because Mississippi's in the South and New Jersey's in the North. I think that the wisest thing any nation can do when it gets itself into any sort of an economic muddle is to pick out some rich nation and declare war, and get licked and then be supported. The folks in the South write because the North has supported us ever since 1865. We had plenty of time to write. . . .

Q. Did you find *Absalom, Absalom!* a very difficult novel to write?

A. Yes'm, it was difficult. I worked on that next hardest to *The Sound and the Fury,* as I remember. Yes, I worked on that for a year and then put it away and wrote another book, and then the story still wouldn't let me alone and I came back to it. Yes, that was very difficult. There was a lot of rewriting in that.

Suggested Reading

Adamowski, T. H. "Children of the Idea: Heroes and Family Romances in *Absalom, Absalom!*" *Mosaic* 10 (Fall 1976): 115–31.

Adams, Richard P. "Work: *Absalom, Absalom!*" In Adams, *Faulkner: Myth and Motion*, 172–214. Princeton, N.J.: Princeton University Press, 1968.

Aswell, Duncan. "The Puzzling Design of *Absalom, Absalom!*" *Kenyon Review* 30, no. 1 (1968): 67–84.

Backman, Melvin. "*Absalom, Absalom!*" In Backman, *Faulkner: The Major Years: A Critical Study*, 88–112. Bloomington: Indiana University Press, 1966.

Bassett, John E. "*Absalom, Absalom*: The Limits of Narrative Form." *Modern Language Quarterly* 46 (September 1985): 276–92.

Batty, Nancy E. "The Riddle of *Absalom, Absalom!* Looking at the Wrong Blackbird." *Mississippi Quarterly* 47 (Summer 1994): 461–88.

Behrens, Ralph. "Collapse of Dynasty: The Thematic Center of *Absalom, Absalom!*" *PMLA* 89 (January 1974): 24–33.

Benson, Sean. "The Abrahamic Mythopoeia of Sutpen's Design: 'No-trespectability' in Search of a Dynasty." *Mississippi Quarterly* 50 (Summer 1997): 450–64.

Bleikasten, André. "Fathers in Faulkner." In *The Fictional Father: Lacanian*

Readings of the Text, edited by Robert Con Davis, 115–46. Amherst: University of Massachusetts Press, 1981.

———. "Faulkner in the Singular." In *Faulkner at 100: Retrospect and Prospect*, edited by Donald M. Kartiganer and Ann J. Abadie, 204–18. Jackson: University Press of Mississsippi, 2000.

Bloom, Harold. Introduction to *William Faulkner's "Absalom, Absalom!"* 1–8. New York: Chelsea House, 1987.

Brooks, Cleanth. "*Absalom, Absalom!*" In Brooks, *William Faulkner: First Encounters*, 192–224. New Haven, Conn.: Yale University Press, 1983.

———. "The Narrative Structure of *Absalom, Absalom!*" In Brooks, *William Faulkner: Toward Yoknapatawpha and Beyond*, 301–28. New Haven, Conn.: Yale University Press, 1978.

———. "Thomas Sutpen: A Representative Southern Planter?" In Brooks, *William Faulkner: Toward Yoknapatawpha and Beyond*, 283–300. New Haven, Conn.: Yale University Press, 1978.

Brooks, Peter. "Incredulous Narration: *Absalom, Absalom!*" *Comparative Literature* 34 (Summer 1982): 247–68.

Brown, Joseph. "To Cheer the Weary Traveler: Toni Morrison, William Faulkner, and History." *Mississippi Quarterly* 49 (Fall 1996): 709–26.

Brylowski, Walter. "Faulkner's Mythology." In Brylowski, *Faulkner's Olympian Laugh: Myth in the Novels*, 11–42. Detroit, Mich.: Wayne State University Press, 1968.

Cohn, Deborah N. "The Case of the Fabricated Facts: Invented Information and the Problems of Reconstructing the Past in *Absalom, Absalom!* and *The Real Life of Alejandro Mayta*." In Cohn, *History and Memory in the Two Souths: Recent Southern and Spanish American Fiction*, 45–93. Nashville, Tenn.: Vanderbilt University Press, 1999.

Cunningham, J. Christopher. "Sutpen's Designs: Masculine Reproduction and the Unmaking of the Self-Made Man in *Absalom, Absalom!*" *Mississippi Quarterly* 49 (Summer 1996): 563–89.

Dale, Corrine. "*Absalom, Absalom!* and the Snopes Trilogy: Southern Patriarchy in Revision." *Mississippi Quarterly* 45 (Summer 1992): 321–37.

Dalziel, Pamela. "*Absalom, Absalom!* The Extension of Dialogic Form." *Mississippi Quarterly* 45 (Summer 1992): 277–94.

Davis, Robert Con. "The Symbolic Father in Yoknapatawpha County." *Journal of Narrative Technique* 10 (Winter 1980): 39–55.

Donaldson, Susan V. "Subverting History: Women, Narrative, and Patriarchy in *Absalom, Absalom!*" *Southern Quarterly* 26 (Summer 1988): 19–32.

Edenfield, Olivia Carr. " 'Endure and Then Endure': Rosa Coldfield's Search for a Role in William Faulkner's *Absalom, Absalom!*" *Southern Literary Journal* 32 (Fall 1999): 57–68.

Egan, Philip J. "Embedded Story Structures in *Absalom, Absalom!*" *American Literature* 55 (May 1983): 199–214.

Forrer, Richard. "*Absalom, Absalom!* Story-Telling as a Means of Transcendence." *Southern Literary Journal* 9 (Fall 1976): 22–46.

Fowler, Doreen. "Reading for the Repressed: *Absalom, Absalom!*" In Fowler, *Faulkner: The Return of the Repressed*, 95–127. Charlottesville: University Press of Virginia, 1997.

Garfield, Deborah. "To Love as 'Fiery Ancients' Would: Eros, Narrative and Rosa Coldfield in *Absalom, Absalom!*" *Southern Literary Journal* 22 (Fall 1989): 61–79.

Godden, Richard. "*Absalom, Absalom!* and Rosa Coldfield; or, What *Is* in the Dark House?" In Godden, *Fictions of Labor: William Faulkner and the South's Long Revolution*, 80–114. Cambridge: Cambridge University Press, 1997.

———. "The Persistence of Thomas Sutpen: *Absalom, Absalom!* Time, and Labor Discipline." In Godden, *Fictions of Labor*, 115–78. Cambridge: Cambridge University Press, 1997.

Gray, Richard. "History Is What Hurts: *Absalom, Absalom!*" In Gray, *The Life of William Faulkner: A Critical Biography*, 203–25. Oxford: Blackwell, 1994.

Guérard, Albert J. "*Absalom, Absalom!* The Novel as Impressionist Art." In Guérard, *The Triumph of the Novel: Dickens, Dostoevsky, Faulkner*, 302–39. New York: Oxford University Press, 1976.

Guetti, James. "*Absalom, Absalom!* The Extended Simile." In Guetti, *The Limits of Metaphor: A Study of Melville, Conrad, and Faulkner*, 69–108. Ithaca, N.Y.: Cornell University Press, 1967.

Gwin, Minrose. "Feminism and Faulkner: Second Thoughts; or, What's a Radical Feminist Doing with a Canonical Male Text Anyway?" *Faulkner Journal* 4 (1988–1989): 55–65.

Hamblin, Robert W. " 'Longer than Anything': Faulkner's 'Grand Design' in *Absalom, Absalom!*" In *Faulkner and the Artist*, edited by Donald M. Kartiganer and Ann J. Abadie, 269–93. Jackson: University Press of Mississippi, 1996.

Handley, George B. "Oedipal and Prodigal Returns in Alejo Carpentier and William Faulkner." *Mississippi Quarterly* 52 (Summer 1999): 421–58.

Hicks, Gina L. "Reterritorializing Desire: The Failure of Ceremony in *Absalom, Absalom!*" *Faulkner Journal* 12 (Spring 1997): 23–40.

Hoffmann, Gerhard. "*Absalom, Absalom!* A Postmodern Approach." In *Faulkner's Discourse: An International Symposium*, edited by Lothar Hönnighausen, 276–92. Tubingen: Max Niemeyer, 1989.

Holman, C. Hugh. "*Absalom, Absalom!* The Historian as Detective." In Holman, *The Roots of Southern Writing: Essays on the Literature of the American South*, 168–76. Athens: University of Georgia Press, 1972.

Hönnighausen, Lothar. "Metaphor and Narrative in *Absalom, Absalom!*" In Hönnighausen, *Faulkner: Masks and Metaphors*, 157–81. Jackson: University Press of Mississippi, 1997.

Howe, Irving. "*Absalom, Absalom!*" In Howe, *William Faulkner: A Critical Study*. 3rd ed., 221–32. New York: Random House, 1975.

Irwin, John T. "The Dead Father in Faulkner." In *The Fictional Father: Lacanian Readings of the Text*, edited by Robert Con Davis, 147–68. Amherst: University of Massachusetts Press, 1981.

Jehlen, Myra. "Death of the Prodigal." In Jehlen, *Class and Character in Faulkner's South*, 47–73. New York: Columbia University Press, 1976.

Jenkins, Lee. "*Absalom, Absalom!*" In Jenkins, *Faulkner and Black-White Relations: A Psychoanalytic Approach*, 177–219. New York: Columbia University Press.

Justus, James H. "The Epic Design of *Absalom, Absalom!*" *Texas Studies in Literature and Language* 4 (Summer 1962): 157–76.

Karl, Frederick. "Race, History and Technique in *Absalom, Absalom!*" In *Faulkner and Race*, edited by Doreen Fowler and Ann J. Abadie, 209–21. Jackson: University Press of Mississsippi, 1987.

Kartiganer, Donald M. "In Place of an Introduction: Reading Faulkner." In *Faulkner at 100: Retrospect and Prospect*, edited by Donald M. Kartiganer and Ann J. Adabie, xiii–xxvi. Jackson: University Press of Mississippi, 2000.

―――. "Toward a Supreme Fiction: *Absalom, Absalom!*" In Kartiganer, *The Fragile Thread: The Meaning of Form in Faulkner's Novels*, 69–106. Amherst: University of Massachusetts Press, 1979.

Kauffman, Linda. "Devious Channels of Decorous Ordering: A Lover's Discourse in *Absalom, Absalom!*" *Modern Fiction Studies* 29 (Summer 1983): 183–200.

Kerr, Elizabeth. "*Absalom, Absalom!* Faust in Mississippi; or, The Fall of the House of Sutpen." *University of Mississippi Studies in English* 15 (1978): 61–82.

King, Richard. "From Time and History: The Lacerated Consciousness of Quentin Compson." In King, *A Southern Renaissance: The Cultural Awakening of the American South, 1930–1955*. New York: Oxford University Press, 1980. 111–29.

Krause, David. "Reading Bon's Letter and Faulkner's *Absalom, Absalom!*" *PMLA* 99 (March 1984): 225–41.

Kreiswirth, Martin. "Intertextuality, Transference, and Postmodernism in *Absalom, Absalom!*" In *Faulkner and Postmodernism*, edited by John N. Duvall and Ann J. Abadie, 109–23. Jackson: University Press of Mississippi, 2002.

Kuyk, Dirk, Jr. "Designs of the Narrative," "The Characters' Design," "The Narrators' Designs," and "Readers' Designs." In Kuyk, *Sutpen's Design: Interpreting Faulkner's Absalom, Absalom!* 28–137. Charlottesville: University Press of Virginia, 1990.

Langford, Gerald. *Faulkner's Revision of Absalom, Absalom! A Collation of the Manuscript and the Published Book*. Austin: University of Texas Press, 1971.

Lensing, George S. "The Metaphor of Family in *Absalom, Absalom!*" *Southern Review* 11 (Winter 1975): 99–117.

Levin, David. "*Absalom, Absalom!* The Problem of Recreating History." In Levin, *Defense of Historical Literature: Essays on American History, Autobiography, Drama and Fiction*, 118–39. New York: Hill and Wang, 1967.

Levins, Lynn G. "The Four Narratives: Perspectives in *Absalom, Absalom!*" *PMLA* 85 (1970): 35–47.

Liles, Don Merrick. "William Faulkner's *Absalom, Absalom!* An Exegesis of the Homoerotic Configurations in the Novel." In *Literary Visions of Homosexuality*, edited by Stuart Kellogg, 99–111. New York: Haworth, 1983.

Lind, Ilse Dusoir. "The Design and Meaning of *Absalom, Absalom!*" *PMLA* 60 (December 1955): 887–912.

Loebel, Thomas. "Love of Masculinity." *Faulkner Journal* 15 (1999–2000): 83–106.

Lurie, Peter. " 'Some Trashy Myth of Reality's Escape': Romance, History, and Film Viewing in *Absalom, Absalom!*" *American Literature* 73 (September 2001): 563–97.

MacKethan, Lucinda Hardwick. "Faulkner's Sins of the Fathers: How to Inherit the Past." In MacKethan, *The Dream of Arcady: Place and Time in Southern Literature*, 153–80. Baton Rouge: Louisiana State University Press, 1980.

Matthews, John T. "Marriages of Speaking and Hearing in *Absalom, Ab-*

salom!" In *The Play of Faulkner's Language*, 115–61. Ithaca, N.Y.: Cornell University Press, 1982.

Miller, J. Hillis. "The Two Relativisms: Point of View and Indeterminacy in the Novel *Absalom, Absalom!"* In *Relativism in the Arts*, edited by Betty Jean Craige, 148–70. Athens: University of Georgia Press, 1983.

Millgate, Michael. *"Absalom, Absalom!"* In Millgate, *The Achievement of William Faulkner*, 150–64. New York: Random House, 1966.

Minter, David. "Apotheosis of the Form: Faulkner's *Absalom, Absalom!"* In Minter, *The Interpreted Design as a Structural Principle in American Prose*, 191–219. New Haven, Conn.: Yale University Press, 1969.

———. "Three Trips to Babylon." In Minter, *William Faulkner: His Life and Work*, 137–64. Baltimore: Johns Hopkins University Press, 1980.

Moreland, Richard C. "Nausea and Irony's Failing Distances in *Absalom, Absalom!"* In Moreland, *Faulkner and Modernism:Rereading and Rewriting*, 23–78. Madison: University of Wisconsin Press, 1990.

———. "Willfulness and Irony's Other Voices in *Absalom, Abalom!"* In Moreland, *Faulkner and Modernism: Rereading and Rewriting*, 79–121. Madison: University of Wisconsin Press, 1990.

Morris, Wesley, with Barbara Alverson Morris. "The Narrative Scene" and "Dialogue." In Morris, *Reading Faulkner*, 176–218. Madison: University of Wisconsin Press.

Mortimer, Gail L. "Significant Absences." In Mortimer, *Faulkner's Rhetoric of Loss: A Study in Perception and Meaning*, 72–96. Austin: University of Texas Press, 1983.

Muhlenfeld, Elisabeth. Introduction to *William Faulkner's "Absalom, Absalom!" A Critical Casebook*, xi–xxxix. New York: Garland, 1984.

———. " 'We have waited long enough': Judith Sutpen and Charles Bon." *Southern Review* 14 (Winter 1978): 66–80.

Parker, Robert Dale. *"Absalom, Absalom!" The Questioning of Fictions*. Boston: Twayne, 1991.

Pitavy, François. "The Narrative Voice and Function of Shreve: Remarks on the Production of Meaning in *Absalom, Absalom!"* In *William Faulkner's "Absalom, Absalom!" A Critical Casebook*, edited by Elisabeth Muhlenfeld, 189–205. New York: Garland, 1984.

Poirier, Richard. " 'Strange Gods' in Jefferson, Mississippi: Analysis of *Absalom, Absalom!"* In *William Faulkner: Two Decades of Criticism*, edited by Frederick J. Hoffman and Olga Vickery, 217–43. East Lansing: Michigan State University Press, 1951.

Polk, Noel. "The Manuscript of *Absalom, Absalom!" Mississippi Quarterly* 25 (Summer 1972): 359–67.

Porter, Carolyn. "*Absalom, Absalom!* (Un)Making the Father." In *The Cambridge Companion to William Faulkner*, edited by Philip M. Weinstein, 168–96. Cambridge: Cambridge University Press, 1995.

————. "Faulkner's Grim Sires." In *Faulkner at 100: Retrospect and Prospect*, edited by Donald M. Kartiganer and Ann J. Abadie, 120–31. Jackson: University Press of Mississippi, 2000.

————. "William Faulkner: Innocence Historicized." In *William Faulkner's "Absalom, Absalom!"* edited by Harold Bloom, 57–89. New York: Chelsea House, 1987.

Reed, Joseph W., Jr. "*Absalom, Absalom!*" In Reed, *Faulkner's Narrative*, 145–75. New Haven, Conn.: Yale University Press, 1974.

Roberts, Diane. "The Ghostly Body in *Absalom, Absalom!*" and " 'But Let Flesh Touch with Flesh': The Terror of the Self-Same in *Absalom, Absalom!*" In Roberts, *Faulkner and Southern Womanhood*, 25–40, 89–101. Athens: University of Georgia Press, 1994.

Rollyson, Carl E., Jr. "The Recreation of the Past in *Absalom, Absalom!*" *Mississippi Quarterly* 29 (Summer 1976): 361–74.

Ross, Stephen M. "Oratorical Voice: *Absalom, Absalom!*" In Ross, *Fiction's Inexhaustible Voice: Speech and Writing in Faulkner*, 212–33. Athens: University of Georgia Press, 1989.

Rubin, Louis D., Jr. "Scarlett O'Hara and the Two Quentin Compsons." In Rubin, *A Gallery of Southerners*, 26–48. Baton Rouge: Louisiana State University Press, 1982.

Ruppersburg, Hugh M. "*Absalom, Absalom!*" In Ruppersburg, *Voice and Eye in Faulkner's Fiction*, 81–132. Athens: University of Georgia Press, 1983.

Ryan, Heberden W. "Behind Closed Doors: The Unknowable and the Unknowing in *Absalom, Absalom!*" *Mississippi Quarterly* 45 (Summer 1992): 295–312.

Saldívar, Ramón. "Looking for a Master Plan: Faulkner, Paredes, and the Colonial and Postcolonial Subject." In *The Cambridge Companion to William Faulkner*, edited by Philip M. Weinstein, 96–120. Cambridge: Cambridge University Press, 1995.

Sewall, Richard B. "*Absalom, Absalom!*" In Sewall, *The Vision of Tragedy*, 133–47. New Haven, Conn.: Yale University Press, 1959.

Simpson, Lewis P. "War and Memory: Quentin Compson's Civil War." In Simpson, *The Fable of the Southern Writer*, 73–95. Baton Rouge: Louisiana State University Press, 1994.

Singal, Daniel Joseph. "The Dark House of Southern History." In Singal, *William Faulkner: The Making of a Modernist*, 189–224. Chapel Hill: University of North Carolina Press, 1997.

Skinfill, Mauri. "Faulkner, Franklin, and the Sons of the Father." *Faulkner Journal* 10 (Fall 1994): 29–56.

Slaughter, Carolyn Norman. "*Absalom, Absalom!* 'Fluid Cradle of Events.' " *Faulkner Journal* 6 (Spring 1991): 65–84.

Snead, James. "The Joint of Racism: Withholding the Black in *Absalom, Absalom!*" In *William Faulkner's "Absalom, Absalom!"* edited by Harold Bloom, 129–41. New York: Chelsea House, 1987.

Spillers, Hortense J. "Faulkner Adds Up: Reading *Absalom, Absalom!* and *The Sound and the Fury.*" In *Faulkner in America*, edited by Joseph R. Urgo and Ann J. Abadie, 24–44. Jackson: University Press of Mississippi, 2001.

Stanchich, Maritza. "The Hidden Caribbean 'Other' in William Faulkner's *Absalom, Absalom!* An Ideological Ancestry of U.S. Imperialism." *Mississippi Quarterly* 49 (Summer 1996): 603–17.

Tobin, Patricia. "The Shadowy Attenuation of Time: William Faulkner's *Absalom, Absalom!*" In Tobin, *Time and the Novel: The Genealogical Imperative*, 107–32. Princeton, N.J.: Princeton University Press, 1978.

Urgo, Joseph R. "*Absalom, Absalom!* The Movie." *American Literature* 62 (March 1990): 56–73.

Vickery, Olga. "The Idols of the South: *Absalom, Absalom!*" In Vickery, *The Novels of William Faulkner: A Critical Interpretation.* Rev. ed., 84–102. Baton Rouge: Louisiana State University Press, 1964.

Wadlington, Warwick. "The House of *Absalom, Absalom!* Voices, Daughters, and the Question of Catharsis." In Wadington, *Reading Faulknerian Tragedy.* Ithaca, N.Y.: Cornell University Press, 1987.

Waggoner, Hyatt H. "The Historical Novel and the Southern Past: The Case of *Absalom, Absalom!*" *Southern Literary Journal* 2 (Spring 1970): 69–85.

Wagner-Martin, Linda. "Rosa Coldfield as Daughter: Another of Faulkner's Lost Children." *Studies in American Fiction* 19 (Spring 1991): 1–13.

Watkins, Evan. "The Fiction of Interpretation: Faulkner's *Absalom, Absalom!*" In Watkins, *The Critical Act: Criticism and Community*, 188–212. New Haven, Conn.: Yale University Press, 1978.

Watson, Jay. "And Now What's to Do: Faulkner, Reading, Praxis." *Faulkner Journal* 14 (Fall 1998): 67–74.

Weinstein, Arnold L. *Vision and Response in Modern Fiction.* Ithaca, N.Y.: Cornell University Press, 1974. 136–53.

Weinstein, Philip. "Precarious Sanctuaries: Protection and Exposure in Faulkner's Fiction." *Studies in American Fiction* 6 (1978): 173–91.

Westling, Louise. "Thomas Sutpen's Marriage to the Dark Body of the Land." In *Faulkner and the Natural World*, edited by Donald M. Kartiganer and Ann J. Adabie, 126–42. Jackson: University Press of Mississippi, 1999.

————. "Women, Landscape, and the Legacy of Gilgamesh in *Absalom, Absalom!* and *Go Down, Moses*." *Mississippi Quarterly* 48 (Summer 1995): 501–21.

Wilson, Deborah. " 'A Shape to Fill a Lack': *Absalom, Absalom!* and the Pattern of History." *Faulkner Journal* 7 (1991–1992): 61–81.

Wittenberg, Judith Bryant. "Portrait of the Artist at Work: *Pylon* and *Absalom, Absalom!*" In Wittenberg, *Faulkner: The Transfiguration of Biography*, 130–55. Lincoln: University of Nebraska Press, 1979.

Young, Thomas Daniel. "Narration as Creative Act: The Role of Quentin Compson in *Absalom, Absalom!*" In Young, *Faulkner, Modernism and Film*, 82–102. Jackson: University Press of Mississippi, 1979.

Zender, Karl F. "Faulkner and the Politics of Incest." *American Literature* 70 (December 1998): 739–65.

Zoellner, Robert H. "Faulkner's Prose Style in *Absalom, Absalom!*" *American Literature* 30 (January 1959): 486–502.